WILDWOOD PHOTOGRAPHERS' GUIDES

A Photographer's Guide to Sussex

Each book is a detailed guide to a well-known tourist area – giving advice and historical details on the places to visit, with recommendations for routes, etc.

The series will appeal especially to all amateur photographers, giving accurate information on how to get the best shots of each location (and advice on light, camera angles and lenses).

These books spell an end to dull, predictable photos of Corfe Castle, Windsor, Brighton and the Tower of London. Now the photographs will live up to your memories.

Early titles in this series will be:

A Photographer's Guide to the Cotswolds
A Photographer's Guide to Yorkshire
A Photographer's Guide to Kent
A Photographer's Guide to Devon and Cornwall
A Photographer's Guide to London

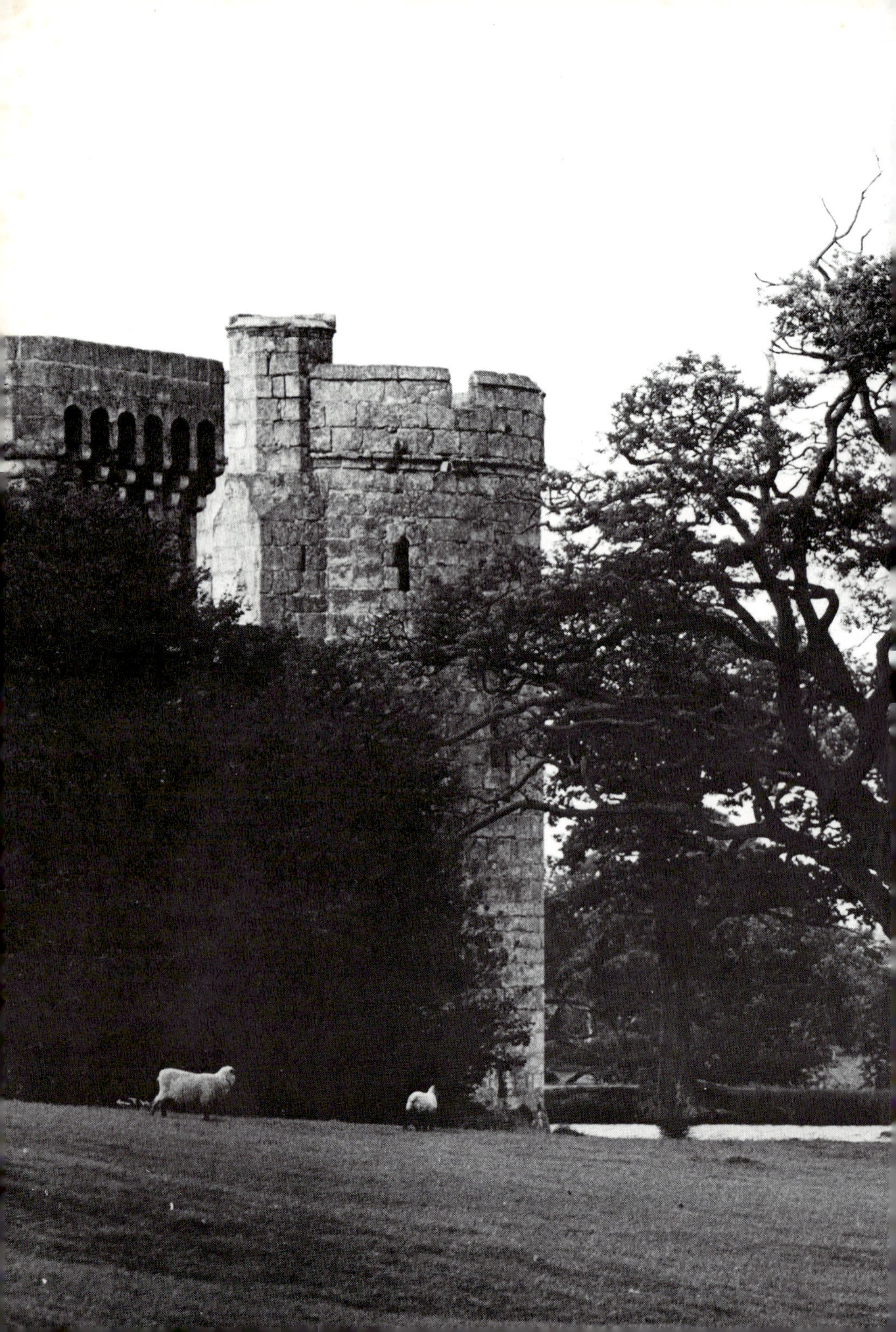

A PHOTOGRAPHER'S GUIDE TO SUSSEX

Kevin MacDonnell

WILDWOOD HOUSE
LONDON

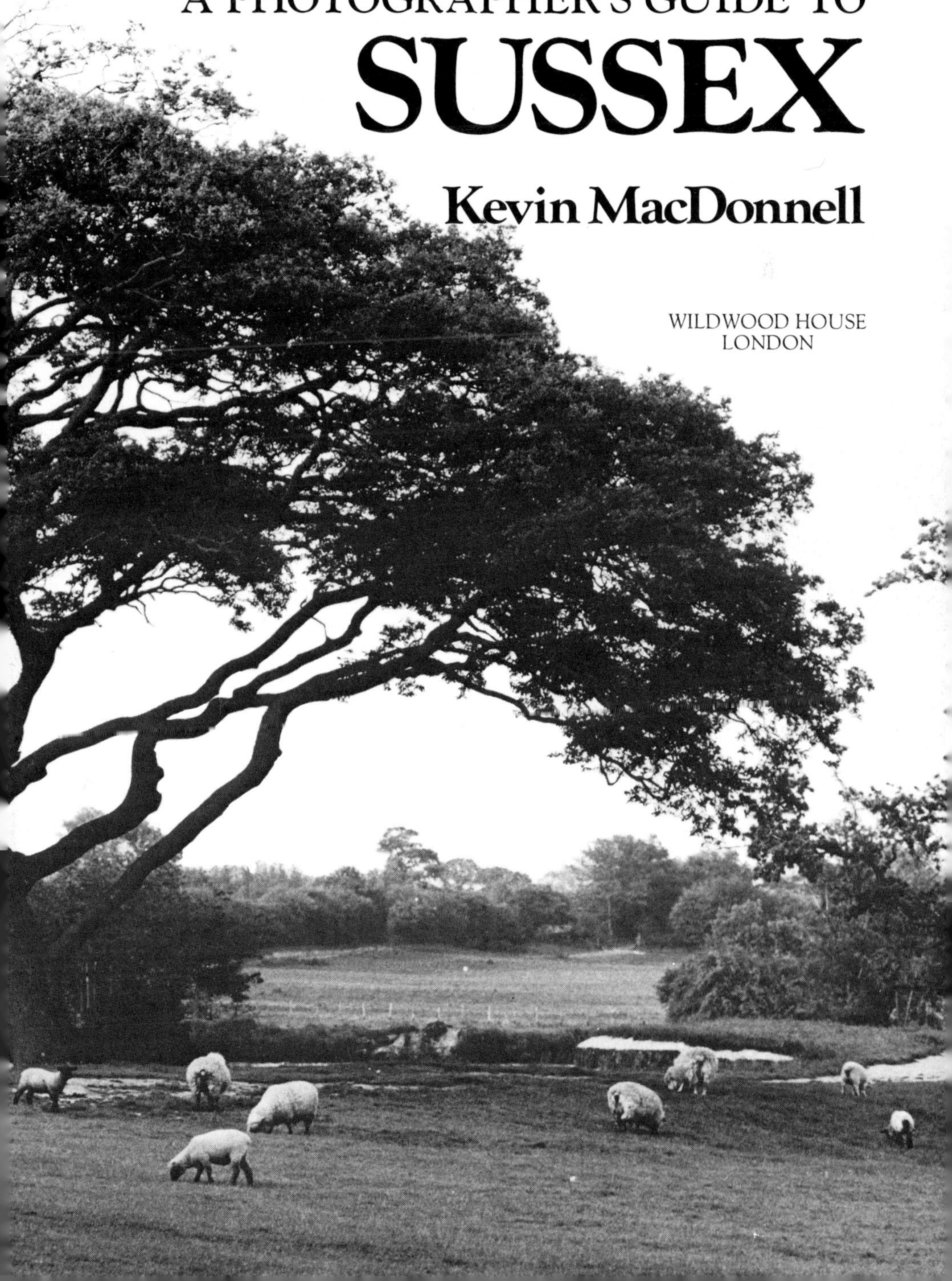

First published in Great Britain in 1984 by
WILDWOOD HOUSE LTD
Jubilee House, Chapel Road, Hounslow, Middlesex, TW3 1TX

Map by Sue Lawes

MacDonnell, Kevin
A photographer's guide to Sussex. – (Wildwood photographer's guides)
1. Travel photography – England – Sussex
I. Title
778.9'4 TR790

ISBN 0 7045 0485 5
Typeset in 10 on 11 point Goudy Old Style by TJB Photosetting Ltd
Printed in Hong Kong by South China Printing Company

Contents

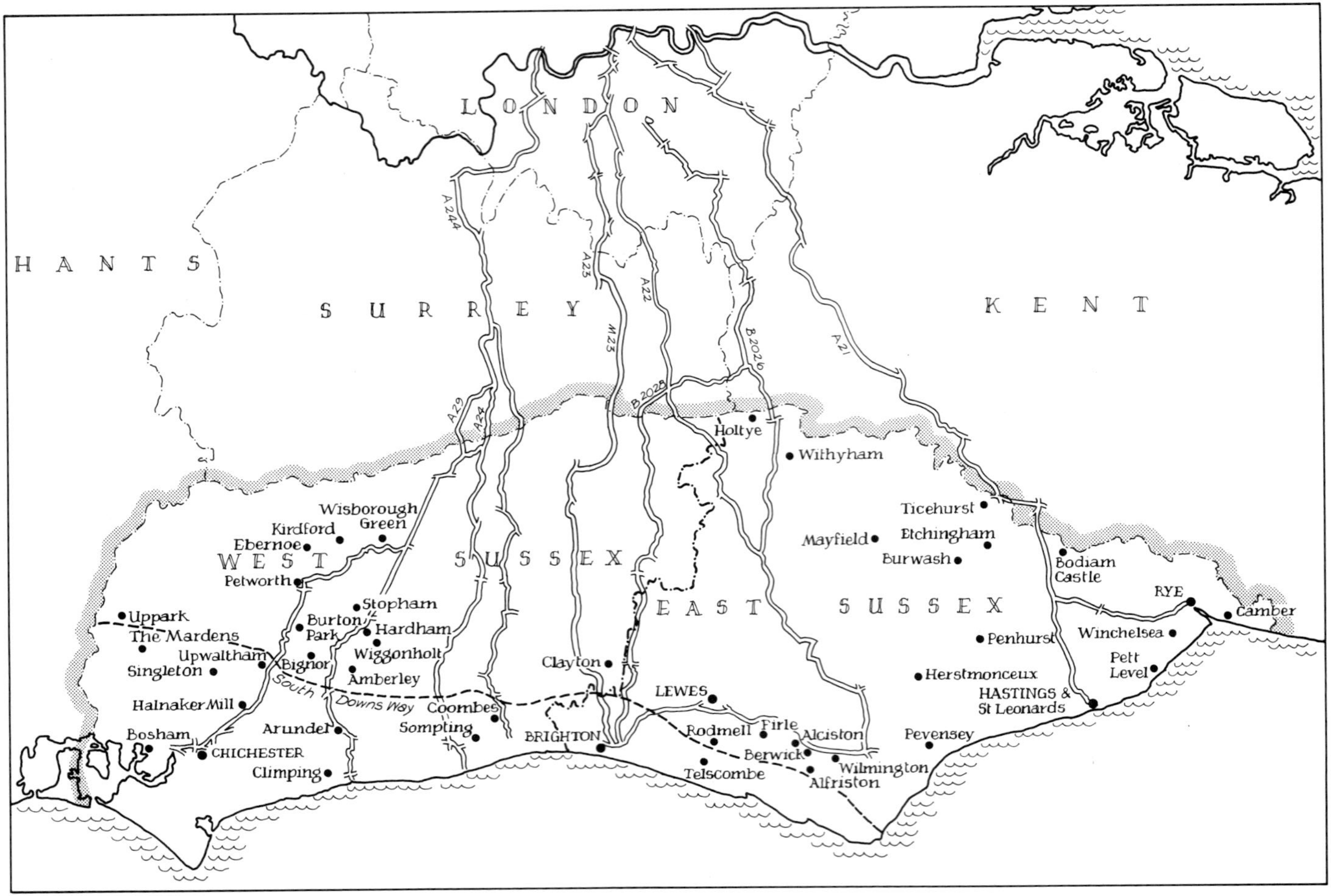

HANTS
SURREY
LONDON
KENT
WEST SUSSEX
EAST SUSSEX
A244
A23
A22
M23
B2026
A21
A29
A24
B2028
Holtye
Withyham
Ticehurst
Etchingham
Mayfield
Burwash
Wisborough Green
Kirdford
Ebernoe
Petworth
Bodiam Castle
RYE
Camber
Uppark
The Mardens
Upwaltham
Singleton
Burton Park
Stopham
Hardham
Bignor
Wiggonholt
Amberley
Halnaker Mill
South Downs Way
Coombes
Sompting
Clayton
LEWES
Penhurst
Winchelsea
Pett Level
Herstmonceux
HASTINGS & St Leonards
Bosham
CHICHESTER
Arundel
Climping
BRIGHTON
Rodmell
Firle
Alciston
Berwick
Telscombe
Wilmington
Alfriston
Pevensey

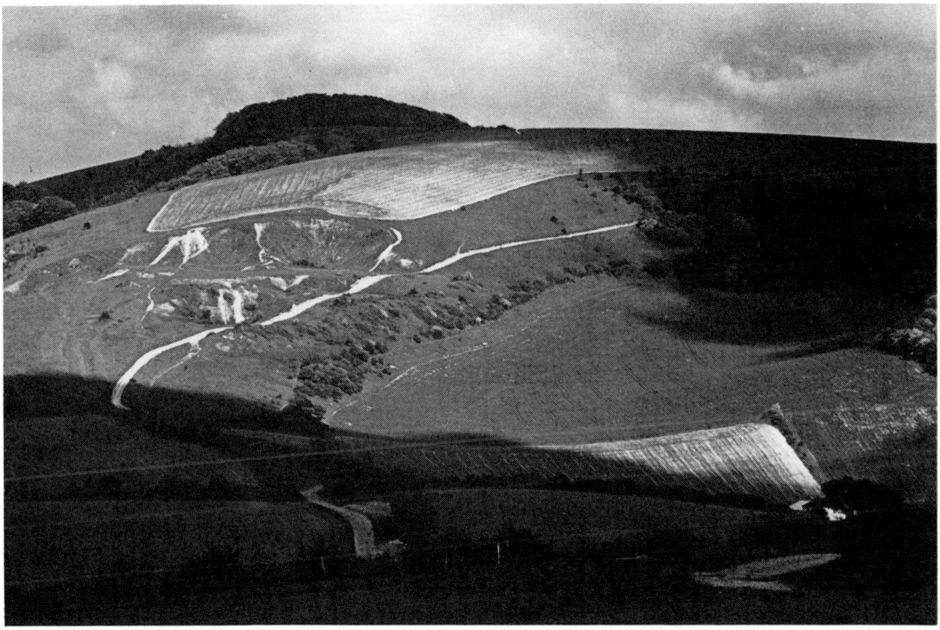

THE SUSSEX SEASONS

The wet South-West winds sweep in towards the coast, rise up over the Downs and deposit their rain in the Weald. As a result, in Sussex you get extraordinary variations in lighting within a few miles. It is a common experience to drive South early on an Autumn morning past woods, hop gardens and orchards which loom out of a dense mist, rise up to the crest of the Downs and look down on a coastal strip brilliantly lit by hard, clear sunlight. Look back from the hills and there lies the Weald covered in swirling fog.

Every season of the year has its own advantages for photographers. In Spring when the trees have a dusting of green you have an uninterrupted view over great distances, flowers start to dot the fields and the orchards burst into blossom. The holiday crowds have not yet arrived and the country lanes are empty.

In Summer you can start your photography at dawn, perhaps at 5.30, and carry on throughout the day until the sun sets; the long days let you cover a lot of ground, but the roads are busy and the tourist areas crowded. In many places Sussex is still thickly wooded and the leafy trees will obscure the view unless you are on high ground. In the Weald the light, especially in the morning, is often soft, hazy and ideal for colour owing to the water vapour drawn out of the earth by the sun, but on the Downs and the coastal strip it can be extremely harsh on a sunny day.

Autumn brings the variation in colour

(above) Along the South Downs Way

and the longer shadows that make many photographers think this is the best season of the year. By late September the roads are quiet once more, pubs and restaurants are glad to greet a customer, the smoke from burning stubble drifts across the fields, the gathering in of the harvest has made country people more relaxed and willing to chat – yes, this is a good time to be in Sussex.

In Winter it is best to explore the Southern side of the Downs and the coast generally since at all times there is more sunshine than in the rest of the country. The light will often give hard-edged shadows that show up detail and texture and is ideal for much architectural work, while if snow falls striking pictures can often be obtained on a sunny day from the Downs looking over the Weald. Because the sun is low in the sky, the light tends to have an orange cast, while the long shadows make objects in a landscape stand out.

Fortunately for us, most holiday-makers only visit Sussex in mid-Summer. Outside this period many country areas slip back into a way of life that hasn't really changed all that much for centuries, while the streets in the towns become pleasant to walk through once more. If you've only seen Arundel or Petworth in August, try visiting them in December; they are completely different places.

You may be surprised at some of the omissions from this book, but many places in Sussex, although well-known, have little to offer the photographer.

Hawkings Hammer Pond, near Horsham

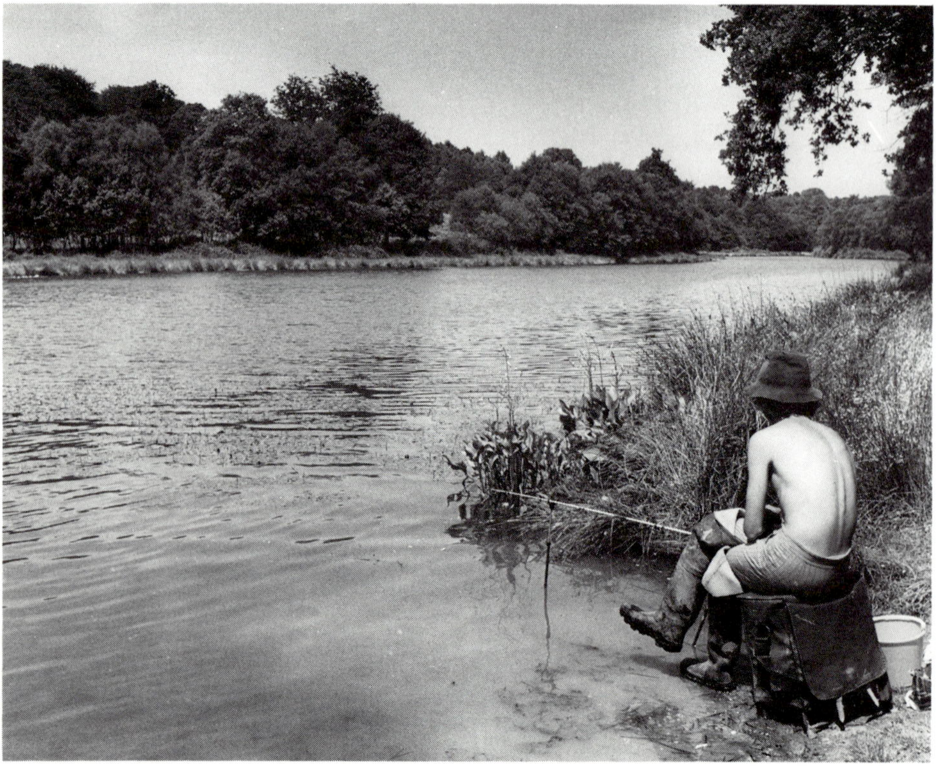

ROUTES FROM LONDON

West Sussex

Starting from Hammersmith Bridge the route follows Castlenau, Rocks Lane, Roehampton Lane and then with a right turn joins the A3, which starts off as the Kingston Bypass and then becomes the Esher Bypass.

Turn left off the Esher Bypass into the A244 (a winding, narrow road) towards Leatherhead. Join the A243, which becomes the Leatherhead Bypass (A24). This joins the Mickleham Bypass, a fine piece of landscaping with views of Box Hill, and becomes the Dorking Bypass, still the A24.

Once past Dorking there is a fast run to Beare Green, where you can branch right on to the A29, a country lane until it starts to follow the Roman Road of Stane Street past the pleasant village of Ockley. Alternatively keep on the A24 past Beare Green to Kingsfold and join the A29 there.

At Billingshurst you carry straight on for Pulborough and Arundel or turn right at the end of the village for Wisborough Green, Petworth and Chichester, a beautiful and often spectacular route.

Central Sussex

Follow the route for West Sussex until you reach Beare Green, when instead of turning right you keep straight on towards Horsham. For the Worthing area take the Horsham Bypass and continue on down the A24.

For a much more pleasant touring route, turn left half-way round the Dorking Bypass into a minor road that goes through Newdigate and Rusper. On the outskirts of Horsham you go over a level-crossing and come to a roundabout; carry on as straight as you can across this. A second roundabout is reached soon after, and here you bear slightly left to reach the main A281. Turn left and after two-and-a-half miles turn right at Monks Gate into a minor road to Nuthurst, where there is a perfect unspoilt pub with roses round the windows and a stone-flagged floor, and on to Partridge Green. Here turn right, then left into the road past Ashurst to Steyning. This is a quiet, beautiful and surprisingly fast way from Dorking.

Brighton

To reach the Brighton area quickly there is no real alternative to the M23, but after crossing the Thames at Vauxhall Bridge the congested part of the A23 can be avoided by turning sharp right as soon as you have passed under the railway bridge, into South Lambeth Road. At Stockwell Tube Station turn right into the A3 (Clapham Road) and after half a mile fork left at Clapham North Tube Station into Bedford Road, which soon becomes Kings Avenue. After two miles fork left into Thornton Avenue and Sternold Avenue.

At the main road (A23) turn right, but keep in the right-hand lane. Fork right into the A216, Mitcham Lane, which becomes first Streatham Road and then London Road. At a triangular junction turn into the A236 (Commonside West) and at the first roundabout keep straight on into the A237. After five-and-a-half quiet miles this joins the main Brighton road (A23), which soon joins the M23.

A pleasant touring route to Brighton with by far the best entry into the town starts at Edenbridge on the Kent/Surrey border. South of the village turn right into the B2028, which passes through Lingfield, Turners Hill and Lindfield on its way towards Haywards Heath. At a fork on the outskirts of the town, keep left and join the B2112 to Ditchling.

Just past Ditchling take a minor left-hand fork to Ditchling Beacon, a steep and winding climb. Once over the hill you come in two miles to a junction. Keep straight on (don't fork left); after running through open suburbs you unexpectedly find yourself at Brighton Pavilion, a surprise entry to the town.

East Sussex

There is no fast route to East Sussex, which has helped preserve its individuality. For the Eastbourne district you can take the Brighton road as far as Sternold Avenue and then carry on down the A23 to Purley Way. At the end of this you join the A22 and keep on it all the way to Eastbourne, passing through East Grinstead and Uckfield on the way. It is probably faster to go to Brighton and then take the A27, which bypasses Lewes and joins the A22 five miles North of Eastbourne.

A slower but more pleasant touring route starts from the Crystal Palace. Drive down Anerley Road, which becomes Elmer's End Road (A214), and keep on this through suburbs until you reach West Wickham. Turn left at the T-junction into Glebe Way (A232) and keep on this for about a mile and a half until you can branch into Baston Manor Way. This joins Heathfield Road (A233), which takes you to Westerham, passing Biggin Hill on the way.

At Westerham you turn left and take the first right (B2026) to Edenbridge, Hartfield and a junction with the A22 at Maresfield, just above Uckfield. From then on take the main road to Eastbourne.

Bosham

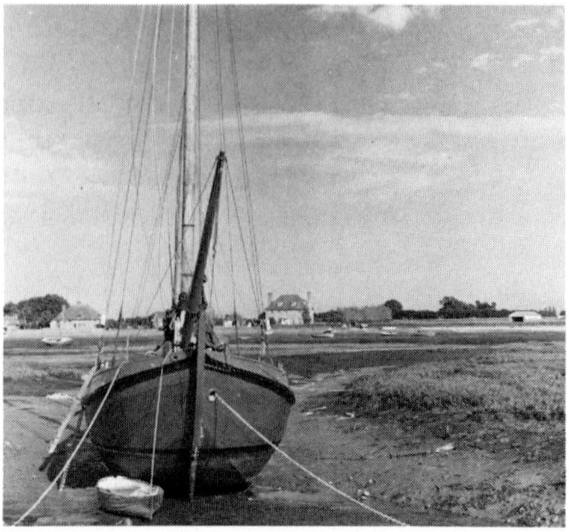

Hastings

For Hastings, reach the A20 either by crossing the Thames to the Elephant and Castle roundabout, where you join the A2 and then the A20 at New Cross, a dreary route, or else by way of the Blackwall Tunnel. Turn right on to the A224, the Orpington Bypass, and join the A21, which becomes the fast Sevenoaks Bypass. At Pembury the A21 becomes narrow, winding and very congested in Summer, but if at Flimwell you turn left at the traffic lights to Hawkhurst and then right at another set of lights in the centre of the village, you can join the A229, a Roman Road which is fast and empty and passes through beautiful country and the show village of Sedlescombe to join the A21 some five miles North of Hastings.

For Rye turn left at Cripp's Corner, about a mile and a half before you get to Sedlescombe, on to the B2089, which runs along a ridge with good views on both sides and brings you conveniently into Rye by a large car park.

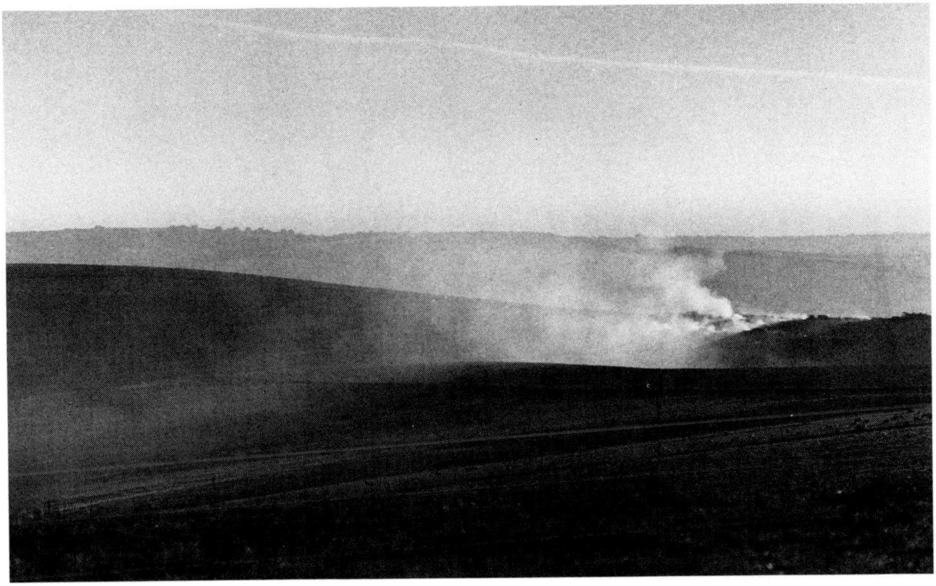

MAPS AND THE PHOTOGRAPHER

This book guides you to some of the places in Sussex which will supply material for your camera, but the real fun lies in trying to find better locations for yourself. The best way to do this is to plan ahead with the aid of an Ordnance Survey map.

The most useful ones are the 1:50,000 'Rangefinder' series, Sussex being covered by 187, 188, 197, 198 and 199. The 1:25,000 'Pathfinders' show more detail and are easier to read but each covers an area of about 6¼ x 12½ miles – fine if you are walking, but you need a lot of them if you are motoring.

Having found on the map the place you are going to visit, the first thing to do is to see which way it faces, so that you can check the direction of the light at various times of the day. Though you don't often want to take pictures with the sun coming from directly behind the camera, one can generalize and say that a building or view that faces East is best photographed in the morning, while a West-facing one should be taken in the evening.

If the subject faces South it can be taken either early or late (but not in the middle of the day when the lighting would be flat); if North, it is wise to choose either a sunny day with big cumulus clouds that will reflect light back into the shadows or else a dull or hazy day when diffused light comes from all directions.

Once you have some idea of the time of day when you will be taking pictures, you study the map to find possible camera positions. The contours will show which is the high ground and which is the low, and

(above) Stubble burning

the location of footpaths and bridlepaths to take you there are also given. You can locate the woods that may obstruct or, if you are lucky, add to the scene and can tell if the trees are coniferous or deciduous – the latter will be bare in Winter and early Spring and the view may be clear.

You can look for a stream or lake to add foreground interest, notice features such as windmills or towers, tell which areas are swampy or reed-covered – the longer you study the map the more you see. Eventually you build up a picture of the place in your mind; though much of it may be wrong when you get there, you will at least have decided on several alternative camera positions and have some kind of working plan. You won't waste time wondering what to do next.

Hop picking

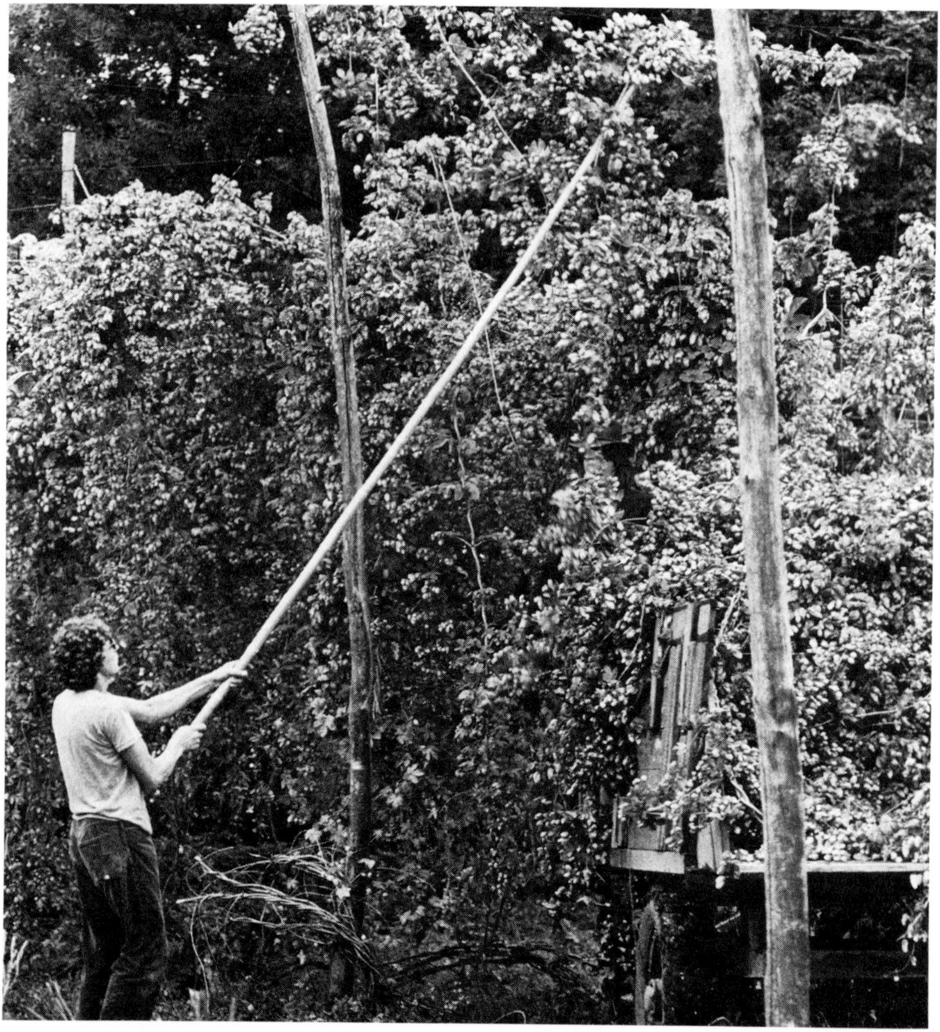

WHAT APPARATUS TO CARRY

In short, the absolute minimum. It's easy enough to think of good reasons for carrying every imaginable item of photographic equipment, but the successful photographer is the one who knows what is really essential and what to leave at home.

If you are travelling by car, you are of course free to take the lot – lenses, filters, spare bodies, tripods, extension tubes, flash guns and so on – even though you'll only use a very small part of the total. However, carrying equipment in a car is quite an art.

Never place a camera, lens or films in the glove locker, for instance, since in many cases this becomes a cross between an oven and a vibration box; films suffer from the heat while screws and lens elements rattle loose. If driving by yourself, rest cameras or gadget bags on the seat beside you, looping the straps over the backrest. If you have to place them on the rear seat, you may not be able to anchor the straps, in which case keep the apparatus in place with coats and jackets to prevent it from sliding on to the floor when braking hard.

Most important of all, remember to lock all equipment in the boot or at least conceal it from view every time you leave the car, no matter where you are. Cameras and lenses are just the kind of small, high-value articles irresistible to a thief and rarely traced.

Films are best carried in a stout cardboard box with a lid. This should never be placed where the sun can fall on it, and loose films should never be left on the rear-window ledge where temperatures can reach surprising heights.

However, you'll never get good pictures until you leave the car and start walking. Then you are in the same position as the person who has to carry his equipment by bus or train, so it's wise to take the absolute minimum in the first place.

The importance of cutting down weight cannot be over-stressed. It is pointless to carry a tripod unless you know you are going to tackle a subject for which it is essential. The same applies to very long-focus lenses, flash guns, extension tubes, etc.

Many experts, in fact, like to carry a camera with a fixed, non-interchangeable lens because they then feel free to concentrate on the things that really matter – the lighting, composition and timing – instead of worrying about what lens or other apparatus to use. They just get on with taking the picture and, of course, hardly notice the weight or bulk of what they are carrying.

On the other hand, if you are using colour film you normally try to fill the frame exactly with the subject and so a single lens reflex with a wide angle and a long-focus lens will be needed. I myself like to use such a camera with a 50mm standard lens with a large maximum aperture (useful in poor light) and with a 24mm lens (approximately half the focal length of the standard one) and a 100mm (twice the focal length) as alternatives, but many people prefer a 28mm and a 135mm – it is a matter of individual taste. Try to have lenses that all take the same size filter; then you need only carry a single one.

Alternatively you can use a single zoom lens with a range of focal lengths between 28 and 80mm, which will cover most subjects. This makes for very relaxed photography, since no time is wasted in lens-changing and bulk is at a minimum. More ambitious photographers may carry instead a 70-150mm and a 24-40mm zoom, thus covering a wider range.

For black and white work a medium-yellow or an orange filter will be needed, the latter giving bolder and more dramatic skies but needing a five-times exposure increase as against a two-times for the yellow. With colour film a 'skylight' filter can prevent a blue cast on dull days.

For dark interiors and for lenses with a very long focal length, a tripod will be useful, though it can often be replaced by a lighter and more easily carried monopod. Make sure it is really rigid and beware of soft rubber feet that can cause a jelly-like shake.

A medium-speed film (about 100 ASA) will be found most useful for general outdoor photography. For hand-held interiors or in dull weather, switch to a fast (400 ASA) material. All colour films vary slightly

A soft, light gadget bag will be much easier to carry than a stiff, heavy one but may not protect the contents so well. A shoulder pad on the carrying strap will spread the load and stop it from sliding off your shoulder. Huge bags full of equipment are impressive but impractical; on the other hand, they should always be big enough for an empty space to be left into which you can deposit the lens you have removed from your camera.

The basic thing to remember is that an outfit that seems reasonably light and compact in your sitting room may become a monstrous burden after you have climbed a few hills; nothing kills enthusiasm for photography more than an aching left shoulder. If at all in doubt about an item of equipment, leave it at home.

Balcombe Viaduct (right)

Hopfield nets (below)

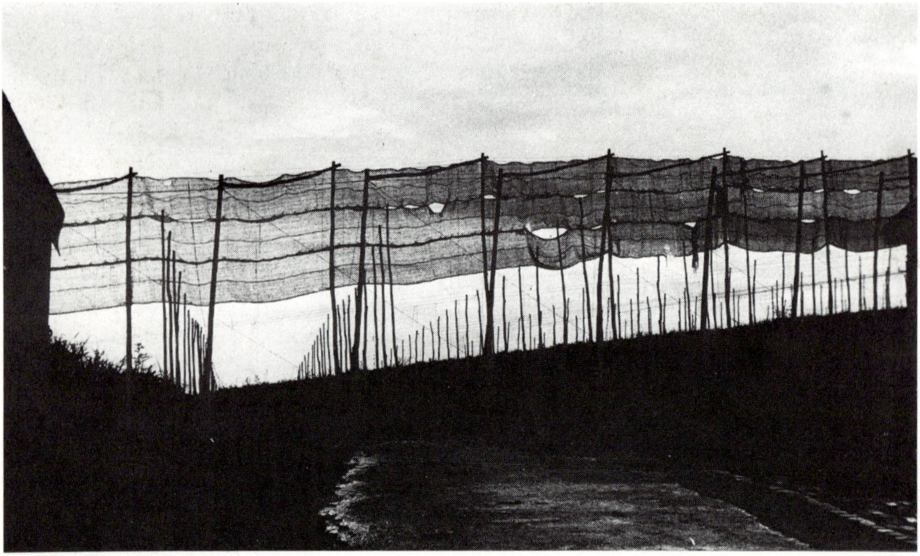

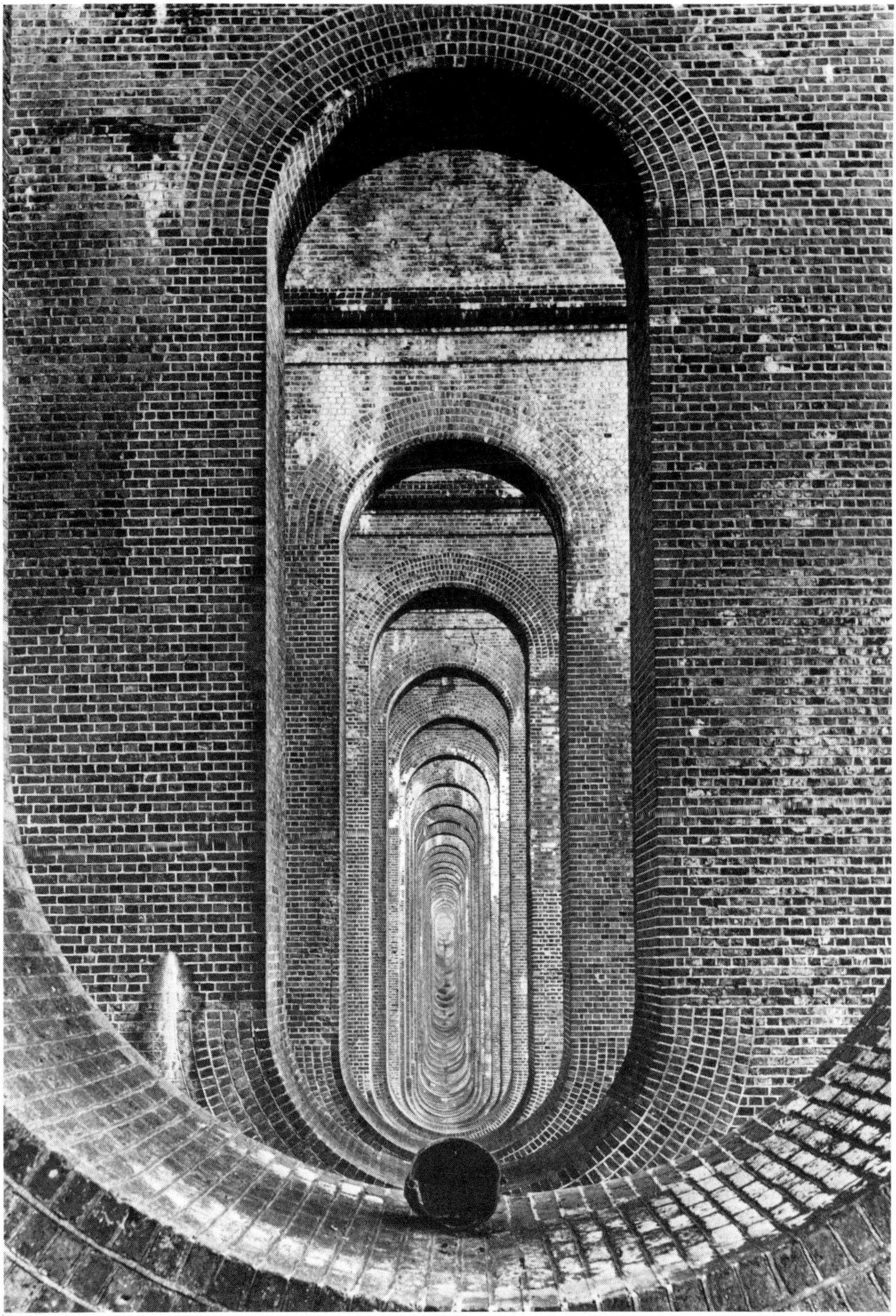

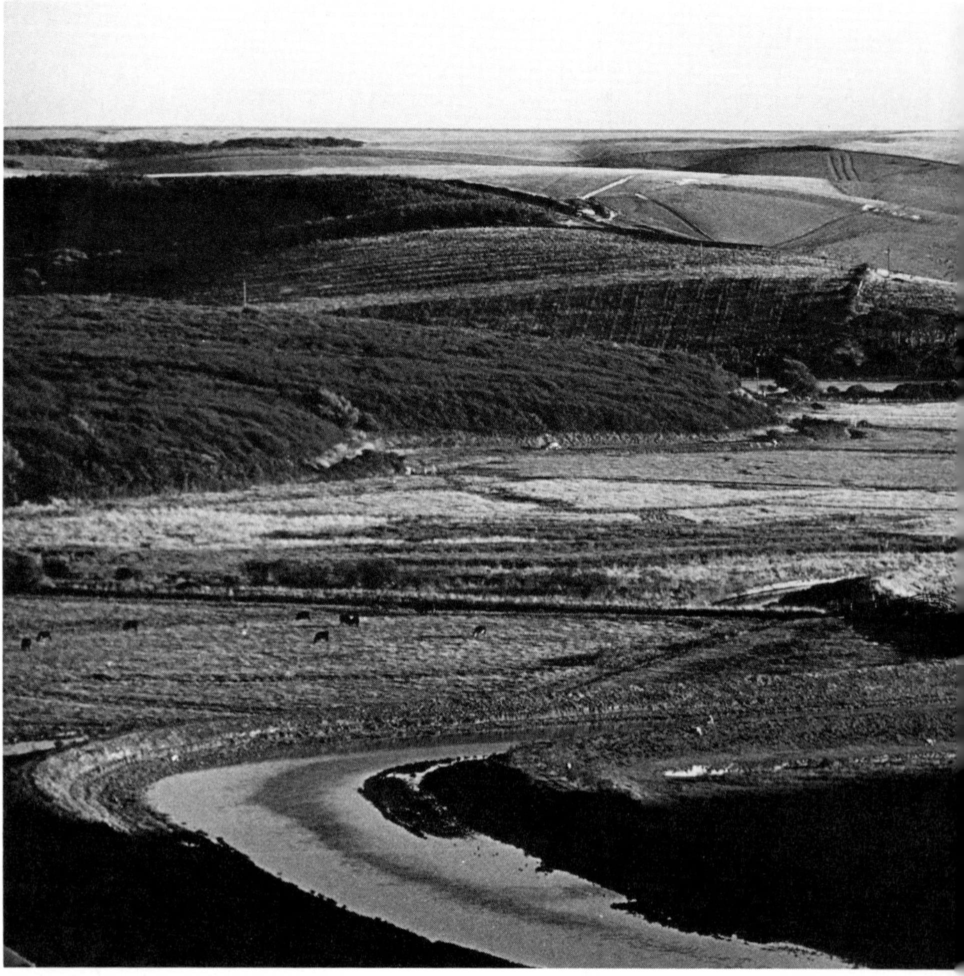

Alciston

One of the string of villages at the foot of the Downs on the Northern side, it is a very quiet and extremely attractive place. The turning off the A27 first passes a pub called Rose Cottage, where on Good Friday there is a skipping race (adult) of unknown origin, then comes Court House Farm next to the 13th-century flint church. In the farmyard is a barn that belonged to the Grange of Battle Abbey (the monks would come here for rest and relaxation); it is one of the longest in Sussex (170 feet) and someone with time on their hands once calculated that there are 50,000 tiles on the roof. There is also a large 14th century dovecote.

The churchyard is round, which makes one think it is built on a prehistoric barrow. The lane past it ends at a farmyard that for me sums up Sussex – flint walls, pond, trees and the Downs beyond.

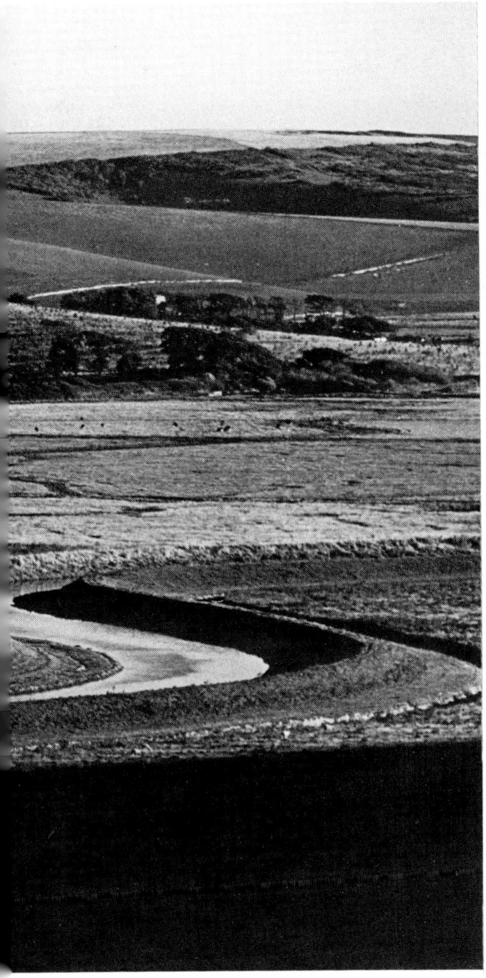

From 'Up and Over', Alfriston

In the village the Old Postman's Cottage, thatched, makes an obvious picture.

Alfriston

Alfriston is the perfect example of the way in which a place can be spoilt by over-popularity. Years ago someone called it 'The Most Beautiful Village in England', a kiss of death that has taken away its self-respect. Tens of thousands of tourists come here in Summer because they feel they ought to, and as a result it has become full of restaurants, boutiques and curio-shoppes with names too embarrassing to mention. Unlike the equally touristy Rye it did not have a strong enough life of its own to stand out against the visitors and has resigned itself to living off them.

Not all that long ago Alfriston really was an interesting and beautiful village, following a traditional way of life. As late as 1932 a local shepherd was buried clutching in his hand a tuft of wool to explain why he had not been able to go to church on Sunday. There was one of the only two market crosses in Sussex to survive the Reformation – vandalized by Canadian troops in the First World War and finally demolished by a lorry in 1955, it is now just a re-built stump.

The Star Inn ('The Star of Bethlehem' when it was built as a hostel for pilgrims going to the shrine of Richard of Chichester in the 14th century) has on the outside unique carvings of bishops, animals and St Michael slaying a basilisk, inevitably called 'St George and the Dragon'. The figurehead of a Dutch ship wrecked in the Cuckmere around 1690 has been added to the woodwork. On the whole it is the best timber-framed house in East Sussex.

The Market Cross Inn was genuinely frequented by a particularly vicious gang of murderous smugglers; the main street has many fine half-timbered houses; the George Inn has Tudor wall-paintings; and the Downs rise on either side. It should be ideal, but my advice is to avoid it if at all possible during the Season, when it is busier and more crowded than Piccadilly Circus.

Outside that time it can still be a delight. At the Southern end of the large and perfect green stands the 14th-century

Clergy House built for visiting priests. Thatched and half-timbered with an in-filling of wattle and daub, it was a labourer's cottage when it was the first building bought by the National Trust in 1896 – for £10. It can be visited from April to October from 11 to 6. An effective photo of it framed by a tree and with open country beyond can be taken from the nearby graveyard.

The church, built like a number of others in the district on a circular Saxon burial mound, is large, majestic and rather dull inside. To the North of it a long wooden bridge spans the Cuckmere and takes you by footpath to the sixteen-foot-square Lullington Church, said to be the smallest in England but in fact just a part of the chancel of a much bigger building.

By climbing the Downs to the East of Alfriston you can obtain good views of the village with its red roofs and church in the morning, while in the evening a climb up to the West provides an equally good location, the tourists and traffic becoming invisible.

Amberley

If you had never heard of Amberley and stumbled across it by chance early in Spring or Autumn you'd probably be enchanted. You might find some of the thatched cottages a bit twee and over-preserved, but the 12th-century church is impressive and the castle on the cliff overwhelming. You'd think it the perfect Sussex village.

The trouble is that people have been stumbling across it for over a century and Amberley has become an artist's and photographer's cliché. In Summer they arrive in coachloads along with the other tourists, and the results hang in every exhibition of watercolours or photographs; because its beauty is so over-familiar many people refuse to set foot in the place.

Yet out of season it is a very interesting village indeed. Walk past the church, past the Bishop's Castle and out on to the Wild Brooks that criss-cross the flat plain below the cliff. Go as far as you can (you'll probably need rubber boots) and then turn and look back. The huge castle wall stretching along the low cliff menaces the whole area and in stormy weather gives an uncanny, sinister feeling. You can obtain impressive pictures in any weather, with any lens, at any distance, especially if you include one of the Brooks in the foreground.

Why 'Wild Brooks'? Some say it's a corruption of Weald Brooks, some because they overflow in winter, but I think it's the way in which they run in all directions.

Back in the village, provided you have chosen a tripper-free day, you can wander around happily enough taking the same pictures of the cottages and the church as did your great-grandfather. You can also obtain that once popular English meal that is becoming a rarity, afternoon tea.

Arundel

The further away you are from Arundel the better it looks. Seen from the high ground to the East on a misty Autumn morning it appears a photographer's dream. The turrets of the castle have a backdrop of beech woods, a huge foreign-looking church dominates even the castle, the thousand-acre Park stretches to the North and the Arun runs at the foot of the hill. Take pictures from this area with your longest-focus lens and don't bother about a filter – it may well destroy the romantic effect of the haze.

Even from the bridge over the Arun the town still appears promising, with the

South Downs Way (right)

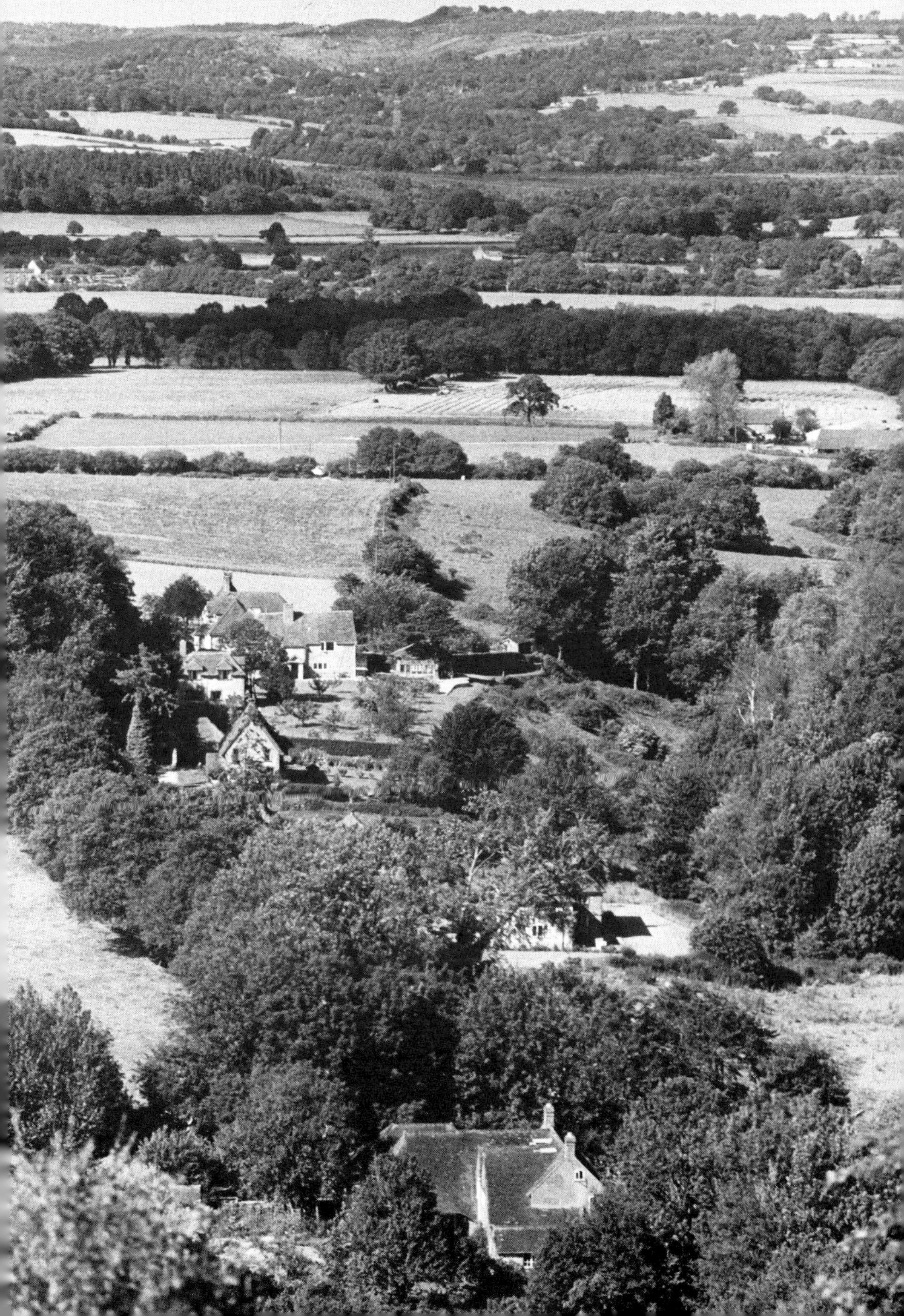

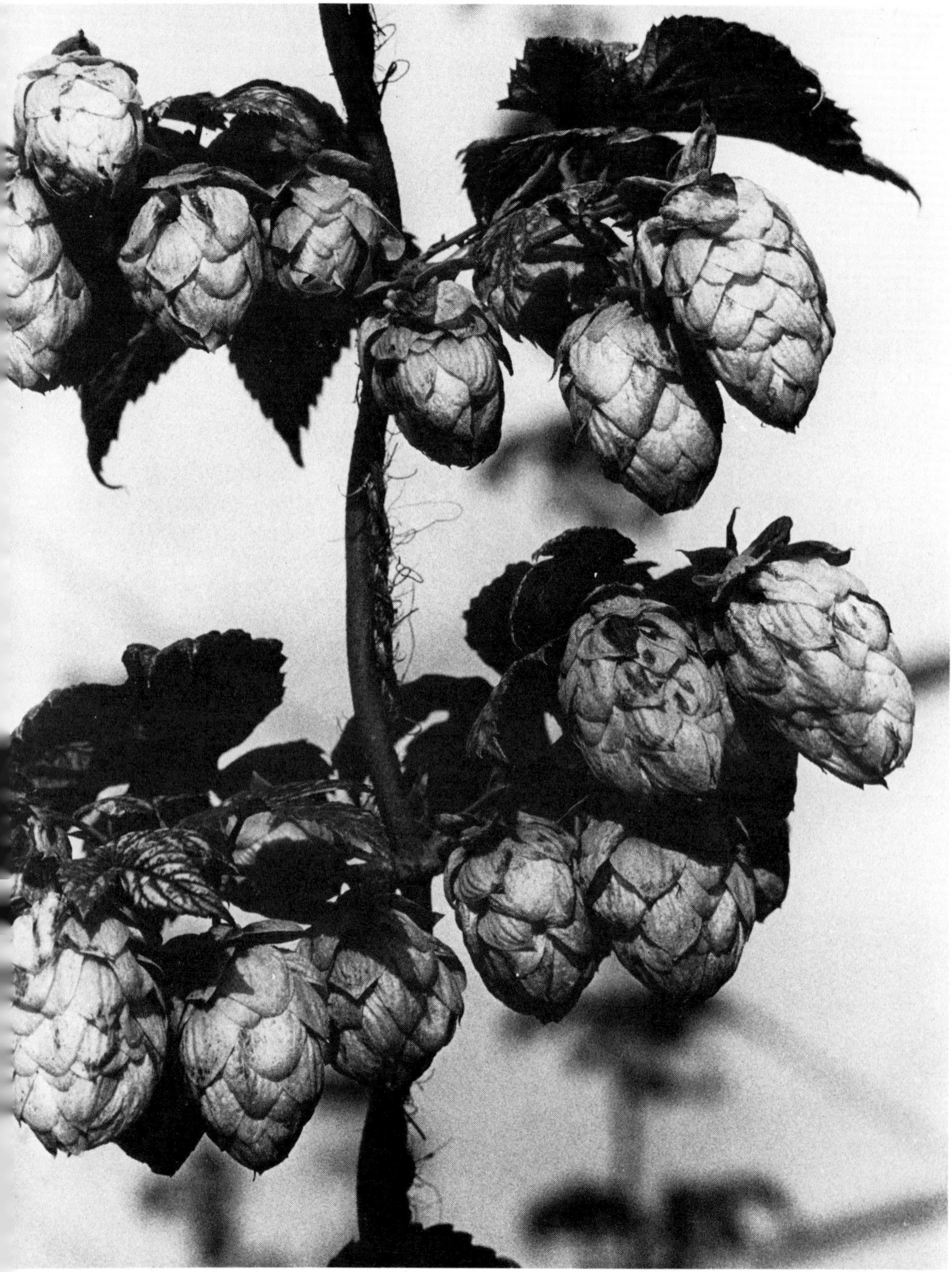

High Street rising steeply up to the castle at the top of the hill, but on closer inspection you will find almost the whole of Arundel is Victorian and much of it mock-mediaeval. Most of the castle dates from 1890 while the vast Roman Catholic Church of St Philip Neri was designed in a kind of 13th-century French Gothic style by the inventor of the Hansom cab; the most impressive thing about it is its size, which would have been even bigger if weak foundations had not prevented the erection of a huge tower and spire.

The castle, and some would say the town, has been the property of the Howards, Dukes of Norfolk, since 1580. Most of it was destroyed during the Civil War by the Roundheads, who hauled cannon on to the tower of the nearby parish church and kept up a bombardment for seventeen days. Attempts were made at restoration in the 18th century but it was not until 1890 that the odd decision was made to build a Victorian castle in the style of the 14th century.

It has been unkindly compared to a Scottish railway station, but parts of it are original – the inner gateway, the outer barbican and the keep, for instance. A long and narrow spiral staircase leads to the roof of the latter from which, and from the battlements, there is a good view of the Arun winding to the sea five miles away and of the Downs to the East.

The castle is open from Easter to October from about 1 till 5. The interior reminds one of those embarrassing tournaments they used to hold in early-Victorian times, all flags and banners, impossibly tall beamed ceilings and a 'Barons' Hall' with huge empty fireplaces. From the castle grounds you can enter one wing of the parish church and see the 'Fitzalan Chapel', which brings us to a very odd situation.

In 1877, after a long and bitter lawsuit, it was decided that the church's Eastern arm belonged to the Catholic Duke of Norfolk, who promptly built a very rough brick wall to cut it off from the remaining, Protestant, section of the church, an arrangement straight out of Jonathan Swift. Only recently has the wall been replaced by a glass screen; the division is worth recording with a wide-angle lens, since as far as I know it is unique.

The Fitzalan Chapel, which cannot be reached through the church, is like a museum of monuments – there are almost too many fine examples to grasp. Perhaps the most interesting, and most macabre, is the tomb of John, the seventh earl, who had his leg shot off by a culverin during the French Wars in 1434, a very early example of the use of cannon in battle. He lies on top of the tomb in armour while his skeleton lies in an open space below. Any one of the tombs would be worth visiting if it were on its own in a country church, but together they make too rich a dish.

The town itself is largely Victorian, though there are some good Georgian facades in the High Street which leads downhill to the Norfolk Arms, a splendid brick coaching inn with the name, in contemporary gold lettering on a white background, worth photographing by itself.

From the towpath that runs upstream along the Arun there are good views of the town, the church and the castle, perhaps with the river and a boat or two in the foreground. Mill Road leads in the same direction past Swanbourne Lake in the vast Arundel Park, then past a Wildlife Reserve and at the Black Rabbit pub a lane turns towards South Stoke; from the pub all the way to the village Arundel makes a superb picture.

The fifty-acre Wildlife Park has over a thousand swans, geese, ducks and other wild birds, and hides are provided for close-up viewing and photography. A lens with a focal length of 200 or 300mm will

Hops (left)

be most useful and great patience is usually needed. When a bird arrives, you will have to work fast; there won't be time to alter stops and shutter speeds, and an 'Automatic' camera is a decided advantage. If the exposure on your camera is set 'manually', do this right at the start and leave it set unless the light changes dramatically. All your concentration will be needed for focusing and composing the picture.

Arundel Park itself is open always and provides plenty of opportunities for the landscape photographer, especially when Autumn brings its browns and golds. Two miles long, there are many paths to follow and you can return from Swanbourne Lake to the Main Lodge at the top of the High Street.

Thanks to a bypass, Arundel is now the peaceful and secure place it once was. The castle is still a great tourist attraction in the Summer, but the photographer will find it better to visit the town in Spring or Autumn when the trees are less likely to obscure the long-distance views.

Berwick

People go to Berwick mainly to see the murals in the 12th-century church, painted during the War by three refugees from the Bloomsbury Group, Duncan Grant, Vanessa Bell and her son Quentin. They show biblical scenes in contemporary terms, Sussex people of the 1940s in a Sussex setting. It is forbidden to photograph them; it is tempting to think that this was at the request of the artists since the figures are sentimental, stilted and quite inferior to their normal work.

In the churchyard there is a Saxon burial mound with a war memorial on top of it, a nice example of continuity. From a footpath on the far side there is a good view of the Downs.

The best thing in the village is the Cricketers Arms, an ideal cottage-pub at the end of a stone-flagged path that leads through a garden. It has literally been featured on the lids of many chocolate boxes but in summer, especially with someone sitting on the bench outside, makes an irresistible picture.

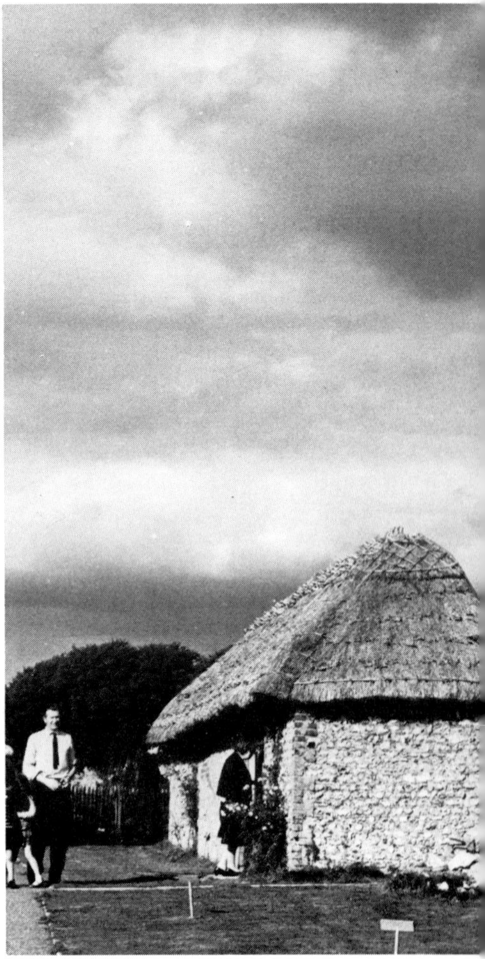

The Roman Villa, Bignor

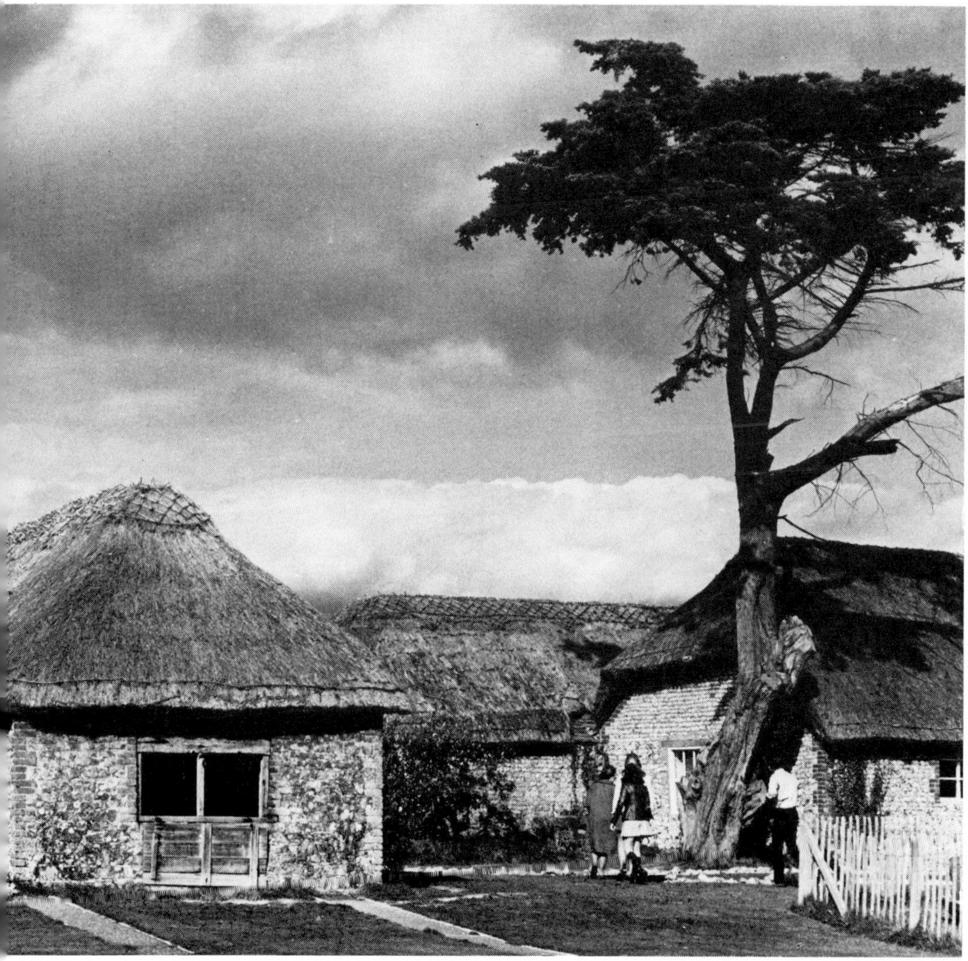

Bignor

In 1811 a farmer named Tupper was ploughing a field called the Berry or Bury that legend said covered a 'Roman Town'. The plough struck a large stone and Tupper stooped to lift it out of the way. Underneath lay a dancing girl, admittedly a mosaic one but nevertheless astonishing in that remote place at the foot of the Downs. He had the sense to report the find to the local Big House and the site was excavated over a period of eight years.

The Roman Villa must have belonged to a very wealthy man, for it covered 4½ acres and was the centre of a 1,900-acre farm. The comfort and luxury would be hard to match today – 60 or 70 compartments, underfloor central heating, a bath block with dressing room and hot, warm and cold rooms, huge mosaic pavements created by a craftsman imported from Switzerland, a location close to Stane Street (the main London to Chichester road) and with superb views of the Downs as far as Chanctonbury. The estate workers, of course, lived in much more humble conditions in an outer courtyard away from the main building – things don't really change much.

Today you reach Bignor by turning off the A29 at Bury, passing through pleasant West Burton, where from time to time they have very enjoyable ploughing matches, and finally reaching the village, scattered around a square of lanes, after 2½ miles.

The Roman Villa (open March to October, Tuesday to Sunday and on Mondays in August, 10 to 6.30) lies on your right just before you get to the village. The remains are covered by a series of thatched wooden huts which, oddly enough, must look very like the dwellings of the Saxons who followed the Roman Occupation. Inside you will find tessellated pavements in remarkable condition – Venus and some cherubs dressed as gladiators, Ganymede and the eagle, a wonderfully cold-looking head depicting Winter, Medusa with fourteen snakes – and this is but a selection of what still remains below the earth.

The museum is owned by Tupper's great-great-grandson and lies in a valley which is still untouched – the view, including Stane Street, is that seen by the Romans. When photographing the pavements, try to raise your camera as high as possible to avoid distortion and use, if possible, 400 ASA colour film. Flash does not give very satisfactory results.

At the East end of the village stands 'the Old Shop', a 15th-century yeoman's cottage that is miraculously unrestored. A wonderful mixture of textures – thatch, timber, brick, plaster and flints – it was once the village store and is irresistible. No matter how often you have photographed it (and it is one of the most overphotographed subjects in West Sussex), you feel compelled to have another go whenever you see it, since it changes appearance so much with the quality of the light. A wide-angle lens is useful.

From Bignor you can continue along twisting, narrow lanes to Sutton and Bar-

The Old Post Office, Bignor

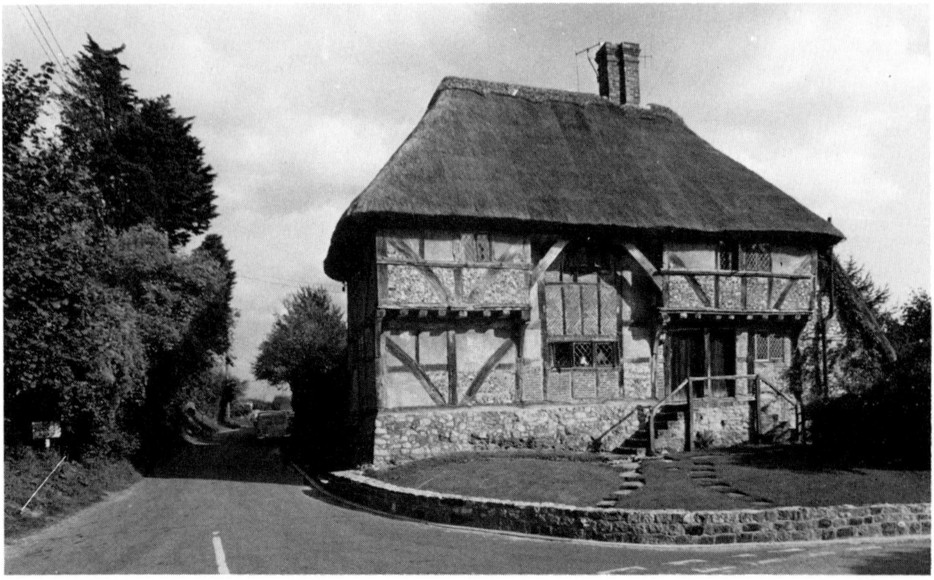

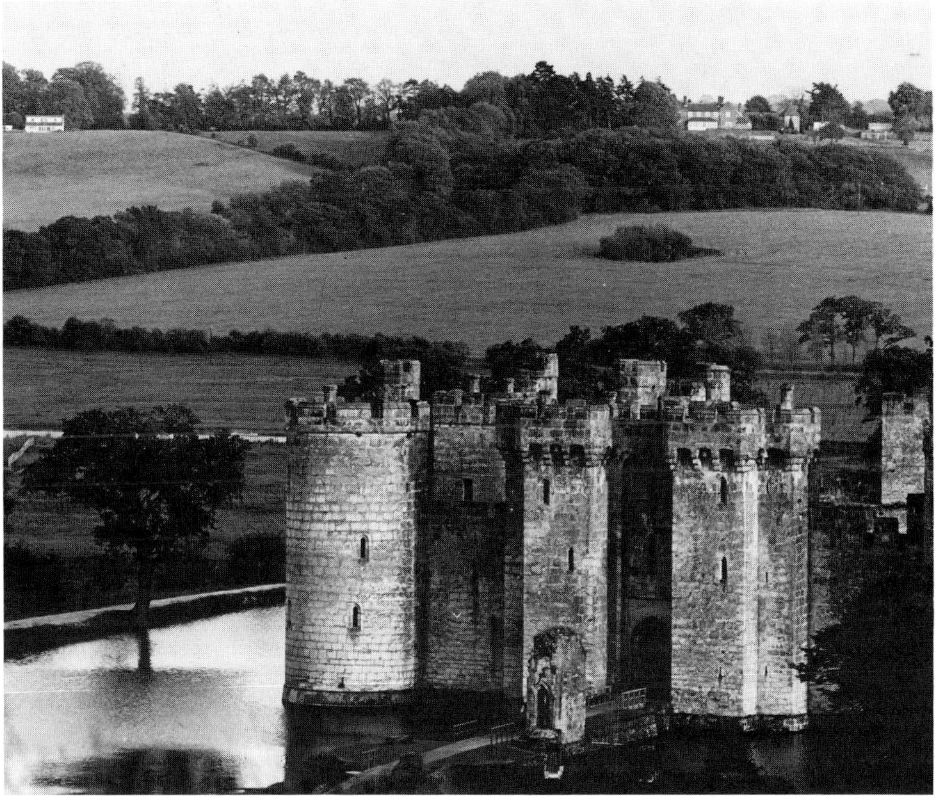

lavington, both picture-postcard villages with the Downs as a background, but remember you are driving along what are basically footpaths which until recently never saw heavier traffic than a herd of cows. In Summer they can become very congested indeed and great care and patience are essential.

Bodiam Castle

Judging by the hundreds of thousands of pictures taken there every year, all film manufacturers owe a debt of gratitude to the 14th-century Bodiam Castle. Though

Bodiam Castle from Court Lodge

the most obvious and over-photographed subject in Sussex, it retains an extraordinary romantic charm no matter how often visited, even though the famous water-lilies in the moat have been cleared away by some visual vandal.

Arrive at dawn and you have the place to yourself apart from some sheep for at least a couple of hours. The standard and very picturesque view is from the South, with the castle framed by the branches of a tree at the edge of the moat – it is best taken with a wide-angle lens, perhaps a 24 or a 28mm. As a curiosity, photograph the Second-World-War blockhouse with the castle as a background; neither, for-

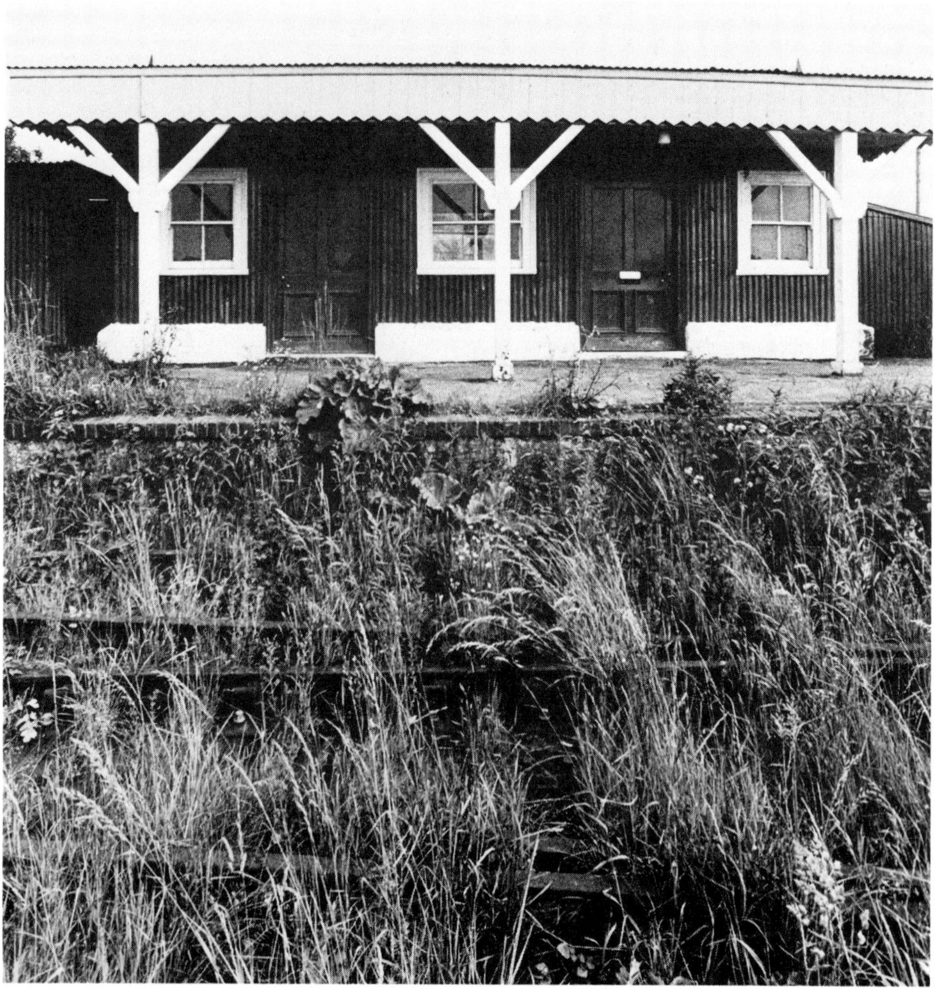

Bodiam Station, deserted

tunately, ever saw action but they make a nice contrast.

In the right-hand corner of the field behind the moat a stile and a path lead uphill towards Court Lodge; from the brow you can look down on the castle, obtaining a tight composition with a 135mm lens. However, you will be shooting against the light and the building will be recorded simply as a silhouette if the sky is clear, so this angle is best used on a day with hazy sunshine when the light is diffused or when big cumulous clouds reflect light back into the shadows.

Cross the bridge over the Rother past the deserted and very photogenic Bodiam Station, once used by the old-time hop-pickers, and turn left up to the over-neat village of Ewhurst Green. Before you reach its centre you'll find a gate on the left leading into a downhill footpath. From this path distant views of the castle and its

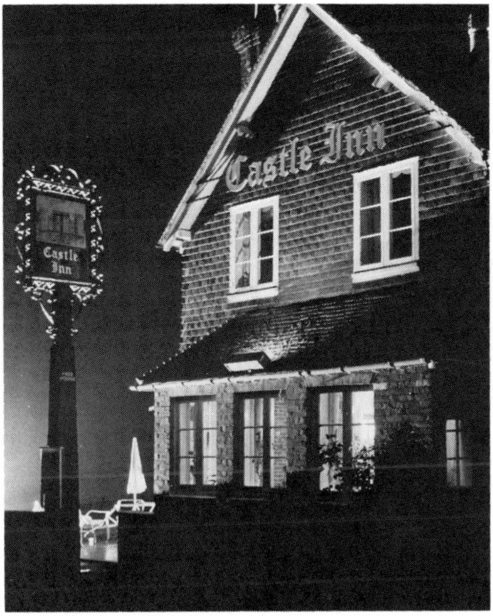

Castle Inn, Bodiam

surroundings can be taken if you have a lens with a focal length of 200mm or more. If using colour film a 'haze' filter will be needed; if black and white, an orange or green. In the early morning there may be too much mist from the river, but the picture can be taken at most times of the day, especially in the late evening (you are shooting from the South), and without interruption.

Back in Bodiam, buy a ticket to the interior of the castle from the friendly and very knowledgeable custodian and photograph the original portcullis, a 15th-century bombard and the view of the Rother Valley from the battlements.

To enjoy Bodiam you must get there early. After 9.30 especially in Summer, it changes abruptly from a magic, deserted castle to a busy tourist attraction, so get your close-up photography done before then and leave it to the visitors for the rest of the day while you concentrate on the long-distance views.

Bosham

Drive west from Chichester along the Portsmouth road and after some three miles turn left towards 'Old Bosham'. Deservedly the most visited of the Chichester Harbour villages, a photographer should go there out of season, since it becomes hopelessly overcrowded in Summer, and when the tide is high. Then the water comes right up to the houses (many of which have mooring rings on their walls) while if you visit the pub you can look out of the window and see the yachts and swans sailing by, seemingly at arm's length. The sun sparkles on the miniature waves and Bosham reminds you of a softer and more prosperous Cornish fishing village.

At low tide a transformation takes place and the harbour becomes a wide expanse of mud and green slime – even the smart boats appear derelict. However, near Quay Meadow, preserved by the National Trust and very beautiful, there is a notice board showing the times of the tide, the strength of the wind and other matters of interest to the hundreds of amateur sailors who potter around Chichester Harbour. If you have the bad luck to arrive at Bosham when the tide is low, study the board and come back when it is high; the effort is well worth while.

The best pictures of the village, the boats and the harbour are obtained by taking one of the two roads that go around the Southern side of the inlet. A little care is needed here since the lower road is submerged at high tide – watching the consternation of visitors who have parked their cars there while they explored the area is a local amusement. At low tide the road is quite safe though patchy with seaweed.

Even in Summer few people come round to the Southern side, from which you get a splendid view of the flint, brick and tile houses lining the water's edge with the

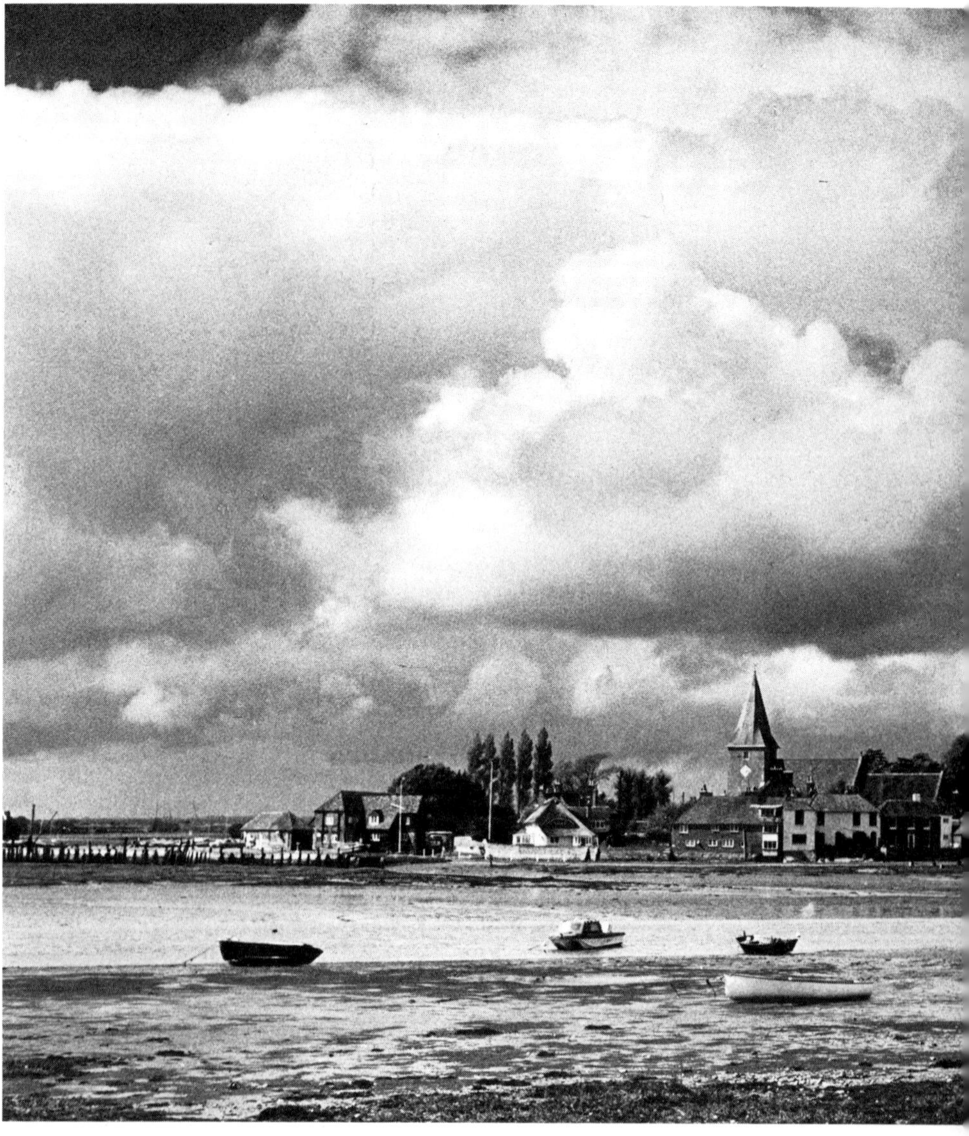

Bosham from the South

Saxon church rising above them and the distant Downs behind. A medium long-focus lens is ideal, with an orange filter to emphasize the clouds if working in black and white. Try to include a boat or better still someone working on them in the foreground to give a sense of perspective.

Back in the village, walk along the short and narrow High Street to the church. It is said to be set on the site of a 4th-century Roman basilica and the layout certainly agrees with this.

When Wilfred of York visited Bosham in 681 he found there the first Christian

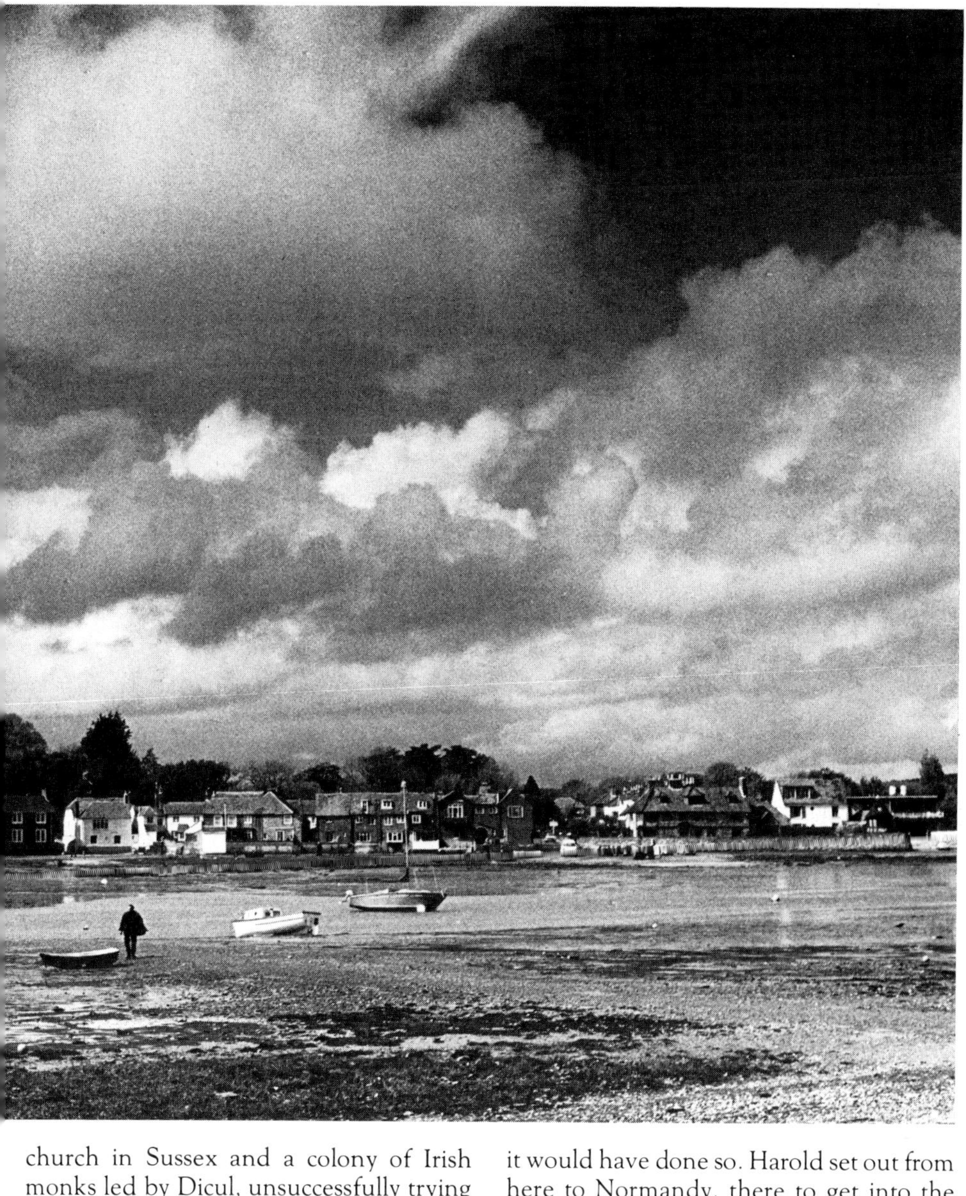

church in Sussex and a colony of Irish monks led by Dicul, unsuccessfully trying to convert the heathen Saxons. Canute buried his little daughter in the church (you can photograph her grave) and it was probably at the harbour's edge that he ordered the tide to go back – I've always thought that if he had timed matters better it would have done so. Harold set out from here to Normandy, there to get into the clutches of William the Conqueror, and is shown in the Bayeux Tapestry riding to Mass in Bosham Church. It is surprising that such a small place has played such an important part in history.

At the bases of the columns in the Northern

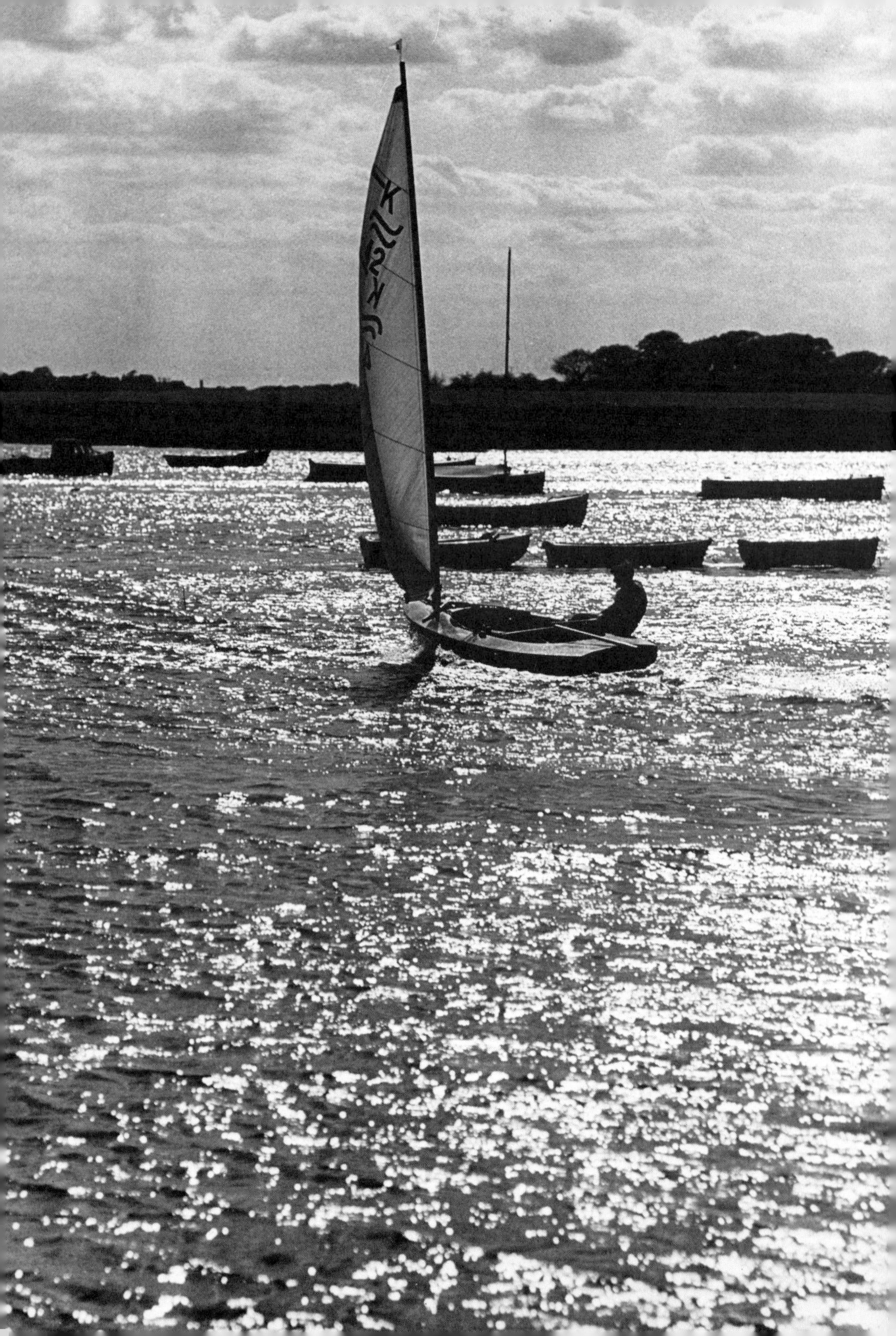

arcade of the church you will find some very photographable eel-like creatures (you'll probably need flash), while if you are a tombstone fancier it is well worth exploring the graveyard.

However, most people come here for the sailing. The nice thing about yachts is that no matter if the sun is behind you or facing you they still make a good picture, but in the latter case try to position the sun behind one of the sails to avoid too much glare. With backlighting the tip of each wavelet sparkles, so include plenty of water in the foreground. The Bosham swans are famous, but a picture of a single one is boring – wait till they go by in stately convoy and include an interesting background.

Bosham at the Western end of Sussex balances Rye at the Eastern tip. Both are beautiful, but both are too popular.

Brighton

Brighton is a bright and sparkling town with a lightness and luminescence in the air that only comes when the sea is close. At any time of the year a visit is a delight – there is a carefree, relaxed atmosphere that is hard to describe but which never fails.

The photographer can choose from a number of Brightons – Flash Modern, Preserved Regency, Sin City, Day-Trip Vulgar, Phoney Antique or Run Down. On the whole I prefer the latter.

Years ago someone described the town as 'a dirty lace ruffle'. At the time the decayed, dilapidated elegance of the Regency and early-Victorian houses that had been rushed up for the waves of Londoners who wanted to live near Royalty by the sea had a slightly sinister charm, but in the centre of the town they have been largely replaced by standardized modern blocks and shopping centres. However, the *Brighton Rock* of Graham Greene can still be found, though the race gangs have disappeared – as a child I knew some of the Italian members and, once away from their working environment of touts and bookies, found them embarrassingly kind and considerate. To get some idea of the Brighton of the Thirties, go up St James Street to the East of the Pavilion and explore the side streets – you'll have to be quick since the developers are moving in and gentrifying the area.

The most relaxing way to arrive in Brighton from London is undoubtedly by train, since Brighton has not really come to terms with the car. Leaving the pleasant Victorian station, bear right as you cross the forecourt into Surrey Street. This becomes North Gardens and then Crown Gardens, charming traffic-free alleys, and then an even

Dinghy sailing at Bosham (left)

Black Lion Alley, Brighton

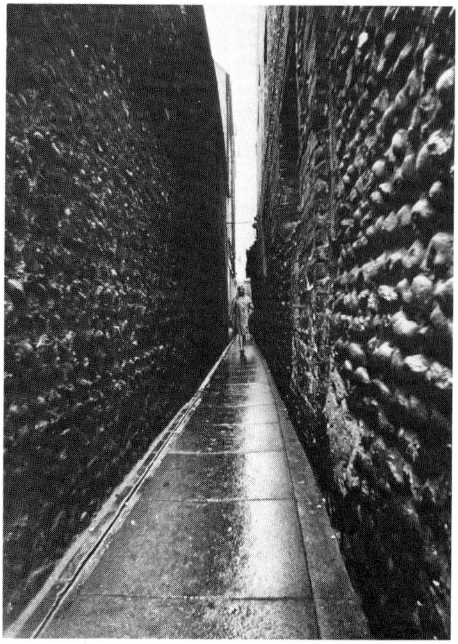

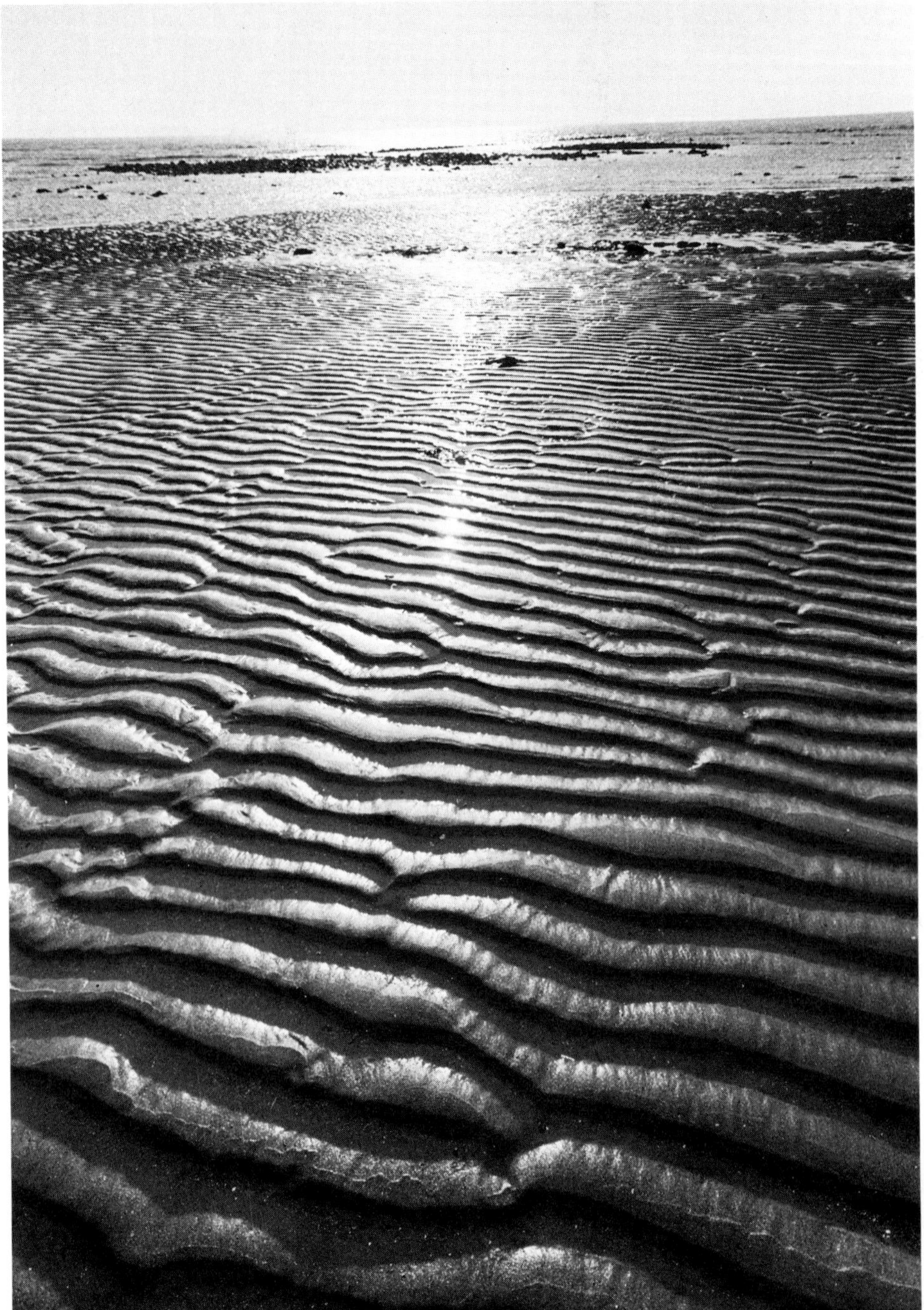

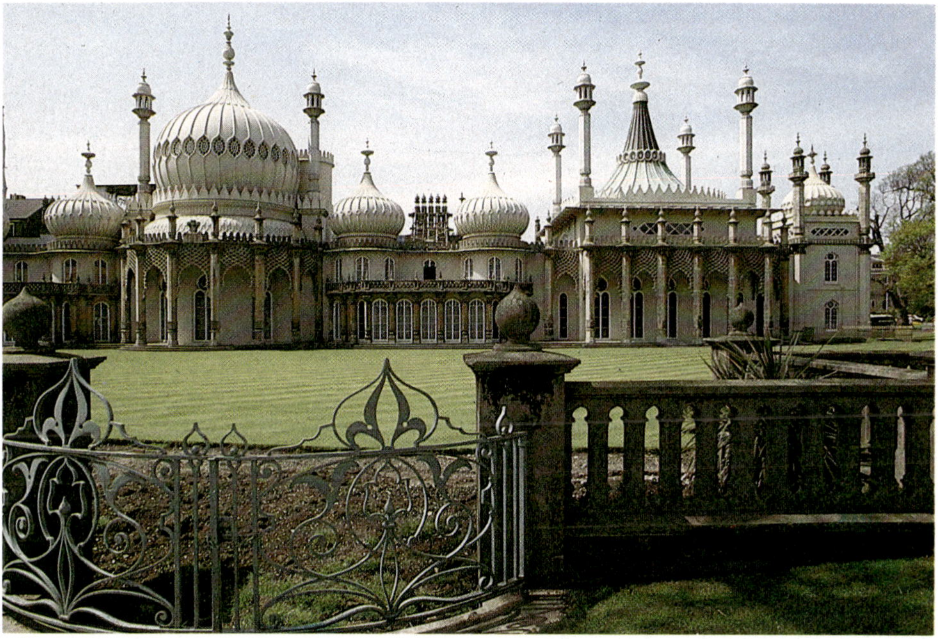

Brighton Pavilion

narrower one brings you out at the Clock Tower, 1888 and obviously designed for a Northern industrial town.

Turn left into North Street. The Pavilion lies a few hundred yards down its slope, but on your way there explore the area on the left round Bond Street. This is where the ordinary working population of Brighton does its everyday shopping, but there are also many junky antique shops where, unlike in tourist Brighton, genuine bargains and curios can still be obtained. This is an especially good hunting ground for the documentary photographer and the collector of photographic antiques. Return down New Street and photograph the Theatre Royal, built in 1807 and very elegant. My wife and I can never see it with the same eyes since we did the front of house pictures of the Brothel Scene from *The Threepenny Opera* there in the days when we were doing theatrical photography. There are some good period shops round about.

Typical Sussex beach at dusk

We have now reached the Pavilion and with any luck you will still have some film left – that's the trouble with Brighton, you set out to photograph some landmark but become so diverted on the way you never get there. The cream-and-green domes and minarets, straight out of a Hollywood production of the *Arabian Nights*, need to stand out against a dark background so, if loaded with black and white, an orange filter and a blue sky will be needed; for colour work a polarizing filter will be useful, but if you haven't got one, choose a clear, hazeless day when the sky is an intense blue and underexpose by half a stop. On an overcast day the Pavilion can seem a little dull and shabby as it merges into the sky, but when floodlit at night the building is transformed. Using a tripod, an exposure of about four seconds at f8 on 100 ASA film will produce fascinating pictures.

The best daylight photos of the exterior are taken from the East in the morning. Flowers and blossom make a good foreground, while a gardener will bring life into the composition (buildings so often appear deserted in pictures). General views will need a wide-angle lens but you can also use a long-focus one to concentrate on architectural detail.

Inside the Pavilion photography and even flash is permitted (I once asked an elderly curator in a museum why flash was banned; 'What, have all that smoke and flame!' he replied indignantly), but tripods are naturally forbidden. It is probably better to photograph parts of a room rather than try to include the whole of it – the chimneys in the Kitchen made to resemble palm trees, the chandelier in the Banqueting Room as heavy as the average car, the writhing dragons and serpents in the Music Room where I once with great difficulty gave a lecture, my eyes wandering as I thought what a great place it would be for a party. Most of the apartments are too big to allow bounce flash to be used and it is best to work with the existing daylight if possible.

The zany good taste of the Prince Regent is stamped on the Pavilion, as indeed on the rest of Brighton. A patron of the arts who collected superb paintings and exquisite furniture, he also used as a shaving mug a priceless gold cup found in a Cornish burial mound; luckily it was rescued at his death and is now in the British Museum. The Dome nearby was once the Royal Stables and a former landlord of the 'Wagon and Horses' in Church Street told me he had visited the tunnel that connected it to the Pavilion – it was very wide and lit with the original oil lamps. I'd like to think it still exists, waiting one day to be photographed.

On the West side of the Old Steine (pronounced *Steen*) which is beside the Pavilion, look out for the house where lived the Prince Regent's wife, the former Mrs Fitzherbert. Inside, it has the original cast-iron staircase up which 'Cripplegate' Barrymore once rode his horse into the attic; two blacksmiths were needed to get it down again and one is inclined to think that perhaps the home life of the lady was not quite as placid and domesticated as is supposed. The house is now the YMCA. . . .

Back in North Street you will see the signposted entrance to the Lanes, once the old fishing village but now a boutiquey pedestrian area full of dubious antiques, gift shops, trendy clothes, cafés and restaurants (some both cheap and good) – it ought to be terrible but somehow or other it is very pleasant and amusing to wander from one shop-lined passage to another. This is wide-angle territory until you reach little Brighton Square in the centre of the maze where you can sit on a balcony with a coffee and photograph the tourists below, some of them very quaint indeed, with a long-focus lens.

The Lanes are always busy at lunchtime during the week as the Brighton workers fill the pubs and cafés; during the Summer and at weekends they are crowded at all times. They are at their best on a sunny morning in Spring or Autumn, though still enjoyable in mid-Winter. As far as I know, there is no other place quite like the Lanes in England.

At the South-West end you will find the bow-fronted 'Cricketers', once the 'Market House', where famous actors used to stay in preference to a hotel – note the list of stabling charges inside the arched gateway at the side. Along the other side runs the extremely narrow Black Lion Passage; both are good subjects for the camera.

Stroll down Ship Street past Henekeys pub with its fake portcullis and imitation beams, in its way as big a folly as the

Pavilion. In the days when it was truly Henekeys we always started our visits to Brighton with a bottle of their extremely inexpensive champagne in the gallery upstairs, but we haven't set foot in it since it became part of the Forte empire. There are probably still pictures to be taken inside.

Work your way down to the front and on to the Palace Pier. Looking back you'll see in Summer an example of the strange British habit of crowding together on a small section of beach with empty stretches on either side. From the pier the buildings along the front make interesting architectural contrasts on a day with hard, clear lighting, but try to include some foreground interest to give depth, perhaps some of the people sitting in deck chairs. But the best subjects are the slot machines, the 'amusements', and, above all, their customers. The light is none too bright in the Palace of Fun and a large-aperture lens may be needed.

Back from your voyage out to sea, as a complete contrast make for the parish church of St Nicholas, not far from the Clock Tower. In the churchyard lies Phoebe Hessell. Born in 1713, she dressed as a man and served in the Army for seventeen years in order to be near her soldier lover; after being bayoneted at the Battle of Fontenoy she ran an apple stall in Brighton, dying at the age of 108. The tomb is closely surrounded by railings and the only way I have found of photographing it is to poke a superwide lens through the bars.

Inside the church is the best piece of Norman carving in Sussex, the famous font. There is little light and I doubt if the use of a tripod is encouraged, but by holding a flash well to one side at the end of a long synchronizing lead the detail in the carving is made to stand out boldly.

In Victorian and Edwardian times the area to the West of the church used to house Brighton's red-light district, catering

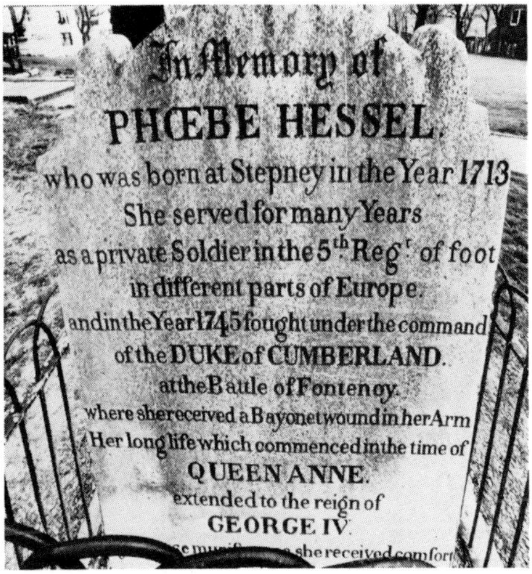

Phoebe Hessell's gravestone, Brighton

for those people who associated a visit to Brighton with sin. Now a district of flats and bed-sitters, it is, I am sure, intensely respectable and is certainly rather dull visually.

To the West. Brighton runs into its prosperous suburb of Hove; to the East lies Kemp Town. Both have magnificently photogenic crescents; facing the sea, they receive the sun from the South for most of the day. However, I find Hove predictable and unexciting; Kemp Town, full of surprises,is just the opposite.

Not the least of these is the Sassoon Mausoleum in Paston Place. This vaguely oriental building, once the burial place of Sir Albert Sassoon and his son, is now the Bombay Bar; I doubt if you'll ever take pictures in a stranger setting. Kemp Town and the district to the East of the Steine have few attractions for the ordinary tourist, but the photographer will find them fascinating.

Brighton is a big town with a quarter of a million inhabitants. It caters for every type of visitor and inevitably there are lots of clip-joint 'clubs', some of them as

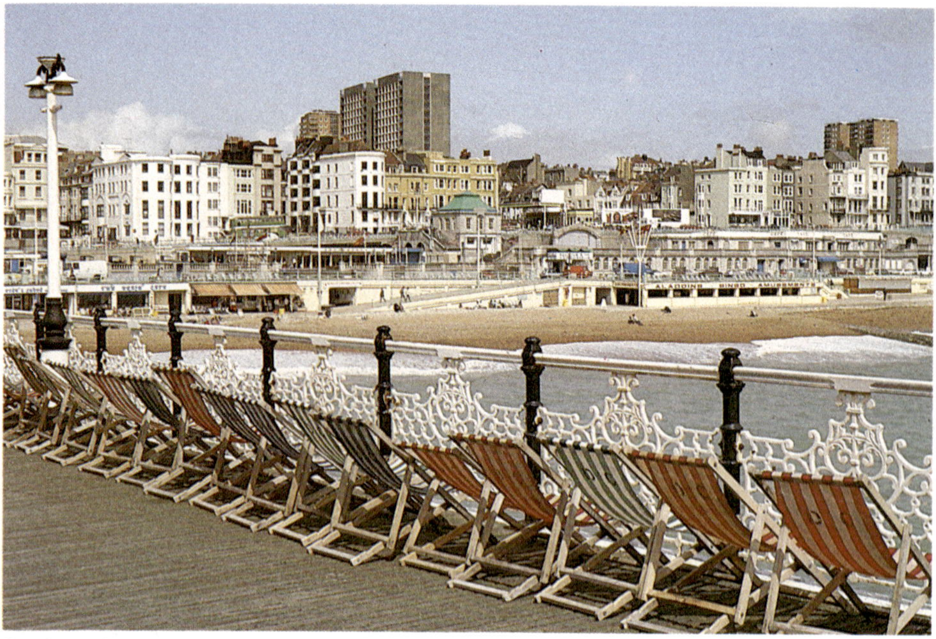

Brighton from Palace Pier
The Cricketers, Brighton

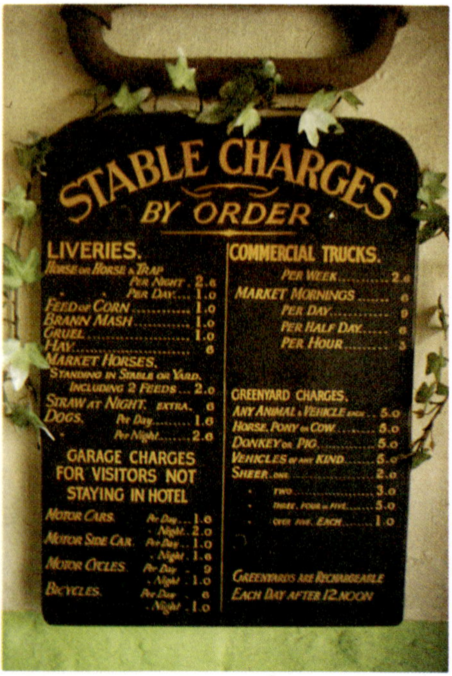

dubious as anything in Soho, pubs with every kind of entertainment and a considerable nightlife in the Season. Somehow or other nothing is quite as squalid as in the inland cities.

Thanks to the University of Sussex out at Falmer there is a very large student population (visiting there once I was confronted in the Buttery by an apparition with long ringlets, beads, ear-rings, medallion, ruffled shirt, fringed jacket and high suède boots; 'Isn't he overdoing it a bit?' I asked the students I was with; 'That's one of our lecturers,' they replied with resignation). There are also fortune-tellers, fishermen on the beach, massage parlours, vegetarian, Indian and Chinese restaurants, treasure-troves of bookshops, beggars, conmen, layabouts, assorted houris, shops selling Brighton Rock, tattooists, saucy postcards, evangelists – in short, if you are a documentary photographer few places will supply more material.

The Lanes, Brighton (right)

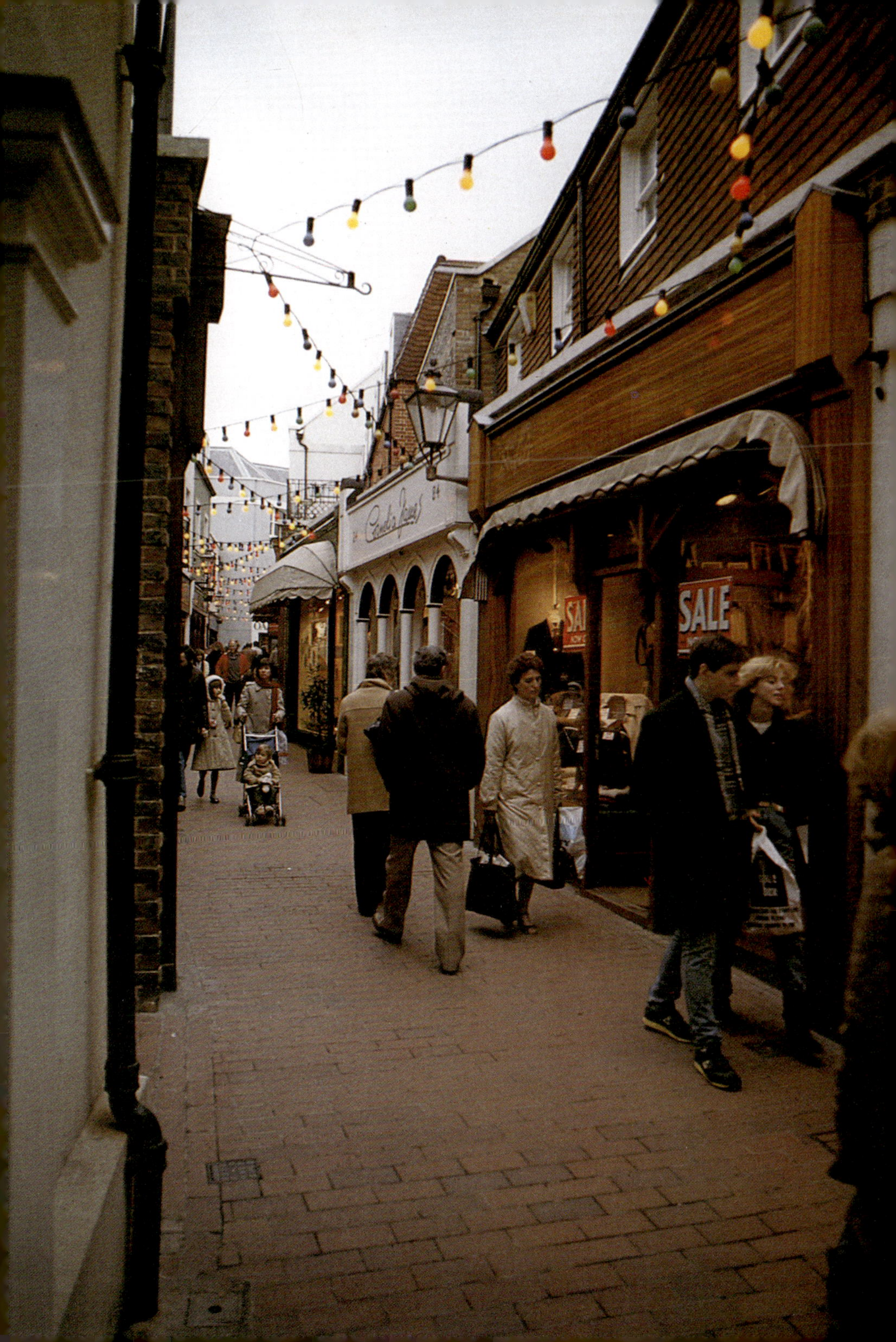
SALE

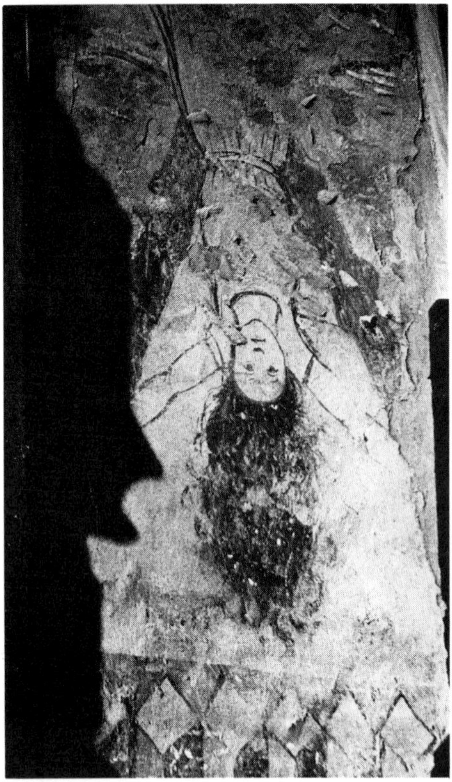

St Uncumber, Burton Park

Font cover, West Burton

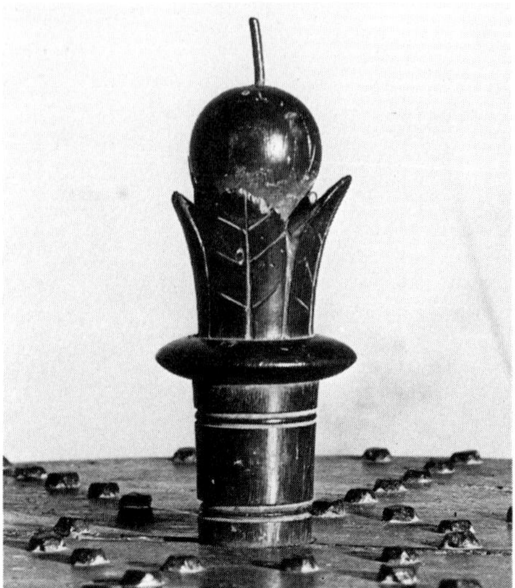

If you want to photograph this side of Brighton life, which I don't suppose has changed much since the rackety days of the Regency, load with 400 ASA film, even on a sunny day, and use either a standard 50mm lens or one with a focal length between 85 and 105mm. Zooms are too slow for this type of candid work since inevitably you'll pause to adjust the focal length and this will cause you to miss the vital moment.

To take pictures of people in the street, find a good setting, perhaps the entrance to a mews, an alley or a flight of steps, set the exposure and the focus and then wait patiently for an interesting subject to come along (you won't wait long in Brighton). Whip the camera up to your eye, press the release and drop the camera again, the whole thing taking perhaps a second; with any luck the subject won't even realize he or she has been photographed.

You cannot possibly cover such an interesting and varied place in a day or even a week. The best plan is to wander round exploring all the side turnings and mews off the main streets rather than concentrating on the known tourist subjects – away from the shopping centres the displays in the windows of the small shops would make a superb photographic essay in themselves.

Many visiting photographers find they spend the day walking from one end of the town to the other instead of taking pictures. The best plan is to select a small, interesting area and concentrate on it.

Burton Park

The best parts of Sussex are the ones least easy to reach; as more and more people become car-dominated, anywhere that can only be discovered on foot is left to the dwindling band of energetic enthusiasts.

Burton Church, set in the middle of Burton Park some three and a half miles South of Petworth, is a fine example. To get there you have to dump your car and walk a mere mile, but that is quite enough to cut out visits from 99% of the Sussex tourists. Unrestored and unspoilt, it is one of the most interesting places in the county. Not unlike one of those Victorian collections of curios, it is a jumble of wall-paintings, brasses, carvings, coats of arms, memorials and so on, any one of which would make a visit worth while; there is almost too much to see.

Tucked away at an awkward angle you'll find a wall-painting of a red-headed female martyr hanging upside-down. Known as St Uncumber, she possessed the useful property of ridding wives of their unwanted husbands on receipt of an offering of oats, a much cheaper and quicker procedure than that of the modern Divorce Courts.

The last major repair was done in 1636 and in the same year a Royal Coat of Arms was installed with the motto 'Obey Them That Have The Rule Over You', in nice time for the Civil War.

The carved wooden apple on the font cover is worth photographing, ancient linenfold panelling has been added to modern benches, there is a good screen, half a dozen brasses, lots of monuments – but make the effort and see for yourself. A small flash with a long synchronizing lead will be useful, as will a lens of about double the normal focal length, but keep apparatus to a minimum – by the end of the mile the weight will have magically doubled.

Burwash

If when young you read *Puck of Pook's Hill* or *Rewards and Fairies*, Burwash and the surrounding area will, no matter how worldly you have become, have a magic about them that will colour your vision. Instead of being merely pretty country full of forests, streams and sudden small hills it will be the place that Kipling wove into the ancient Sussex stories told to him by an old woodsman. If you dislike the way in which he over-compensated for his lack of physique and self-doubts by adopting a bullying, Jingoistic style for much of his work, come to Burwash and get a truer picture of the shy and rather tragic romantic who lived there.

Most photographers are as ungregarious as Kipling, so come early in the morning before the pilgrims arrive from all over the world. Burwash is a delightful village ruined by traffic – the trees that line the main street are pollarded so that their branches will not interfere with the passing lorries (myself, I'd rather pollard the lorries). Tourists park their cars at random, shops are tourist-orientated. But in Summer the place retains its character until well into the middle of the morning while in Winter it is worth a visit at any time.

Walking along the main street you pass a good variety of village shops and houses, many built during the prosperous days when Sussex supplied the country with iron. The fine brick house named Rampyndene (1699) makes a good picture while in the church further on is the earliest known cast-iron grave slab, a fact that may or may not interest you. Earthy photographers will appreciate the information that in the pub opposite they sell a beer made in the small Lewes brewery, a pleasant change from the pasteurized chemical beverage sold by the big concerns.

A lane beside the church runs down to Batemans, built by a Sussex ironmaster in 1639 and lived in by Kipling for thirty-four years. With any luck there'll be a couple of donkeys hanging about to provide a foreground to the picture; after midday the front of the house is in shadow. The interior has been left untouched and you feel the writer has just walked up to the village for a minute.

A tragedy lies over the house, for in the First World War Kipling's short-sighted and unathletic son was pushed into the Irish Guards by his father and shortly after arriving in the trenches wandered into no-man's-land and was shot. Kipling never really recovered.

Try to arrive at Batemans shortly before it opens and perhaps you'll have the house to yourself for half an hour. We were lucky enough once to be shown around on our own by an elderly gentleman who had been in the Dover Patrol in the 1914-18 affair and whose tales would have provided Kipling with much material.

To see the country of the stories, go a couple of miles West to Burwash Weald, take the minor road opposite the Wheel Inn, cross Willingford Bridge and after three-quarters of a mile the hill on your left is Pook's Hill – this, the original name , was misheard by a map-maker who called it Park Hill and now it is Perch Hill (we had a great picnic there once). Carry on to the obelisk built by Mad Jack Fuller and then perhaps continue to Penhurst and Ashburnham.

Alternatively take the road that leads back towards Burwash but branch off right and seek Glydwish Wood (sometimes called Gladwish), which is or was haunted by the ghost of David Leary, a farm labourer wrongly hanged in 1825. A number of people claim to have seen the tattered thing that roams and moans around the wood but unlike you they weren't carrying a camera....

Farm cart

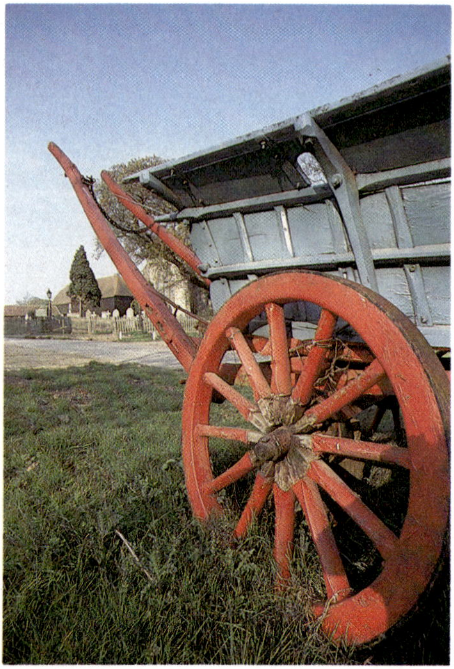

Camber

If from Rye you drove through Camber on the way to Lydd you'd probably accelerate at the sight of the caravans, the chalets and the holiday camp. But behind the sandhills lies the finest stretch of beach in Sussex, mercifully hidden from the inland squalor.

It is at its very best on a wild Winter's day, when for mile after mile the firm empty sands stretch into infinity. As you walk along the water's edge you see exotic-looking shells, tree branches weathered into strange shapes, glass floats torn away from nets and all the debris of the sea. The Winter sky is often spectacular, the air makes you feel immortal and you could easily imagine yourself the last person left on earth.

Batemans, Kipling's home (right)

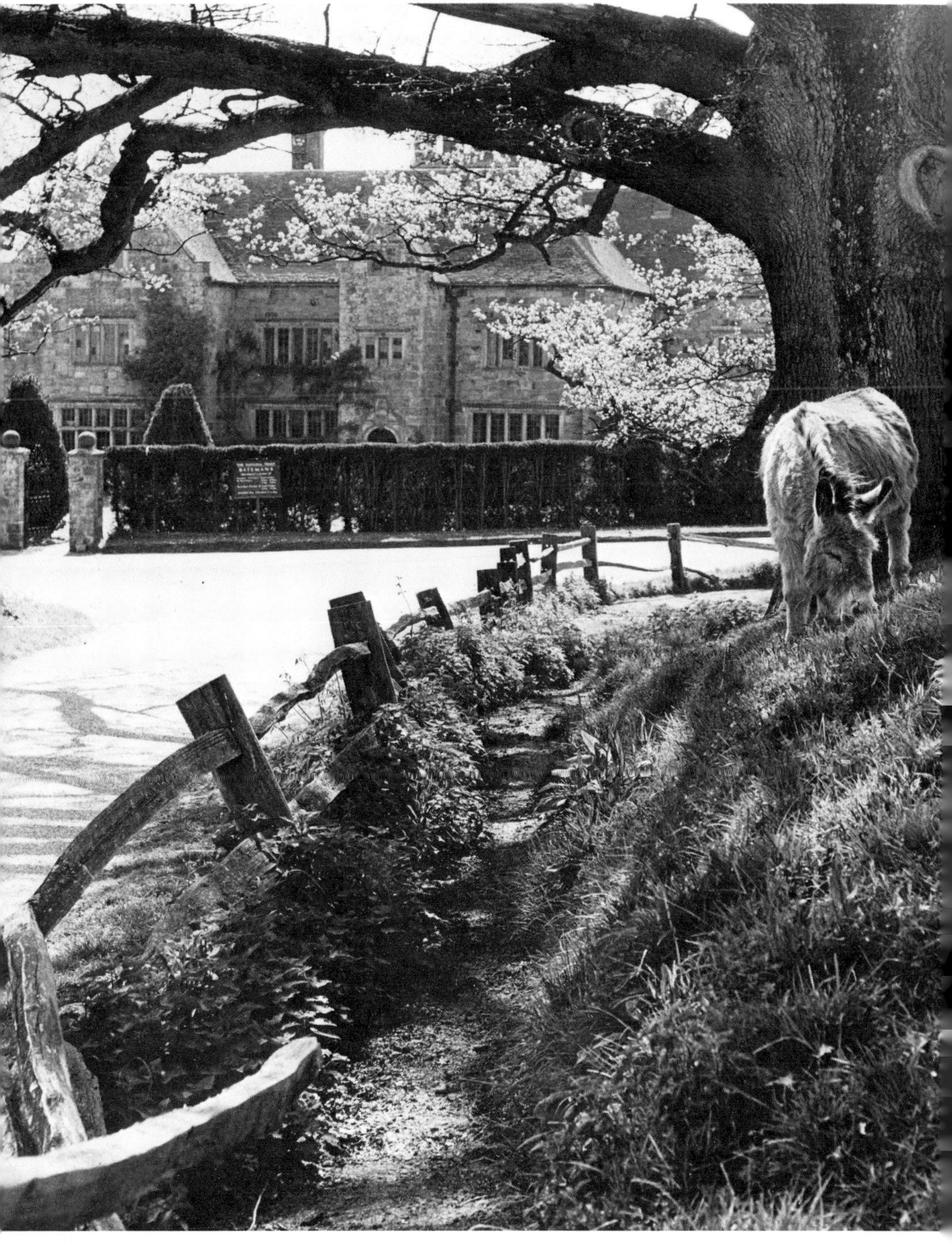
BATEMANS

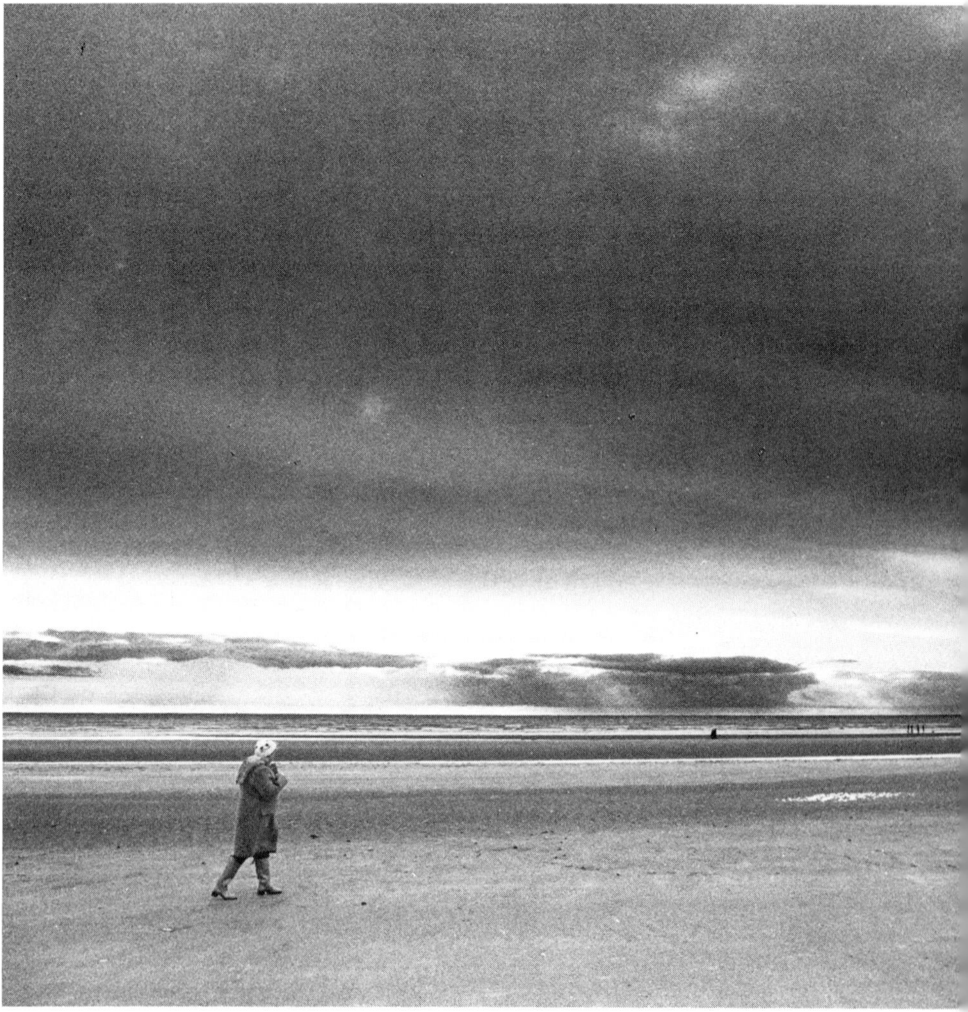

Camber Sands in Winter

To capture the space and emptiness you'll need a wide-angle lens; the smaller objects cast up by the sea are best recorded with a lens with a long focal length that will focus down to a close distance.

Camber Castle, on the other side of the Rother, lies on a track that runs between Winchelsea and Rye. Part of Henry VIII's protection for the South Coast, it seems to be permanently under repair and is best photographed from a considerable distance.

Chichester

I never see the spire of Chichester Cathedral without thinking of the child who was travelling by train with her governess towards the town in 1861. 'Look, dear!' said

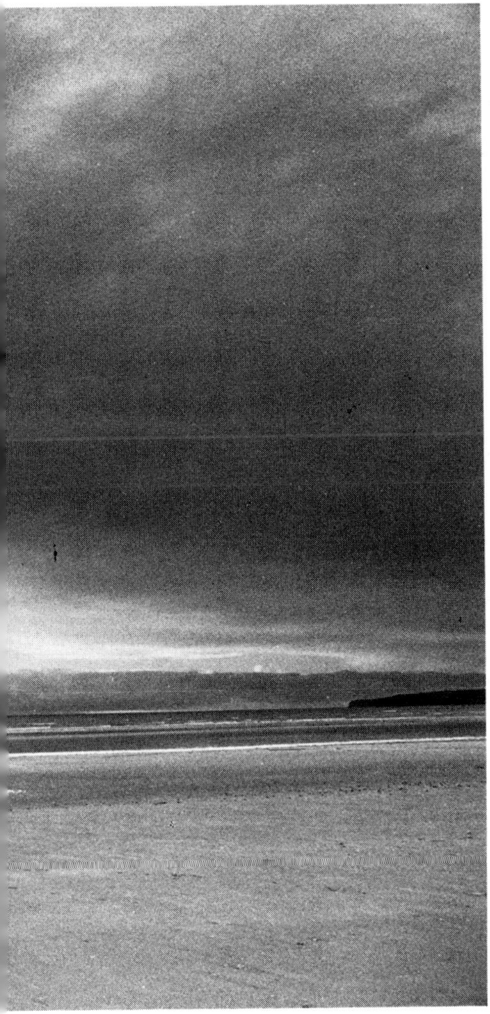

the governess, 'Look at the spire of Chichester Cathedral!' The little girl looked at the spire, which promptly collapsed. It must have affected her for life.

By 1865 it was rebuilt and the largely Norman cathedral remains the focal point of the town – unlike most others it is not separated from the world by a close but is bang on the main street like a village church though it is a huge place, only slightly smaller than York Minster or St Paul's. Inside, it is not all that interesting photographically speaking, thanks to the Puritans who destroyed all the monuments, the organ and just about everything else they could reach, but two stone panels, which were hidden behind the choir stalls, survived; one shows the Raising of Lazarus, the other Christ with Martha and Mary. Oddly modern-looking, they are probably early 12th-century though some say they come from the vanished cathedral at Selsey which has been under the sea for nearly a thousand years. The only way to photograph them is to use flash from one side on the end of an extension lead, preferably getting someone to hold it well back.

However, you could spend a very long time indeed photographing the exterior since as you explore the town or the country for miles around you keep seeing different and interesting compositions with the spire forming a centre of interest – it is in fact the only cathedral that can be seen from the sea.

The centre of Chichester, which was laid out by the Romans, is the Market Cross dating from around 1500. It was of course damaged by the Puritans, a bronze bust of Charles I was added after the Restoration and an out-of-place cupola and clock in the mid-18th century, but it is still one of the very few comparatively original ones left. It stands where North, South, East and West Streets meet and used to cause a perpetual traffic jam but is now the middle of a very large pedestrian area. This has made life easy and pleasant for the photographer who can wander about in the middle of the road without having to wait for traffic to move out of the picture – the people usually add to it.

On the whole the side with the bust of the King looks best, but this means getting up early on a Summer morning to photograph it when the light comes from the East – no hardship, since Chichester seems designed to be explored with a camera. It

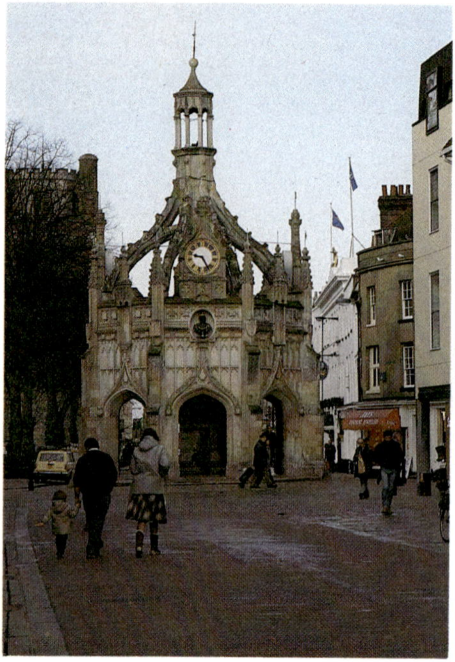

Market Cross, Chichester
Behind Chichester Cathedral

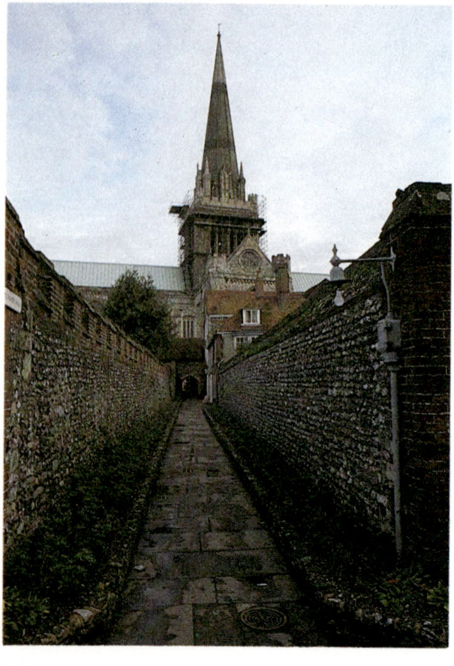

is worth including the ornate painted sign of the 'Olde Punch House' on the left to add some depth.

Most visitors like to start off with pictures of the cathedral and the best plan is to start walking from the cross down South Street, turning right first into Vicars Hall and afterwards into Canon Lane. From the former you reach the Cloisters and the Bishop's Palace Garden – out of season you will probably be the only person there. It's impossible to tell you from which position to photograph the cathedral since everything will depend on the state of the trees, shrubs and flowers that either add to or obscure the view, but always the spire is there in the background.

Canon Lane, leading to the Deanery, passes narrow St Richard's Walk on the right, a short cut for clerical traffic and for Chichester folk generally. Lose yourself in this very pleasant maze and before taking a picture wait for someone to walk into the right position – with luck you may get some quite remarkable characters.

At the bottom of South Street you come to the busy ring-road; if you turn right here you can obtain views of the whole of the cathedral across Westgate Fields with a good stretch of the original Roman City Wall in the foreground. Around midday the lighting will be flat; pictures are best taken in the morning or evening.

Walk back up South Street and after you pass Canon Lane turn right into an area known as the Pallant. In spite of a series of admittedly useful and well-kept car parks this is a very rewarding place for the photographer. At the cross-roads in the centre you will find Pallant House, known locally as 'Dodo House'. It was built in 1712 for a wine merchant named 'Lisbon' Peckham who had risen to riches and wanted, typically, a coat of arms. Ostriches, he thought ponderously, would provide a good pun on his surname, and writing from Africa to his architect he described the

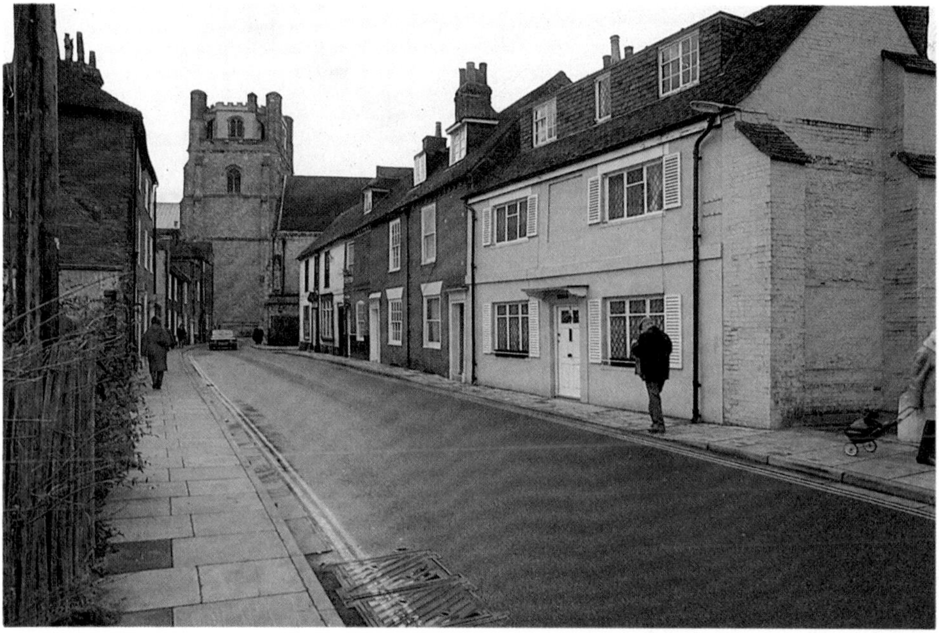

Chichester

bird, obviously not very accurately since the two carved birds on the gate-posts were thought by the people of Chichester to be either pelicans or dodos; hence their name for the house. Some people think it was designed by Wren, but then they say this about almost any surviving house of the period.

Spend some time wandering round the whole of the Pallant, since every so often you'll come across some really fine piece of architecture; look out for the view of the cathedral spire from West Pallant. In a way, with one main street running North/South and the other East/West, it is very like Chichester in miniature.

Back at the Market Cross, continue on up North Street, pleasant but without any outstanding buildings. A bookshop on the right was formerly the church of St Olave; if you turn right just past it into Lion Lane you come to St Martin's Square, formed by the low frontage of a remarkable place called St Mary's Hospital. An archway takes you into the Middle Ages, into the only almshouse in Britain in which the pensioners live in apartments in the aisles of a church. Founded in 1158, it has been ever since the concern of the Dean and Chapter of the Cathedral – one thinks of Trollope's Barchester.

Inside, its beamed roof makes it look very like a tithe barn, with eight dolls' houses in the aisles to hold the pensioners. The chapel is separated from the rest of the building by the best oak screen in Britain, carved in 1290. Twenty-four misericords of the same date are superbly decorated with various figures and natural-looking foliage, and the whole thing is an extraordinary and quite unexpected survival. Opening times vary but are posted up outside the entrance arch.

St Martin's Square runs into Priory Park, where you can walk along the top of a good stretch of the old Roman Wall (about a mile and a half survives in all) or alternatively, if you return to North Street, you can stroll back to the cross enjoying the freedom from traffic.

West Street passes the cathedral on the left behind an avenue of limes and the detached Bell Tower with its eight bells, of which there is a good view from Tower Street on the right. Facing the cathedral is a stylish black and white 18th-century coaching inn, the Dolphin and Anchor, with an original cobbled courtyard; further on there is not a great deal to photograph.

Back in East Street the Olde Punch House, whose sign we have already included in a picture of the cross, has a good bowed 18th-century plastered front but it is really Tudor underneath, like so many Chichester buildings. As with most cathedral towns there are a great many pubs; in fact, writing at the turn of the century the naturalist W.H. Hudson said it was the most drunken town he had ever encountered. This is no longer true, I am assured, but the pubs remain and some are well worth recording.

East Street has many good shops and can interest the documentary photographer, especially since one can stand where one likes without dodging traffic, but nothing is outstanding.

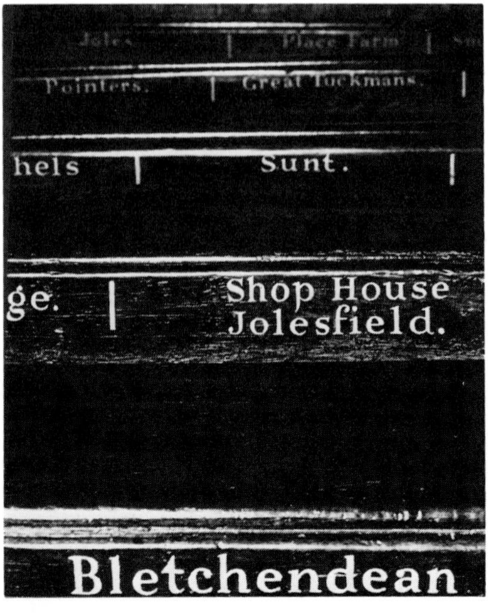

Farm names on pews

Chichester should be explored at leisure. If you are pressed for time you will inevitably rush around trying to photograph as many places as possible and producing good results from none of them. Ideally you should stay there for a week or so, photographing the interesting and beautiful town, the life of the cathedral, the Roman Palace at Fishbourne, Bosham and all the villages scattered throughout the magnificent country to the North. The town can give you as good a holiday as you will find in the South of England.

Clayton

Clayton is reached by the A273 from Haywards Heath, by the B2112 from Ditchling or from a turning off the main A23 that goes through Hurstpierpoint. Though it is a very small place, it holds a wealth of material.

The church, for instance, which lies at the foot of a steep slope in the appropriately named Underhill Lane, appears very unpretentious from the outside with a little shingled bell-turret and patched-up walls, but it contains paintings unique in England for their brilliance, age and extent.

Examples of true fresco, the colours being mixed with wet plaster before being applied, guesses at their date vary between the late-11th century and the 13th, most authorities settling on about 1150. They represent the Last Judgement, with archbishops being pushed away from the Cross by angels, Satan on a hell-horse trampling the damned souls, St Peter and his keys and, above the Saxon chancel arch, Christ in Judgement. With small heads and long bodies the figures have a Greek Byzantine appearance and may well be rather older than is generally assumed. The quality of the colour is astonishing and must have stunned Kempe when he discovered them in 1895.

As with all murals, they are not easy to record well. If you are very lucky, conditions may be just right with bright, even lighting, but the exposure needed will probably be too long for the camera to be hand-held and a tripod or monopod will be called for. Alternatively, the camera can be pressed against something solid, when exposures of at least a second can be given, though difficulty may be experienced in composing the picture – walls and pillars never seem to be in quite the right place.

In spite of their claims, most small flash units give rather uneven lighting and do not give satisfactory results if pointed directly towards a wall. In addition they are not powerful enough to be used for 'bounce flash' in a large building, a technique which would otherwise give very even results.

Any lens can be used to record the murals, a wide-angle one showing their impressive extent and a long-focus one, preferably a zoom, letting you pick out interesting individual figures. The interior of Clayton Church is something you will never forget.

Outside, cross the road and move around until you get a good view of the extraordinary entrance to Clayton Tunnel, through which run all the London-Brighton trains. It's the Victorian idea of the entrance to a castle, all crenellated turrets, loopholes, battlements and an entrance arch, built out of yellow brick in 1840. Even more astonishing, someone later on built a small house between the two turrets, slap over the tunnel entrance, where the endless stream of trains must jar it all day and most of the night.

It's not difficult to take a straightforward picture looking down on this curiosity from the road (it faces North and the light is fairly even), but more interesting results can be obtained by placing the camera on a tripod, stopping the lens down as far as it will go and making a long exposure just as a train emerges from the arch. The resulting blur will give a sense of speed and action; a fast shutter speed would freeze the movement and the train would appear to be standing still.

When looking at the tunnel and at the cutting that leads into it, remember that the whole of the London-Brighton line was constructed by men working only with picks, shovels and wheelbarrows. They lived rough, cooking their meals in the open air where they worked, drank heavily and terrified the local Sussex people.

They also invented the best way yet discovered of cooking bacon and eggs. A shovel is positioned so that the blade lies at an angle just over the edge of a fire and strips of bacon are laid across it. The fat runs down and fills the hollows on either side where the handle joins the blade and an egg is broken into each to cook gently. What in the world has this to do with photography, you ask? Nothing at all – I just thought you'd like to know.

From the church a footpath leads steeply uphill to Clayton's best-known tourist attraction, the twin windmills called Jack and Jill, but if you haven't got the energy drive half a mile South down the A273 and turn left up a lane that leads to a car park close to them.

Jack is a black tower mill without any sails, Jill is a white-painted post mill with four sweeps. She has an interesting history, being built in 1821 and dragged by oxen across the Downs from Brighton's Dyke Road to her present location in 1850. They stand on private ground and there is a house between them, but from footpaths, including the South Downs Way, good angles can be obtained and I don't suppose anyone would mind much if you walked over the nearby fields provided no crops are being grown.

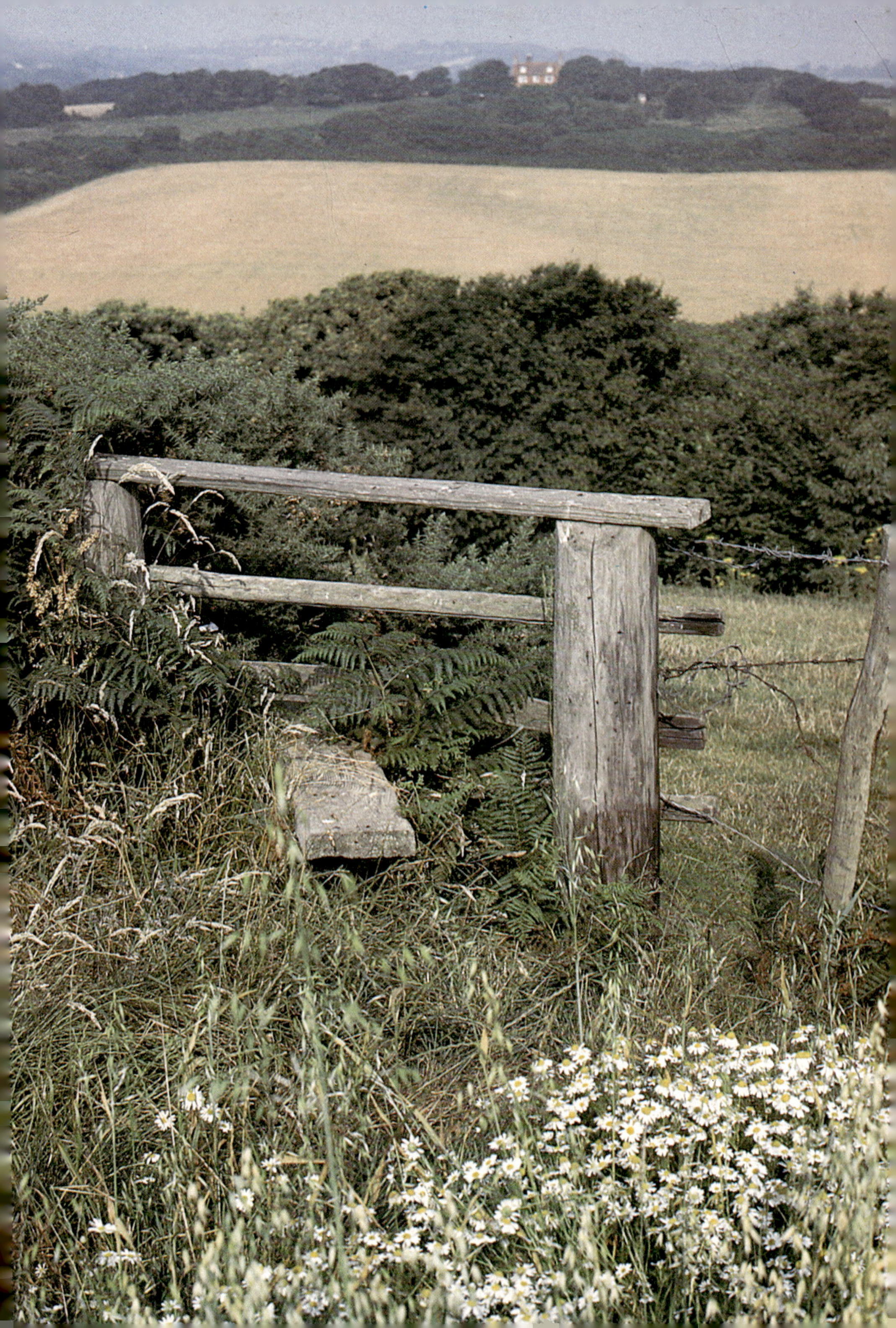

Climping

Drive West from Littlehampton along the A259 and two miles after crossing the Arun turn right into the lane marked Climping and Ford. Climping Church is unchanged from when it was built in 1220, incorporating an earlier Norman tower. This is forty-five feet high, has walls four feet thick and, judging by the grooves on either side of the door, may have had a drawbridge – it was obviously built for defence.

The saying 'Climping for perfection' refers to the design and proportions of the church, possibly the finest village church in Sussex. Inside you'll find an ancient chest with a slit for offerings; on the 31 December 1199 the Pope ordered such chests to be placed in churches to enable poor knights to go on crusades – people tend to forget how expensive such expeditions must have been.

Return to the main road, turn right and after half a mile turn left to Atherington. A leafy country lane leads down to the sea; it is sad to think that this beautiful beach with the fields behind it is the only piece of coastline between Selsey and Brighton that is not built up. The photographs you take will show what much of the Sussex coast looked like a century ago. There are some thatched flint barns and a squat windmill with its sweeps intact.

A little way inland is Baliffscourt, an architectural curiosity. The fragment of a 13th-century chapel stood there until 1935, when Lord Moyne decided to build an exact reproduction of a big mediaeval house with several cottages around it. Some buildings were brought from far away and reassembled; others were built from scratch using period materials. The result is quite indistinguishable from the real thing; it is now a hotel.

Sussex country scene (left)

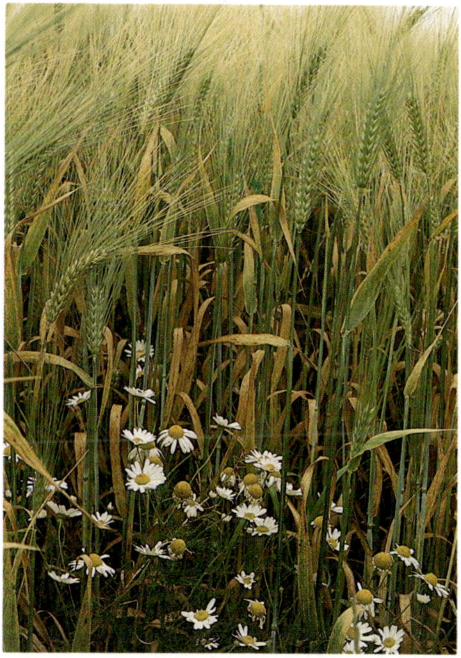

Barley field

Coombes Church

Coombes Church takes some finding but is worth the effort. Go from Steyning towards Bramber and take a right-hand turning into a lane that runs towards St Botolphs. After about 2½ miles a track on the right goes through a farm to Coombes.

You pass through a 'Tapsell gate' which rotates about a central pivot. Many earnest and learned people have tried to find the origin of the name and many interesting theories have been put forward. The explanation is simple enough; it was made by Mr Tapsell, an 18th-century carpenter who made similar ones at Friston and East Dean. At weddings they were tied shut with white ribbons and the groom had to lift the bride over them.

There are usually some sheep grazing

between the gate and the little low 11th-century church. Across the field stands the priest's house and it is possible that the church was once surrounded by a hamlet. Everything seems incredibly old and unchanged until you look across the Adur towards the vast, overpowering cement works. The contrast is extraordinary.

Inside the church are some wall paintings. We were present when they were first uncovered and excitement mounted as week after week more and more plaster was removed to show the dim figures of the past. It looked as though Coombes was going to be famous, but then the pictures ended abruptly and Coombes Church went back to sleep.

Mediaeval murals, Coombes Church

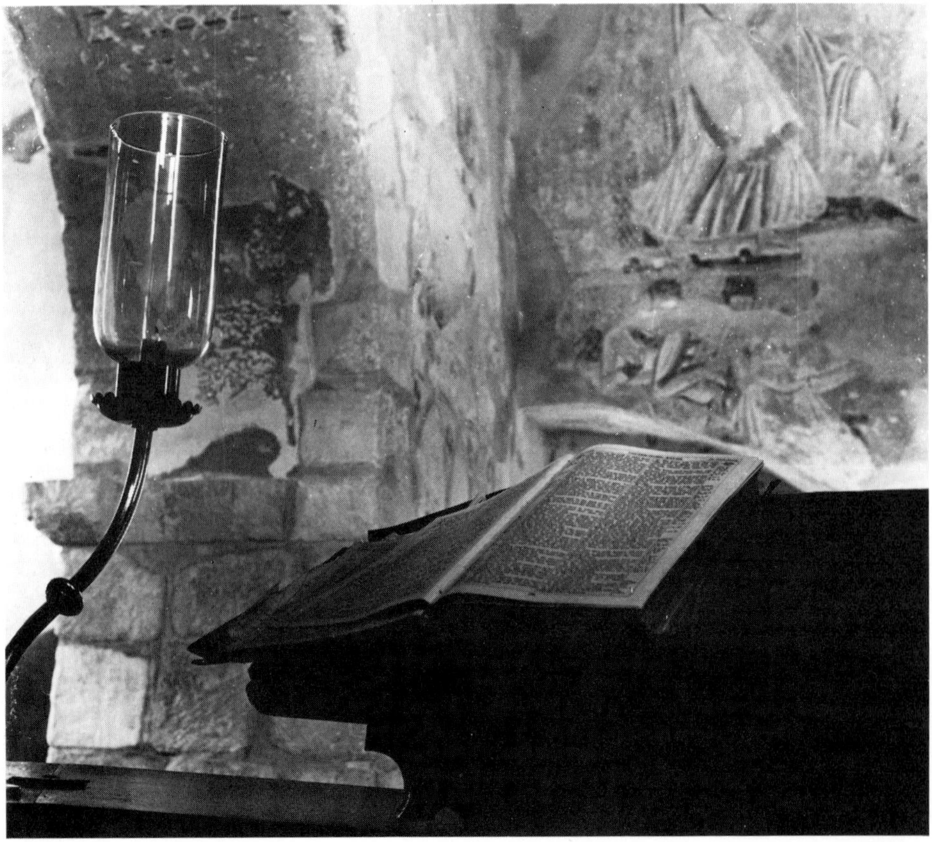

Ebernoe

For 364 days of the year Ebernoe is an empty, enchanted district. This is how much of Sussex must have been in Edwardian times, but the peaceful atmosphere is hard to record on film. Then on St James's Day (25 July) comes the Ebernoe Horn Fair.

It probably started in the Middle Ages, but no one knows exactly when. Around

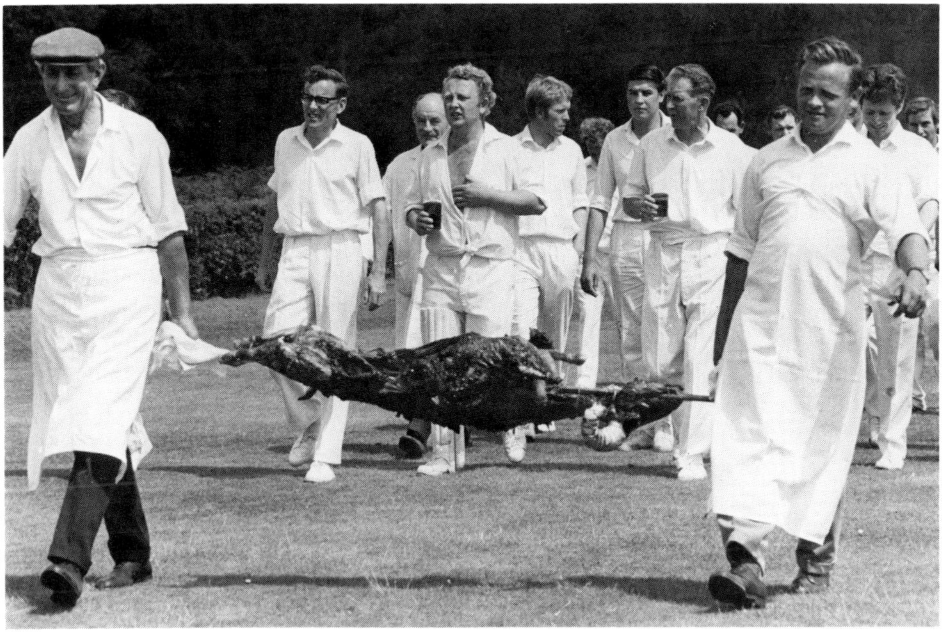

dawn they start to roast a sheep whole over a fire-pit – the spit and its supports are at least a century old. A cricket match begins, Ebernoe against the rest of England, ancients sit on straw bales criticizing the play, a little travelling fair starts up, the beer tent opens and stays open for the rest of the day; and then comes lunch.

The team carries in the roast sheep, escorted by every dog in the district, and after much eating and drinking an extremely uninhibited game is resumed. At the end of the match Lord Egremont presents the player who has done best with the sheep's skull, horns silvered. Dancing and the fair continue into the night; few days in Sussex are better.

For the cricket a long-focus lens, perhaps a 200mm, will give you close-ups of the action with a background of cottages. For general pictures of people at the fair, something between 85 and 105mm is most useful, while in the tents and marquees a normal or wide-angle lens is best. As dusk

Bringing in the roast sheep, Ebernoe Horn Fair

falls, 400 ASA film and a lens with a maximum aperture of at least f2 will be needed.

Lord Egremont presents the Horns

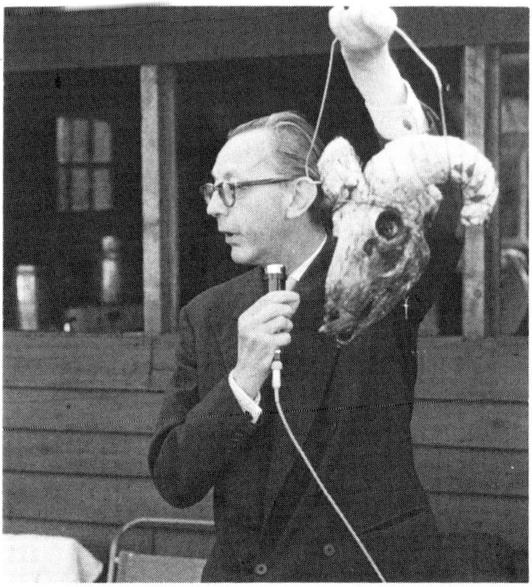

Etchingham

Though Etchingham is a pleasant village surrounded by good country, most people go there to see the church, an unspoilt example of the decorated style built in the 14th century. Since there is a busy road and a row of trees in front of it, the standard picture is taken from inside the churchyard with a wide-angle lens. But if you walk towards the pub and the village store you will see a small bridge crossing a stream. Two footpaths lead from it in an uphill direction; take the one on the left going towards a group of trees on the hillside.

From this position you obtain a good view of the church with a field gate in the foreground; the branches of the trees can be used to frame the scene. A long-focus lens will be needed and a 70-150mm zoom will let you compose the picture tightly in the viewfinder without having to move back and forth too much.

Inside the church are some fine brasses and what are perhaps the best stained-glass windows in the country.

Firle

From Lewes take the Eastbourne road (A27); after 4½ miles a turning right goes to Firle, usually called West Firle to distinguish it from East Firle. The latter ceased to exist 700 years ago, but you can't be too careful.

The village is dominated by Firle Place, the home of the Gages for the last 500 years, and is still vaguely feudal. The Gages have a very interesting history – one introduced the greengage into this country while another, by losing the Battle of Bunker Hill, helped America to leave the Empire; opinions vary as to which was the greater service.

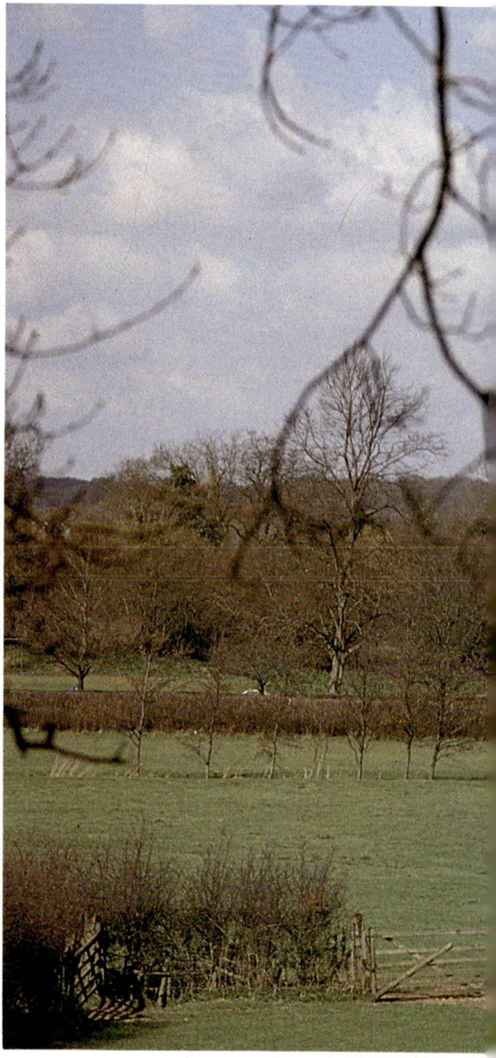

Etchingham Church from the South

Firle, together with Alciston and Berwick, lies at the foot of the Downs on a dead end, but all three villages were once joined together by a coach road running from Brighton to Alfriston. Deserted, it became a grassy track along which flocks of sheep were driven to market; if you follow it today, muddy and rutted, you will pass a

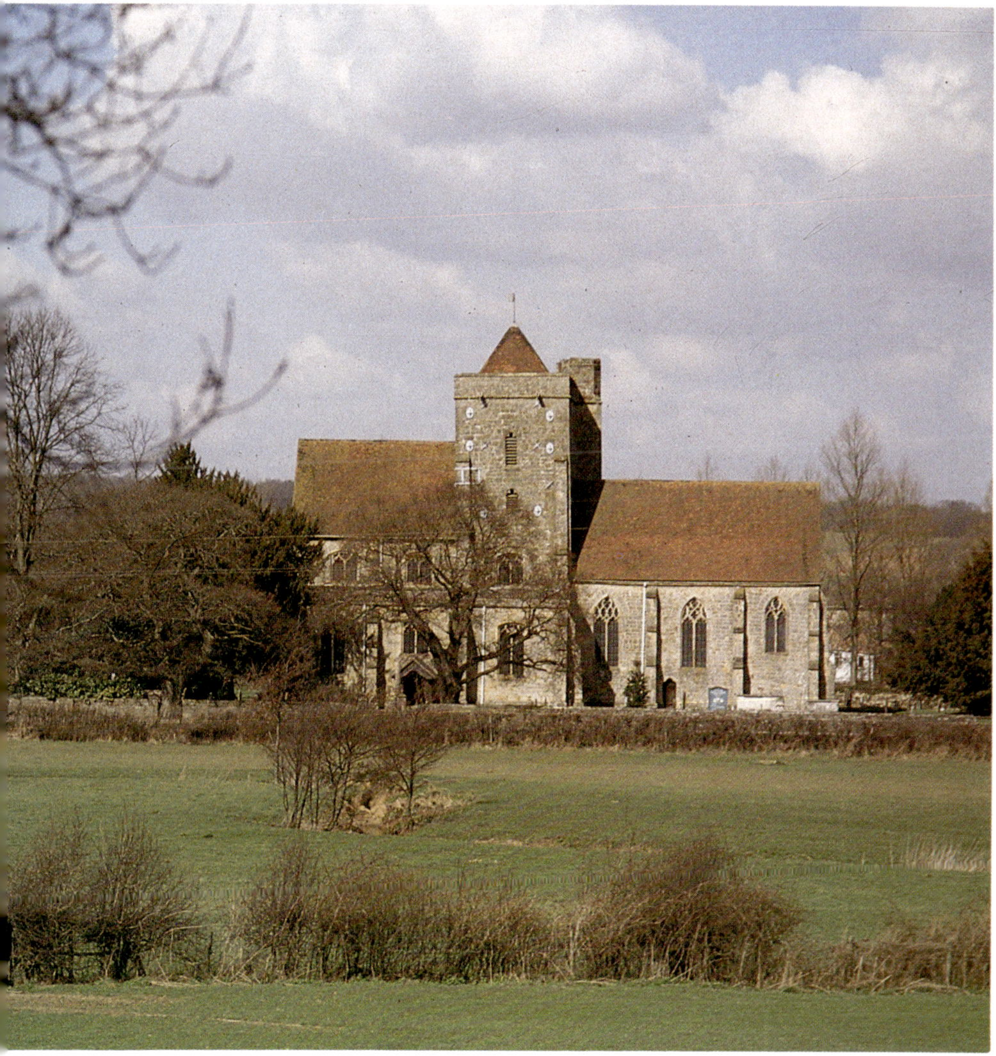

number of houses that were once drovers' inns.

In Firle we used to play toad-in-the-hole at the Ram Inn, a game I have not seen elsewhere. Big brass counters are thrown, with luck, into a hole cut in a large block of lead; the noise is very satisfying. The village, bright with flowers, is as unchanged as any in Sussex, while the church is full of brasses and memorials to the Gages – the alabaster one to Sir John Gage and his wife (he is in armour with his feet resting on a ram) is outstanding.

A War Memorial lists nine Firle men who were killed in the First World War – the loss to such a very small community must have been shattering. But then all over Britain you come across these tragic reminders of the end of an age.

A road leads up to a car park near Firle

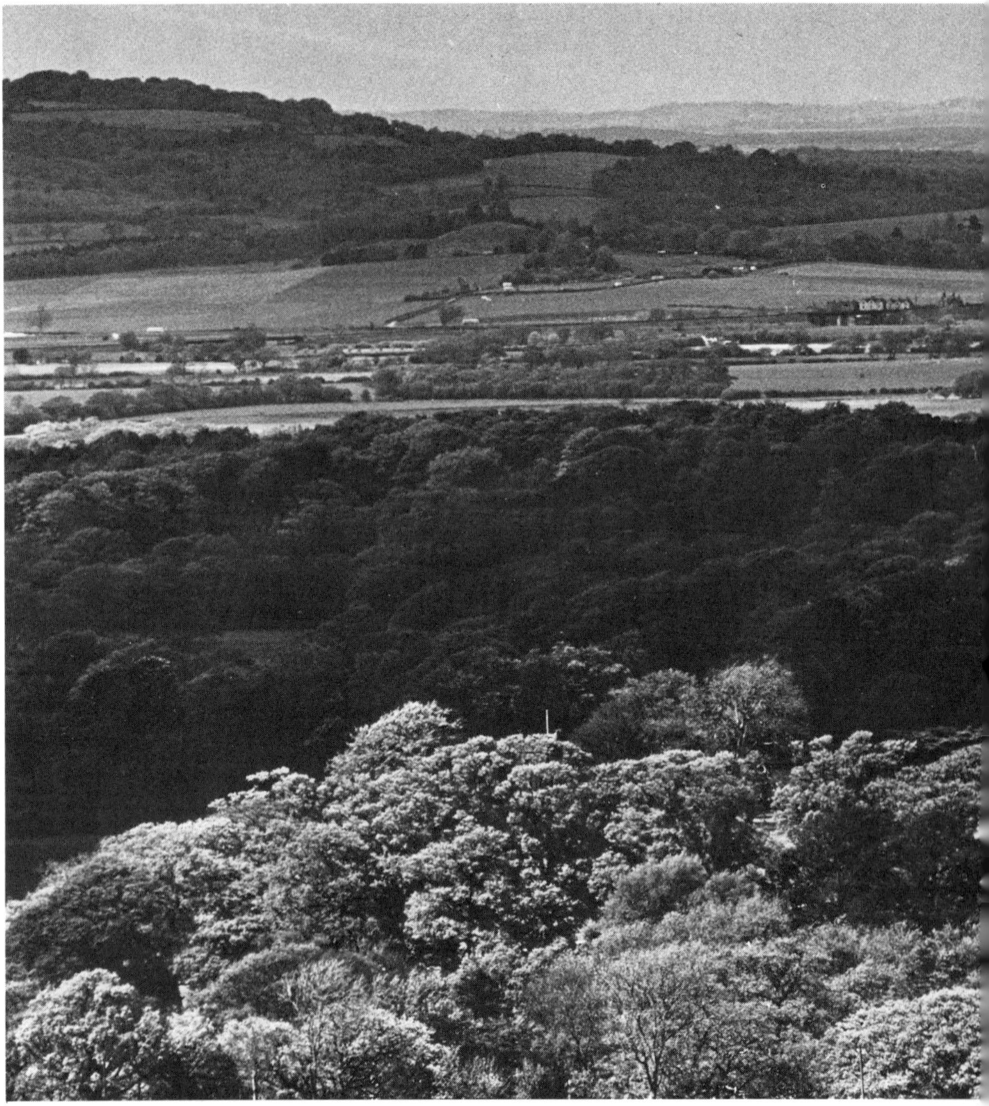

Firle Place from the Downs

Beacon, a mile walk bringing you to the 713-foot summit where a beacon once signalled the coming of the Armada. The view of East and Central Sussex on a clear day is astonishing and in Summer you may well see gliders in action. The country's first gliding contest was held on this ridge in 1922, the second prize being won by a man who fitted a wing off a Fokker DV11 to the fuselage of a Bristol Fighter; he had bought them for 25p each. An exhilarating three-mile walk along the top of the Downs past a great number of prehistoric burial mounds brings you to Alfriston.

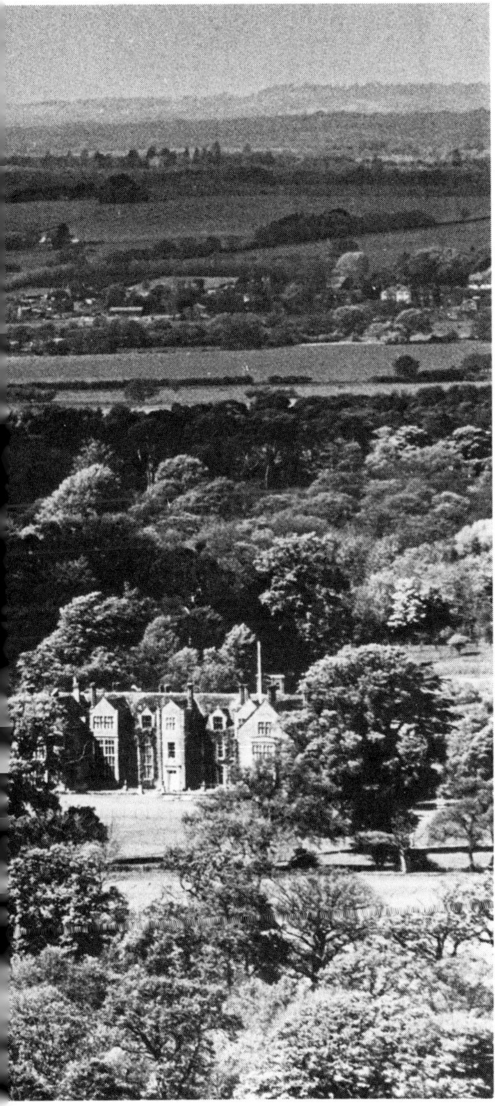

Firle House stands at the Southern end of the vast Firle Park, which is crossed by various footpaths. Georgian with a Tudor core, it contains a fine collection of paintings, porcelain and furniture and is open in Summer on Wednesdays, Thursdays and Sundays from 2.15 to 5.30. Photographically speaking, the inside is not very inspiring, but the exterior provides good pictures from the garden terraces. A footpath from the left of the main drive goes West towards the village, coming out at the Post Office.

Firle has a lot to offer – big house, magnificent park, picture-book village, friendly pub, long-distance views from the Downs and a peaceful and more relaxed atmosphere. Go there in the morning and stay for the rest of the day.

Halnaker Mill

If you travel along the road from Petworth to Chichester (A285), you will find it curves round a hill on your right just before you reach the straggling village of Halnaker. A footpath leads from Warehead Farm at the bottom of the hill past a few cottages and then starts to rise. You are walking along Stane Street, the Roman road that ran between Chichester and London – the distance as the crow flies is 55 miles and yet the engineers made the road so straight that it was only 56½ miles long.

Stane Street carries on round the base of the hill, but our footpath swings left up a steep slope. There are two stiles and 420 feet to climb before you reach the Mill, perched on an outpost of the Downs. Built from brick in 1750, with white sweeps and fantail, it has a rustic appearance that blends perfectly with the surrounding fields and hedges.

You can start your photography long before you reach the Mill, using the path to lead into the subject, and as you come closer there is a gate and a hedge to provide a foreground. A long-focus lens can be used to start with and a wide-angle one when you reach the top of the hill.

The Mill is probably best photographed in a hard early-morning light that will show up the texture of the brickwork. The view

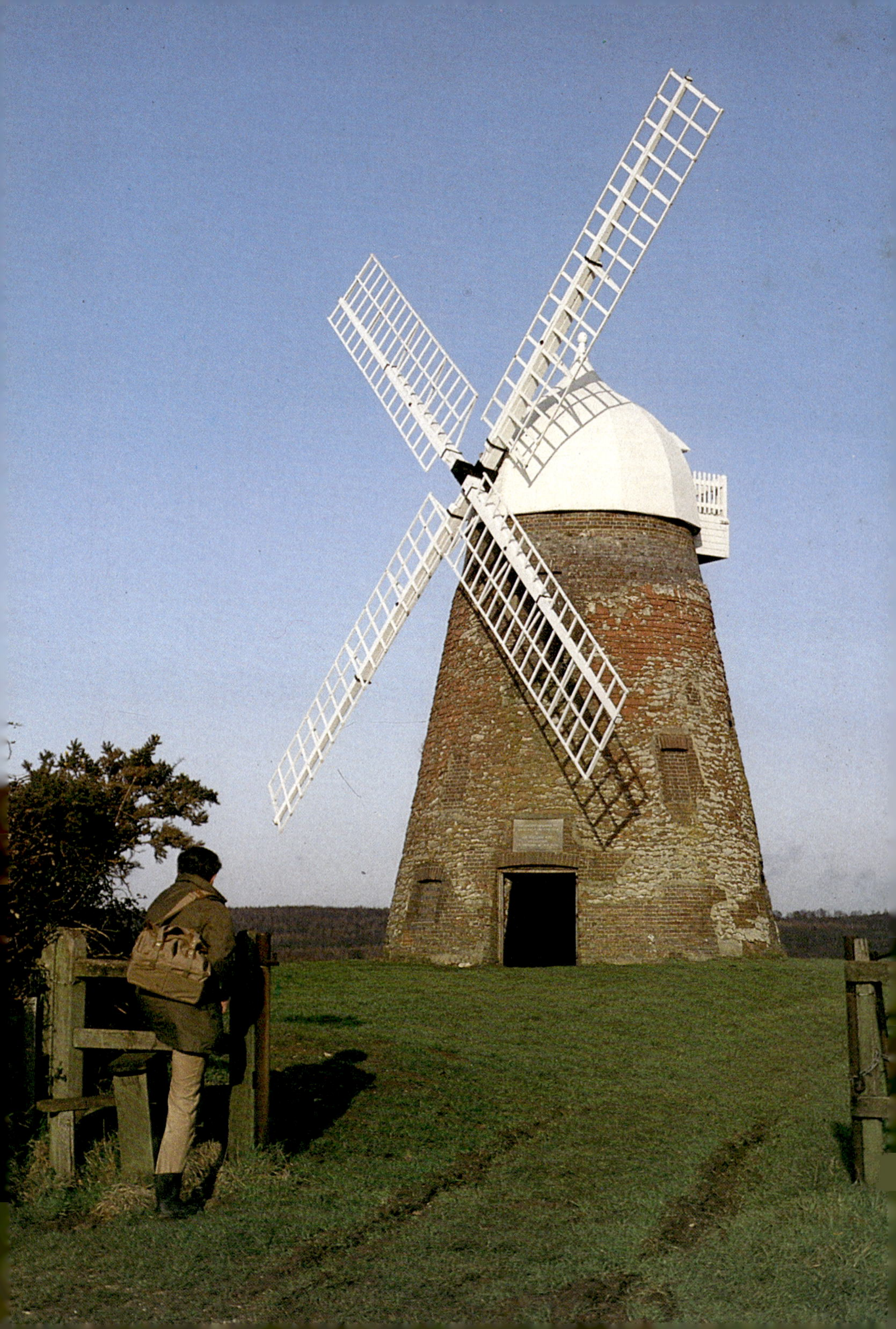

from the hill is spectacular – you can pick out Chichester Cathedral, the houses of Bognor and the prehistoric earthworks of the Trundle. Even in Summer the climb daunts most visitors and the chances are, especially in the morning, that you'll have the whole place to yourself.

Hardham

From Pulborough cross the Arun on the A29 and travel South for about a mile. On the left a narrow turning leads to the hamlet of Hardham – unless you keep a sharp look-out you are almost bound to miss it. In the middle of the row of cottages stands the 11th-century St Botolphs.

The small windows allow little light to enter and at first you can see nothing. Then as your eyes grow accustomed to the gloom you realize the walls are covered with faded brown and yellow paintings; Eve milks an enormous cow in Eden, Adam and the Serpent can be seen, St George slays a Dragon, Fiends and Devils torment sinners – the effect is extraordinary as the scene gradually reveals itself.

The artist was at work shortly after the church was built, but for some odd reason the murals were covered up by the 13th century – why, I wonder? It is interesting to realize that these were probably the only pictures ever seen by most of the congregation at the time, and their effect must have been very powerful.

We were once there in a thunderstorm and the interior of the church was pitch-black except when a flash of lightning lit the murals brilliantly – it was rather uncanny. You can supply your own lightning with an electronic flash, but if possible it should be connected to the camera by means of a long synchronizing lead and held by a companion as high as possible

Halnaker Mill (left)

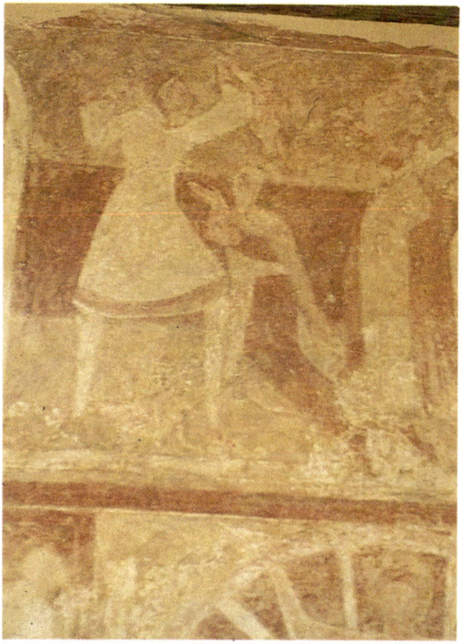

Stane Street, Eartham
Mediaeval mural, Hardham

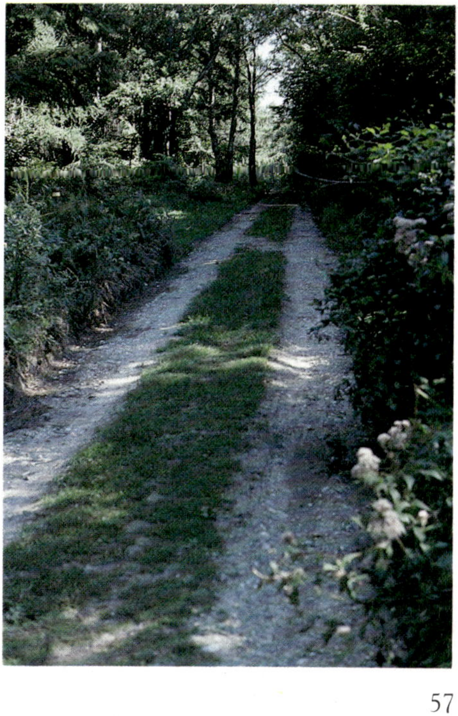

and well behind the camera. This will give much more even lighting than if the flash were in its normal position.

A zoom lens will allow you to include the whole of a scene or to concentrate on a single figure. With flash, of course, a tripod will be unnecessary and your only real problem will be the low contrast of the paintings; if using black and white film it will probably be necessary to print on the hardest grade of paper.

Hastings and St Leonards

Because so much of the main road from London is narrow and twisty, Hastings is not popular with day-trippers and has retained a briny Edwardian charm that makes it unique among the coastal towns of Sussex. There are a number of obvious photographic subjects – the Net Sheds, the Fishing Fleet, the Castle, the Old Town and so on – but the everyday life of Hastings with its visitors, its residents and the fishermen is also well worth recording.

Let's start in the prosperous Western suburb of St Leonards, which has much the same relation to Hastings as Hove has to Brighton. Photographically speaking, it is not very interesting, but if the tide is really low, archaeological photographers will want to see the outline of the 17th-century Dutch merchantman sunk in the mud off Bulverhythe, while the architectural worker will make for the extraordinary Masonic Temple standing in the road running parallel with the Promenade – the huge pillars would be considered ostentatious on the Bank of England. Documentary photographers can concentrate on the retired colonels and their ladies in the colonnaded shopping parade.

Hastings Old Town (left)

The main part of Hastings is a pleasant enough seaside town with fewer 'amusements' than most and the side streets and markets are worth exploring with your camera. Further East lies Pelham Crescent, Regency, elegant, but almost impossible to record satisfactorily even with a super-wide lens. It has presented a challenge to photographers for generations; perhaps you can find a solution to the problem.

Climb up to the not very impressive castle ruins on top of the cliff behind it; from them you get a fine view of the Old Town and the boats on the beach. Make for them – we've kept the best till last.

It's odd how the Old Town has retained the atmosphere of a fishing village, because there is no harbour, the luggers having to be hauled on to the steeply shelving beach by winch. It makes for exciting pictures at high tide as they charge the shore to get as far up as possible before the cable is attached – study the tide-tables to see when

Hastings Old Town

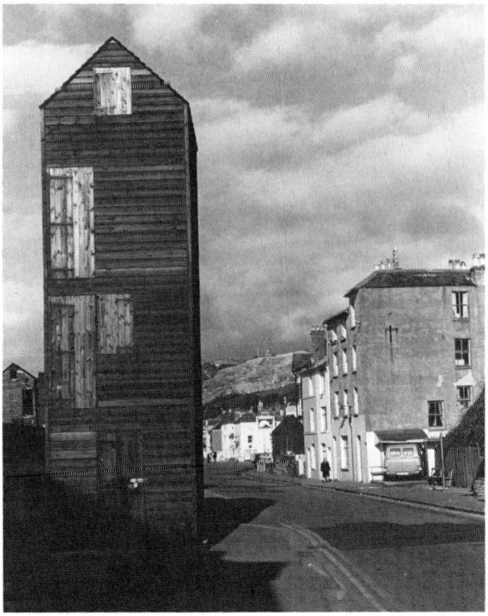

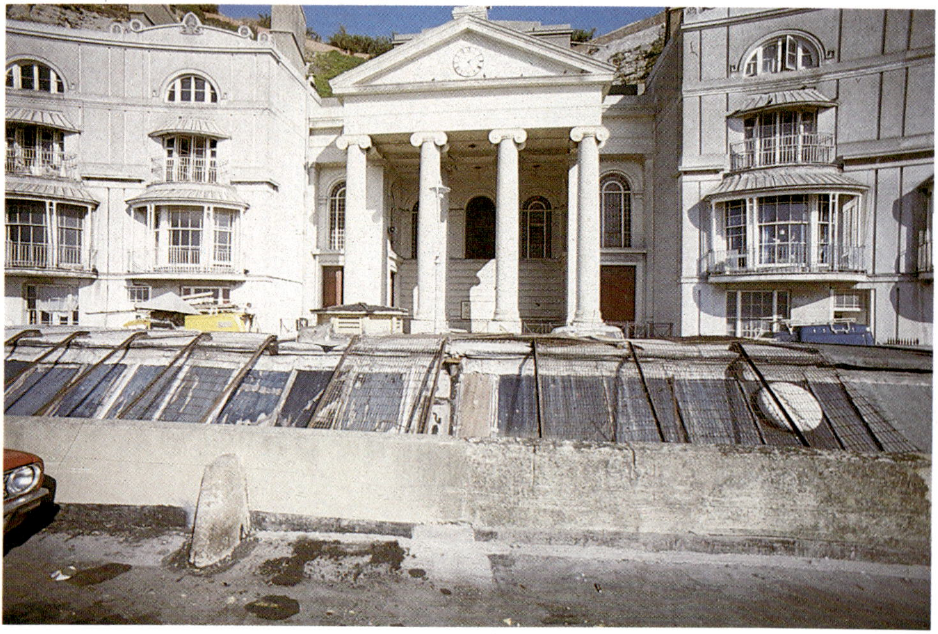

Pelham Crescent, Hastings

this will happen and use a long-focus lens to compress the perspective between the approaching boat and the men waiting for it on the beach.

Turner painted the strange Net Sheds that look like tarred sentry boxes and though it's doubtful if you'll do as well, try photographing them either from the East by early-morning sunlight or from the West in the evening. Amongst the sheds are booths where fish can be bought that were in the ocean an hour before; they can also be bought straight off the boat.

The fishing community tends to keep apart from the rest of the community and has a foreign look about it; until recently they used to intermarry with French families from across the Channel and you can still hear the occasional anglicized French word in their conversation.

Two centuries ago the main occupation along this stretch of coast was smuggling and there are still far-fetched stories of cheap brandy and cigars being available to those in the know, but anyone who has ever had dealings with the fishermen of Hastings knows they would never be associated with anything so illegal.

The tangle of narrow streets leading inland from the Old Town beach contains a fascinating mix of junk shops, ships' chandlers, chapels, odd little amphibious pubs, cockle and whelk stalls, fish shops selling lobsters at half London prices, weather-boarded cottages and ancient timber-framed houses – it's quite impossible to suggest a route and the fun lies in wandering around on your own with a camera fitted with a short-focus lens (the streets really are very narrow). On the whole it's best to load with fast film since so many subjects are either in shadow or indoors.

Romantic-sounding Tamarisk Steps and the Tackleway are photographically disappointing; make instead for the High

Hastings Front (right)

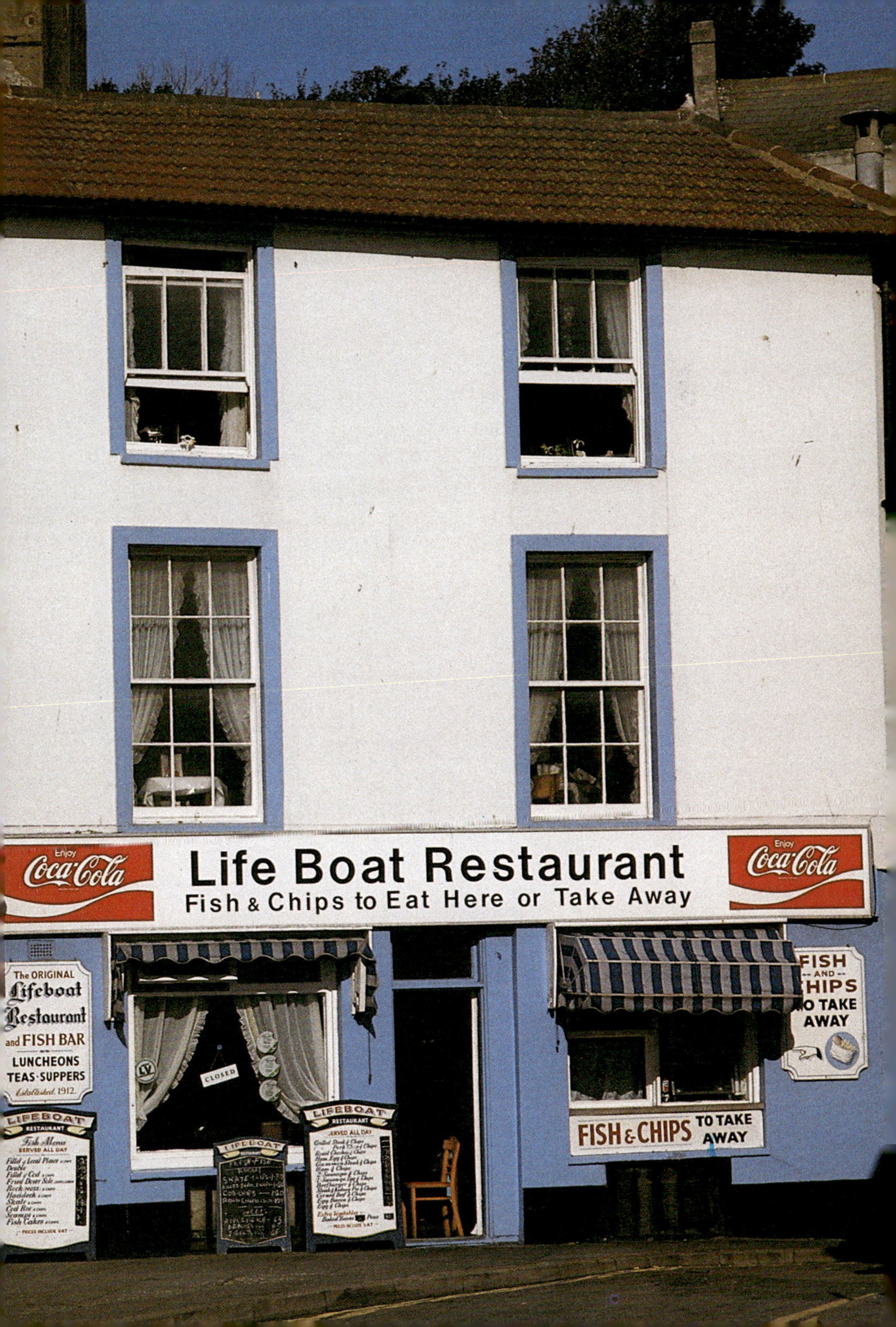
Enjoy Coca-Cola
Life Boat Restaurant
Fish & Chips to Eat Here or Take Away
Enjoy Coca-Cola
The ORIGINAL
Lifeboat
Restaurant
and FISH BAR
LUNCHEONS
TEAS·SUPPERS
Established 1912
CLOSED
LIFEBOAT
RESTAURANT
LIFEBOAT
LIFEBOAT
RESTAURANT
SERVED ALL DAY
FISH
AND
AWAY
FISH & CHIPS TO TAKE AWAY

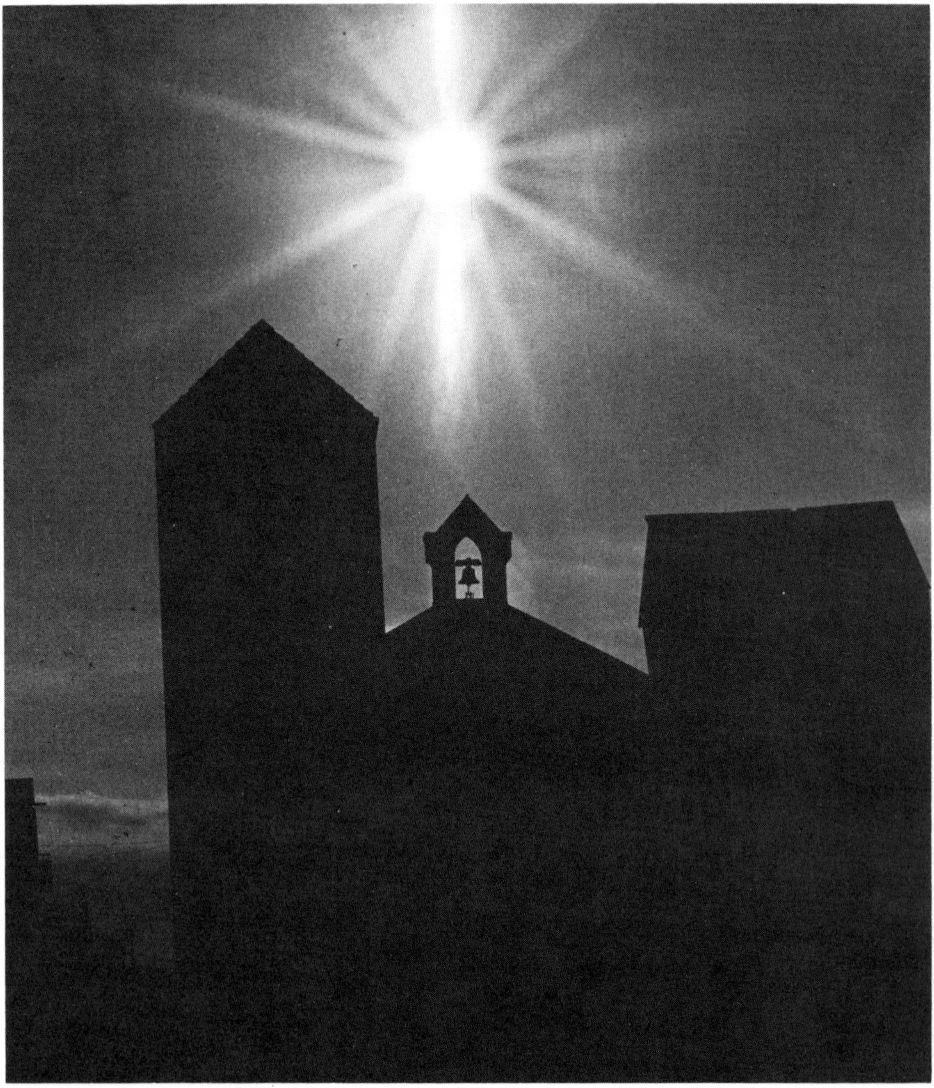

Sunrise, the Net Sheds, Hastings

Street, All Saints Street and their twittens, which sound like unintelligent young cats but is a Sussex word for alleys. Though very picturesque, the area isn't at all phony or tourist-orientated and most of the people you see are ordinary Hastings folk going about their business.

Try if you can to visit Hastings on Mid-Lent Sunday (check the date in your diary) when the ceremony of 'Clipping the Church' is performed at the 15th-century All Saints, which lies in All Saints Street not far from the half-timbered Cloudesley Shovel House, a popular camera subject with

Waiting for the catch, Hastings (right)

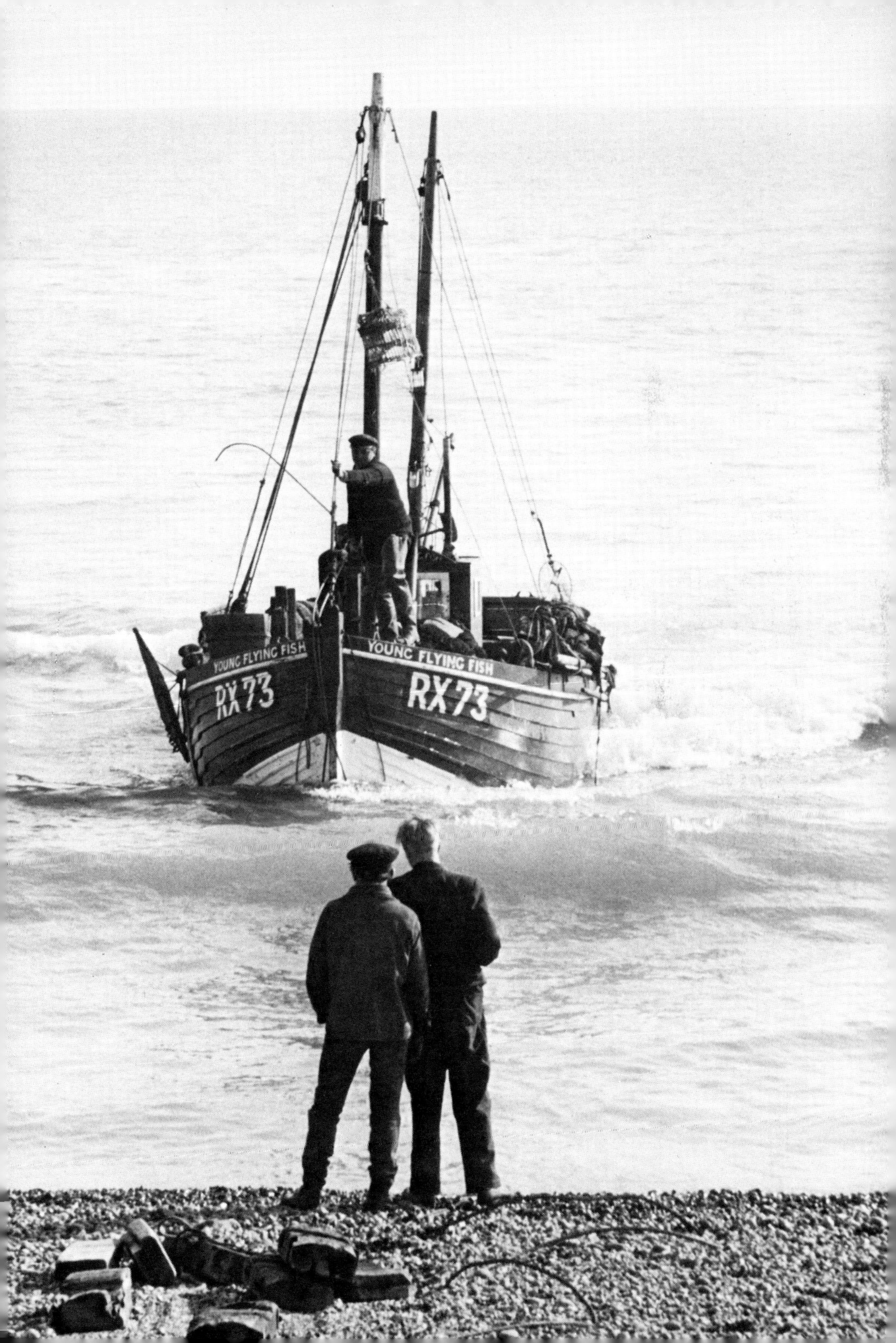
YOUNG FLYING FISH
RX 73
YOUNG FLYING FISH
RX 73

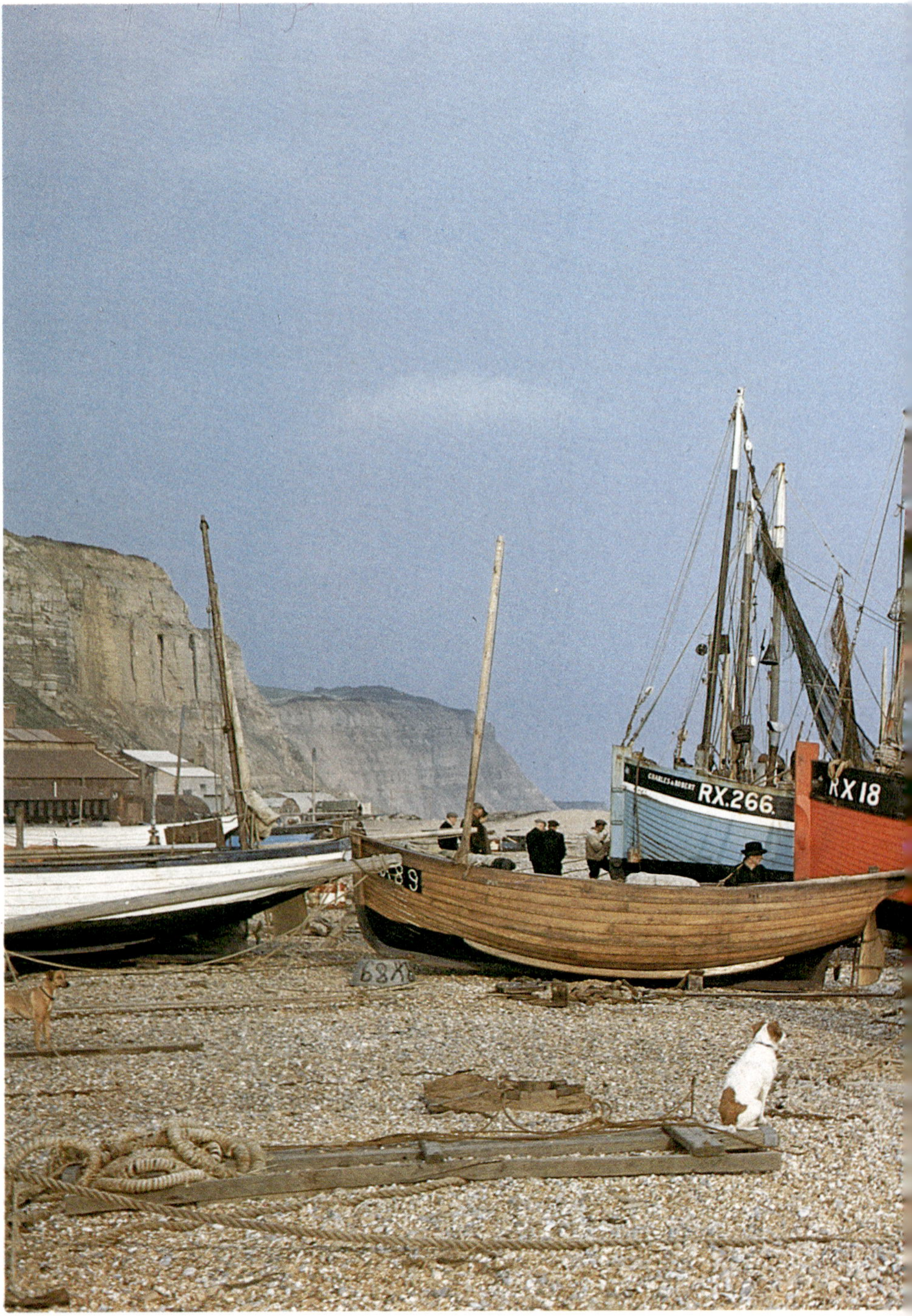
CHARLES & ROBERT RX.266.
RX 18

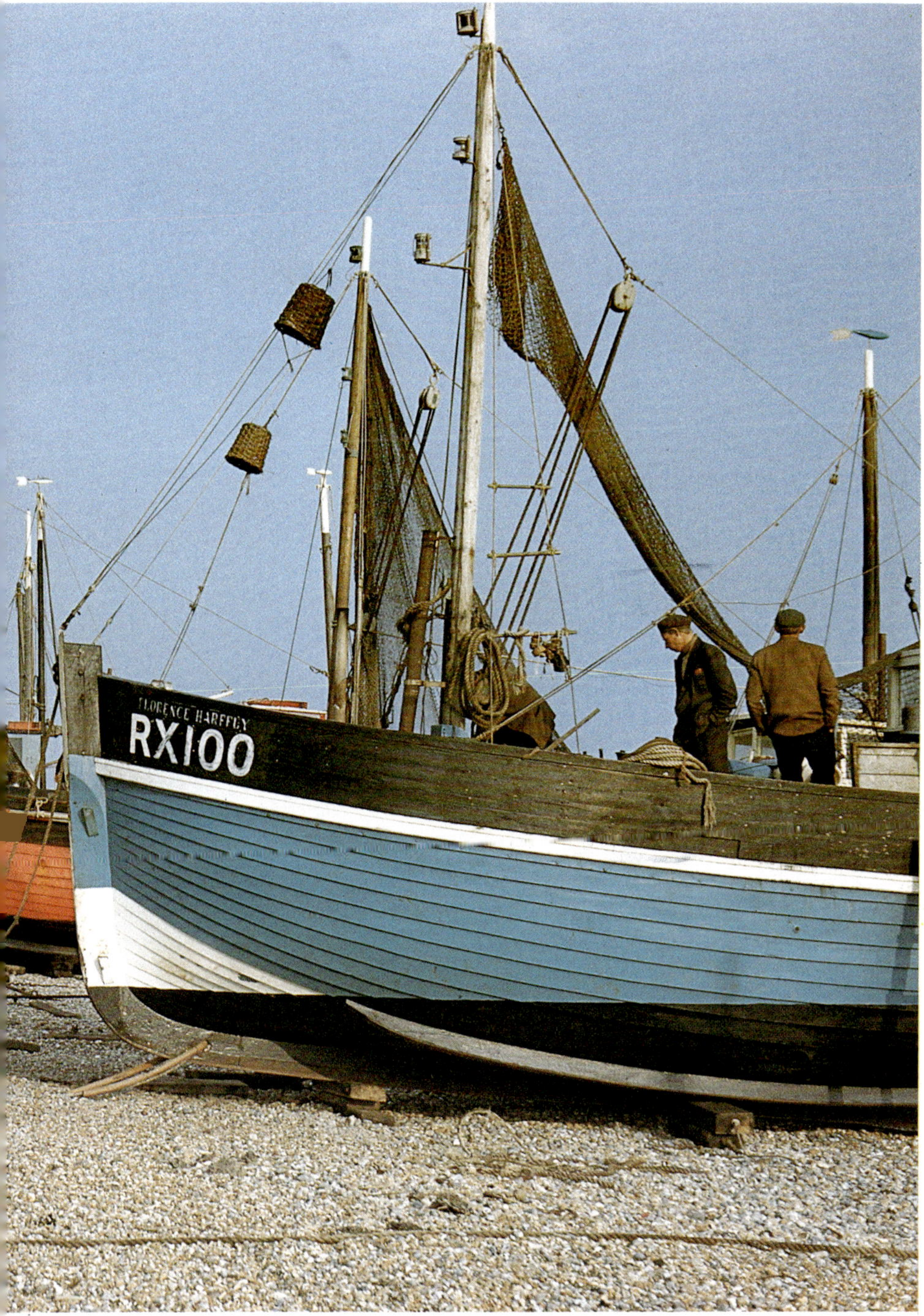

Hastings fishing boats

visitors. On that day the parishioners join hands and encircle the church while singing a hymn; use your widest-angle lens and see if you can think of a reason for the custom. No one else has.

Energetic people will make for the lift which runs up the face of East Cliff like a funicular railway and at the top will take the path to the East, the start of a walk that will take them down glens, past miniature waterfalls, up gorse-covered hills, all the time with the sun on their right turning the sea into a sheet of jewels. They'll end up at the Fire Hills, so-called because of the flaming yellow gorse criss-crossed with the wide turf rides and cliff-edge paths. This is probably the best stretch of Sussex coast left – it's tragic to think that not all that long ago such a happy marriage between land and sea was the rule rather than the exception.

There's a lot of scrambling up and down on this walk, which is slippery after rain, so keep equipment to a minimum. If you start from Hastings in the afternoon or evening you will have the sun behind you lighting up the spectacular views, but avoid weekends in Summer if you possibly can.

Herstmonceux

The village of Herstmonceux lies along a busy road, but it is worth stopping to photograph the trugs, gardening baskets with a chestnut frame and a willow base, for which the place is famous. Their design only dates from the Great Exhibition of 1851, but they can be seen all over Britain. Stacked together outside the shops, they can make an almost abstract picture.

However, all the visitors come to see the castle, reached by a lane to the East of the village which passes through the pleasant and photographable hamlet of Flowers Green. The home of the Royal Observatory, which moved there from Greenwich due to air pollution and the reflection of the lights of London, the castle is closed to the public, but the grounds are open regularly in Summer (check locally) and should be visited if possible.

Built by a hero of Agincourt, Sir Roger Fiennes, in 1440, the rose-red castle rises from a water-lilied moat to contrast splendidly with the green fields and ancient chestnut trees. Ducks paddle about while under the surface lurk legendary carp. You can walk in an Elizabethan garden and follow a stream to lakes and woods. It's an idyllic scene, almost over-romantic.

On a still day the reflection of the castle in the water is a popular subject and so are the six steel and copper domes and the silver-topped tower of the observatory. Once when writing an article about astronomy we were given a conducted tour in early Spring and discovered that the interior of the domes housing the telescopes has to be at the same temperature as the atmosphere outside to avoid air movement – I have never been so cold in my life.

The great Gatehouse faces South and can be photographed from several angles. If using black and white film, an orange or deep-yellow filter will lighten the brickwork and give more detail as well as helping it to stand out against a dark sky. Notice the round loopholes for early guns, placed to cover the draw-bridge which has now been replaced by a brick one.

Any camera can be used to photograph the Gatehouse, but a wide-angle lens will be needed to include the whole of the

Herstmonceux Castle (right)

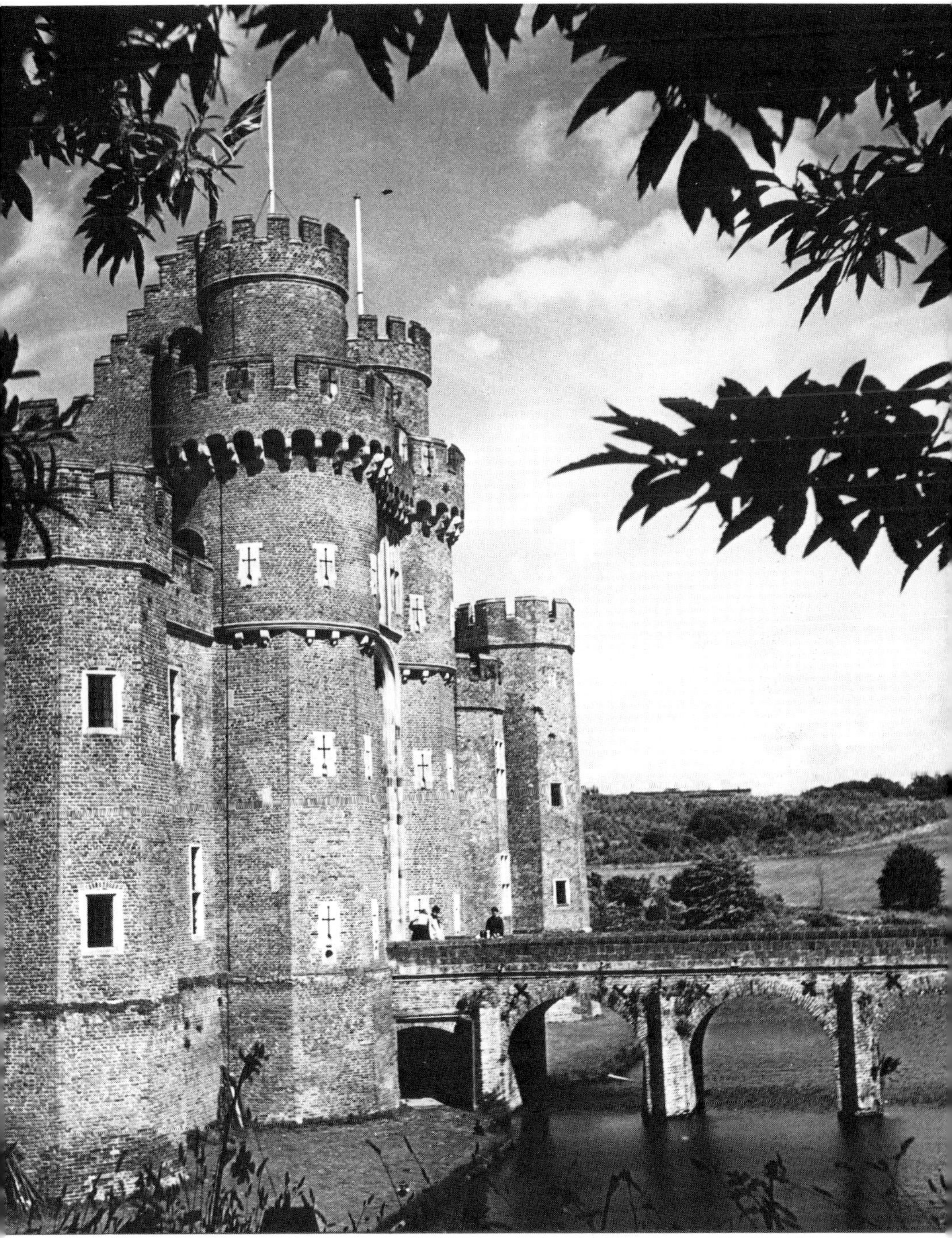

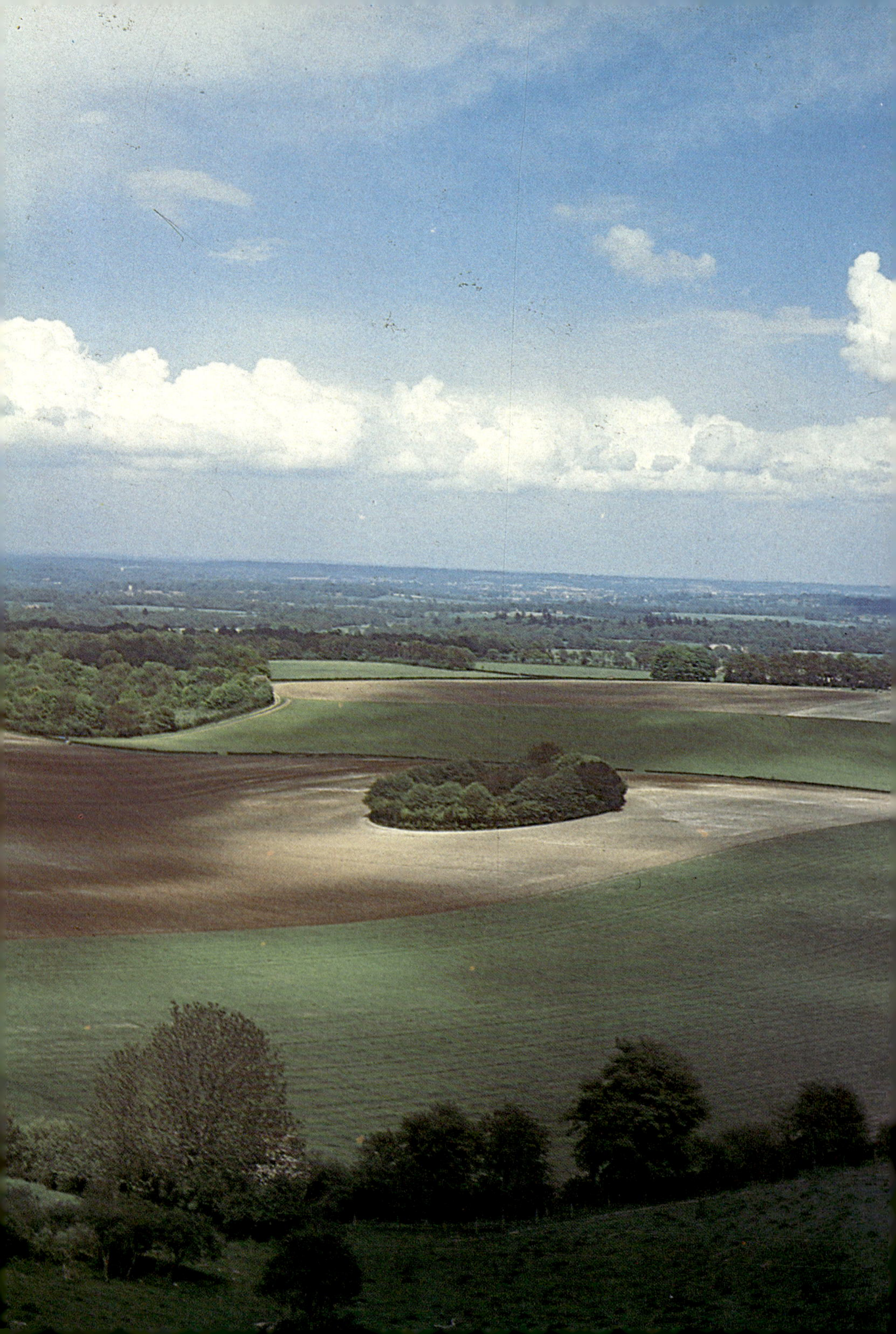

castle. Whenever you are photographing buildings it is essential to keep the back of the camera upright to avoid 'converging verticals', the effect that makes a tower look as though it is falling over backwards if you tilt the camera to include the top.

However, this often means you have to include a lot of boring, unwanted foreground. Fortunately Herstmonceux is a classic example of the way in which a foreground, the moat with its reflections, can add considerably to a picture.

The castle was the first important brick building to be constructed in England since the Roman occupation and was really designed as a home first and a castle second. Of course, it wouldn't be complete without a ghost – in this case that of a nine-foot-high drummer – and I was privileged to be the first person to photograph the path on the battlements along which he walks. Unfortunately he didn't put in a personal appearance and cynics say he was an invention of the smugglers who wanted to frighten away strangers when using the castle as a dump for contraband when it was deserted towards the end of the 18th century. This may well be true since a ton of tea was seized there in 1776.

On a rise in the ground a quarter of a mile to the West stands Herstmonceux Church with a shingled spire. There is an impressive tomb to Lord Dacre and his son with two figures in armour; it is now thought that it was bought cheap when Battle Abbey was dissolved and that it was originally a memorial to Lord Hoo and his son who died a century before Dacre – it's as though someone bought a second-hand tombstone to save money. Lately restored, it now glows with colour and makes a fine picture, best taken by the existing light though a tripod or monopod will probably be needed.

From the South Downs Way (left)

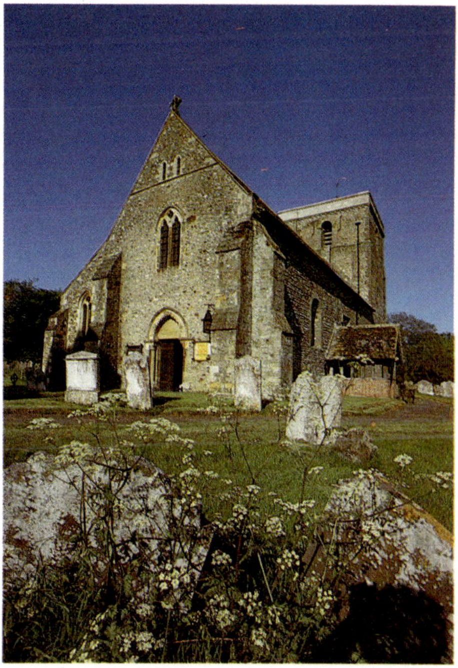

Typical Sussex church

Note also the thin wooden wands at the ends of the pews, each carrying a single candle; they make a good close-up foreground. Near the church you will find a 14th-century tithe barn.

It is impossible to avoid a lot of other visitors when the grounds are open since the castle is a magnet for tourists, but if you get there early there is enough space for them not to interfere with your photography.

Holtye

Want to photograph a Roman Road complete with the wheel-marks of the carts and chariots? Take the A264 from Tunbridge Wells towards East Grinstead, pass under the railway bridge at Ashurst and after some four miles start to look out for the White Horse Inn on your left. Three hundred yards before it there is a sign-posted track to the Roman Road.

Dating from about 100 AD, it is surfaced with iron slag from the 'bloomeries', the iron-smelting furnaces of the time, because the local stone was too soft; it was discovered when the metal was struck by a lightning bolt. The average track between the cart wheels is 4 ft. 6½ ins., 2 ins. narrower than that of the British Rail.

To show the construction of the metalled surface use a wide-angle lens from a low and close position, stopping well down to obtain good depth of field. If you are feeling energetic you can follow the track down past the exposed section of the road to Bassetts Manor Farm, Hartwell and Hartfield.

Polling Station, Stag Inn, Balls Cross

Kirdford

Around Kirdford you can still find the remnants of the forests of huge oaks that once covered the whole of the Weald. Unique survivals, these giants are well worth recording, and dramatic pictures can be taken if strong backlighting is used with the sun itself shielded from the lens by the trunk or branches while the beams of light filter through the leaves.

Opposite the locked church you will find on the wall a plaque listing the horrifying effects of alcohol – it was set up by a hard-drinking 18th-century vicar, presumably suffering from a hangover. It is best photographed on an overcast day; otherwise tree-shadows may produce patchy lighting.

Walk up the main street to the Foresters Arms, a superb example of natural grouping that developed gradually between the 16th and 19th centuries; if using black and

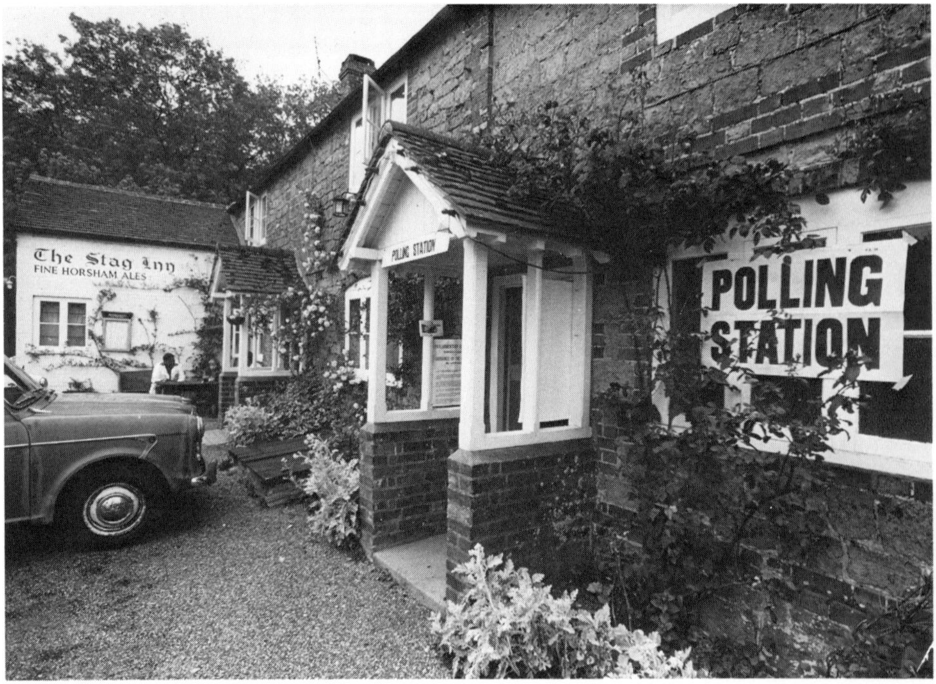

white film, an orange filter will bring out the detail in the tile-hung front. In spite of having read the plaque, enter and ask for 'Sausage in the Basket' – it sounds a joke, but the sausages, made by the butcher in Petworth, are the best in Sussex. They should be eaten to the music of a heavenly choir but all you'll hear if it's a weekday is the solemn tick of a grandfather clock. Saturday night, when 25lbs of sausages are eaten, is rather noisier. Both inside and out, the Foresters provides at any time a lot of subject matter.

A mile and a half to the West lies the hamlet of Balls Cross. While the cottages are attractive, unique pictures can be obtained at election time, since the Stag is the only pub in England that is also a polling booth; it's surprising how many of the scattered electorate are overcome by a desire to vote during licensing hours.

Lewes

The first thing you see as you come into the town from Brighton is the grim bulk of the Victorian prison on your left – I remember the President of the Irish Republic, Eamon DeValera, once telling me about his experiences there as a guest of the establishment in 1916. This is a down-beat introduction to an airy and exciting hillside town.

The first thing of interest in the High Street is St Anne's Church on the right, the best of the six parish churches in Lewes. Photograph the Norman font, carved like a basket, and the cell in which lived a 13th-century female hermit – you can look into it through a window on the South side of the chancel (that's the part of a church in which the altar is placed).

Then on the left comes Shelley's Hotel. This started life as an inn called the Vine in

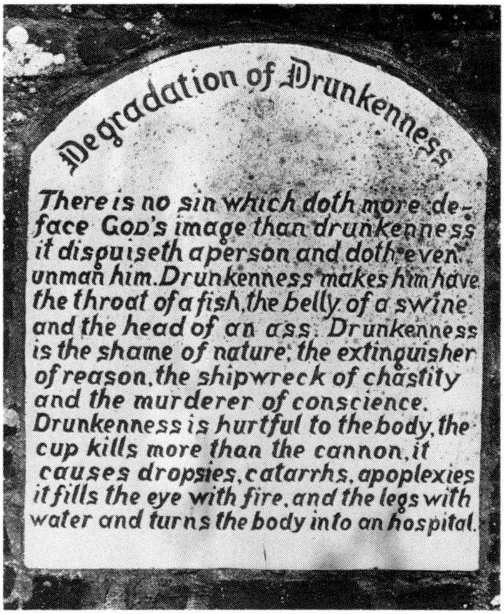

Temperance Notice, Kirdford

Elizabethan times – there are still paintings of the period on the walls of one of the rooms – was taken over by the Shelley family as a home in 1663, fitted with a new Georgian front and then became a hotel. Apart from making a picture, it is a good place to stay now that heavy traffic has been diverted to the bypass.

Next, cobbled Keere Street runs down a 3-in-1 hill on the right. Now for pedestrians only, the story goes that while attending Lewes Races the Prince Regent in a moment of elation drove a coach and four down it, but this is hard to believe. It's a difficult enough task to go down the hill on foot and my guess is that he was driving the light post-chaise in which, a superb whip, he held the London to Brighton record. If he really did drive down Keere Street there was obviously a lot more to him than the fat voluptuary of history.

The upper half has a central gutter that could be mediaeval and the street, running North/South, is evenly lit from midday to the early afternoon. There are some good houses and cottages in Keere Street and at the bottom lies the Tudor Southover Grange with gardens open to the public.

Climb back up to the High Street. Just a few yards along is Bull House, a place of pilgrimage for the unlikely combination of tourists from the United States and revolutionaries, for it was once the home of Tom Paine. The author of *The Rights of Man* and *The Age of Reason*, he was in part responsible for the American War of Independence. Married to a woman from Lewes, he was both a tobacconist and an exciseman, which must have caused comment.

The house itself was built in 1450 and has later carved satyrs on the front which can be picked out with a long-focus lens. A wide-angle lens will be needed for the building (open from 3.30 to 5.30 on Wednesday, Thursday and Friday), which is always in shade and is best photographed on a day when big white clouds reflect light back from the sun.

On your way along the High Street you will pass a photographic studio called 'Reeves'. Pause respectfully – in the course of research on early-Victorian photography I came to the conclusion that this is the only studio in Britain, and possibly in the world, that has been in continuous use since 1850. When I visited it, the original daylight studio, resembling a large greenhouse, was unchanged.

Next on your left you come to the castle and the Barbican House Museum (where the huge negatives taken by the Reeves family covering the whole of the Victorian period are stored). The Barbican, the outer gate, faces South and can be photographed from the front or, better, from the right. The castle (weekdays 10 to 5.30; Sundays 2 to 5.30) has views from the top of the keep as far as the sea at Newhaven in one direction and to the hills around Crowborough in the other, but the photographer will prefer the red roofs and trees of Lewes.

In the 16th century when Christians were executing each other to prove the superiority of their own brand, seventeen Protestants were burnt at the stake at the top of steep School Hill, the continuation of the High Street. Lewes has never forgotten and on 5 November there is an event which is unlike anything else in England. Pagan fire rituals, the Gunpowder Plot and anti-Popery are all combined in a night which no photographer will ever forget.

All roads close at 5.30, so get there early. The six Bonfire Societies of Lewes parade in elaborate fancy dress on which each group has been working for the past twelve months; they carry torches, fireworks explode, bonfires blaze and the Cliffe Society burns the Pope in effigy. The rivalry between the societies is deep and bitter and things can become very animated indeed.

Flash will destroy the unique atmosphere of smoke, flame and flickering shadows. Use instead 400 ASA slide or colour-print film in a camera with a lens that has a maximum aperture of at least f2. Set the shutter speed at 1/30th, the slowest that can with care be hand-held, though it is wise to brace yourself against a tree or wall to steady the camera as much as possible. Lewes on Bonfire Night is an unimaginable experience.

However, at any time the town is a cheerful and photographically rewarding place. When Henry VIII divorced his lucky wife, Anne of Cleeves, part of the alimony was a house in Southover High Street, to the South of the town (open February to November, weekdays, 10 to 5.30). She never lived there, but it's full of interesting things including the eight-sided table made from black Sussex marble on to which the assassins of Thomas à Becket threw their

Spring daffodils (right)

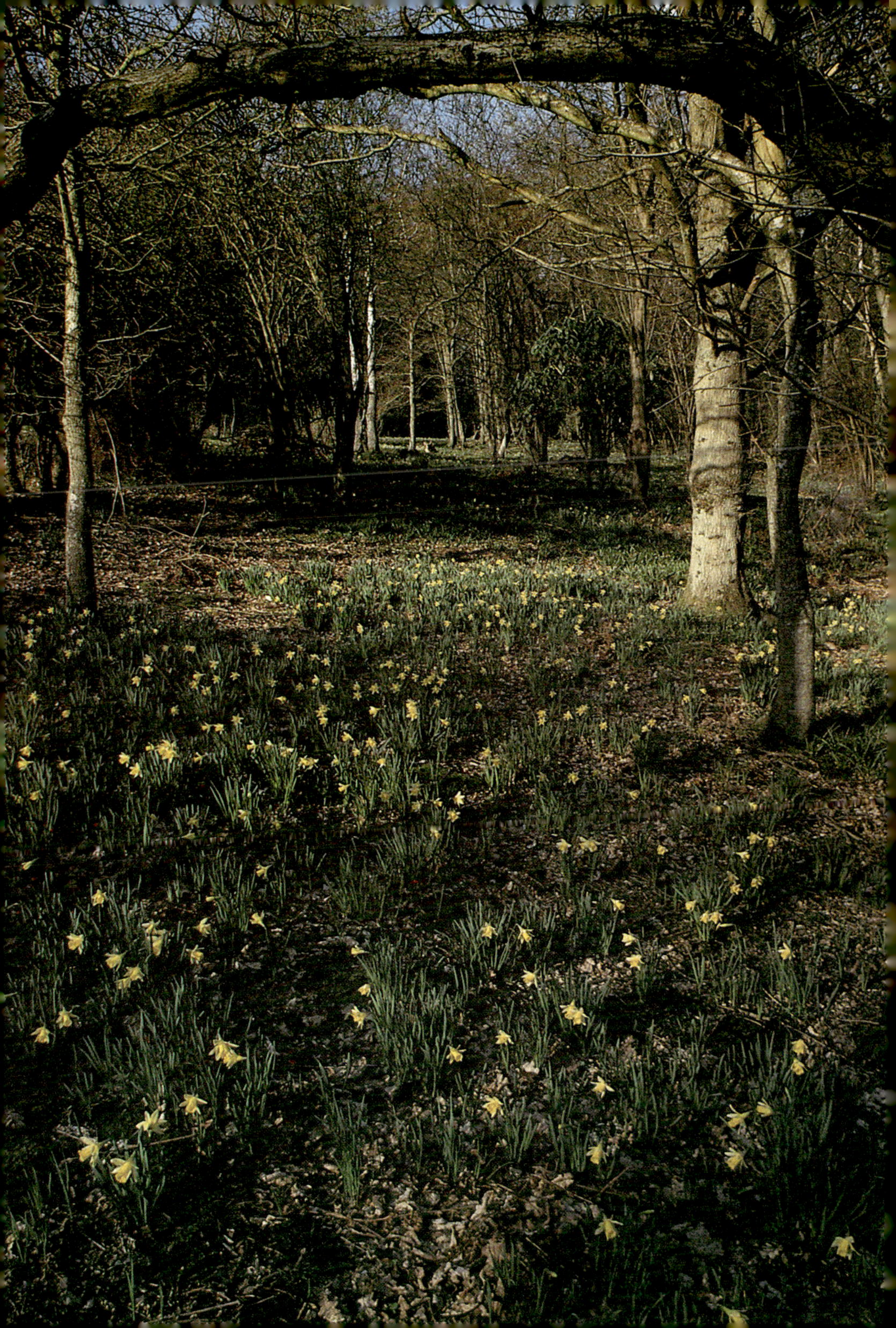

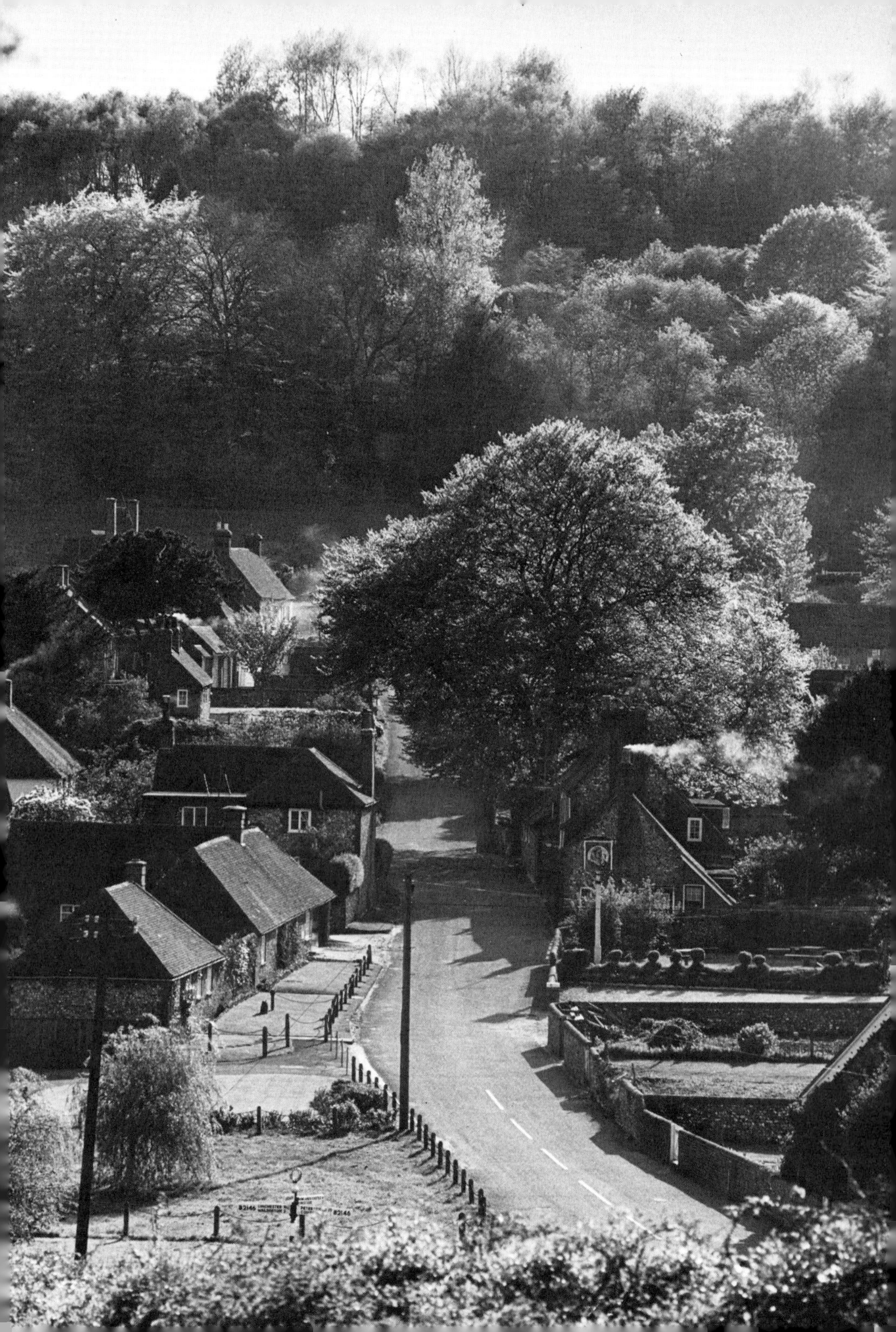
B2146
B2146

weapons during their escape from Canterbury; it promptly threw them off again – poltergeists are nothing new.

As with all Sussex towns, the best plan for the visiting photographer is to get lost – literally. There's a cattle market on Mondays, you can see the tombstone of William the Conqueror's daughter Gundrada in Southover Church, and the White Hart Inn, where Tom Paine was the noisiest of the 'Headstrong Society' that met there, is full of lawyers and their clients at Assize time (Lewes is the County Town of East Sussex), when the bar becomes something straight out of Dickens.

The town is hardly a mile wide in any direction and can easily be explored, perhaps ending with a walk that continues down the High Street, crosses the River Ouse, goes down Cliffe High Street and continues along a footpath that climbs Cliffe Hill, giving a magnificent overall view of the town and castle that is best photographed in the morning, and which leads on through glorious country to Mount Caburn, Glynde and Glyndebourne.

West Marden (left)

The Mardens

East, West, North and Up Marden; two of them are villages and two consist of just a church and a farm. All are quiet and beautiful places in a very remote part of Sussex; it is almost impossible to believe they are only some fifteen miles from Portsmouth. Though the four places are only a few miles apart by footpath, you have to drive a long way on narrow roads to see them all, and the chances are that without an Ordnance Survey map you will miss the two churches in the farms since they are hidden from the road by trees.

The most conventionally pretty – 'picture postcard' if you like – is East Marden. The centre of the village has a small 13th-century flint church with a stumpy weatherboarded tower standing above a miniature green surrounded by a handful of cottages. There are beehives in the churchyard, and in the church a small, highly gilded organ which once belonged to Prince Albert.

East Marden (below)

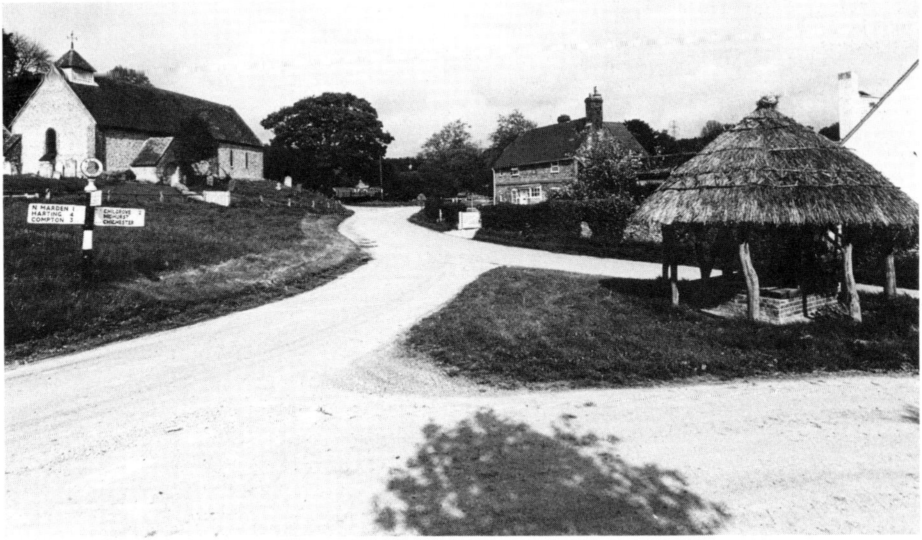

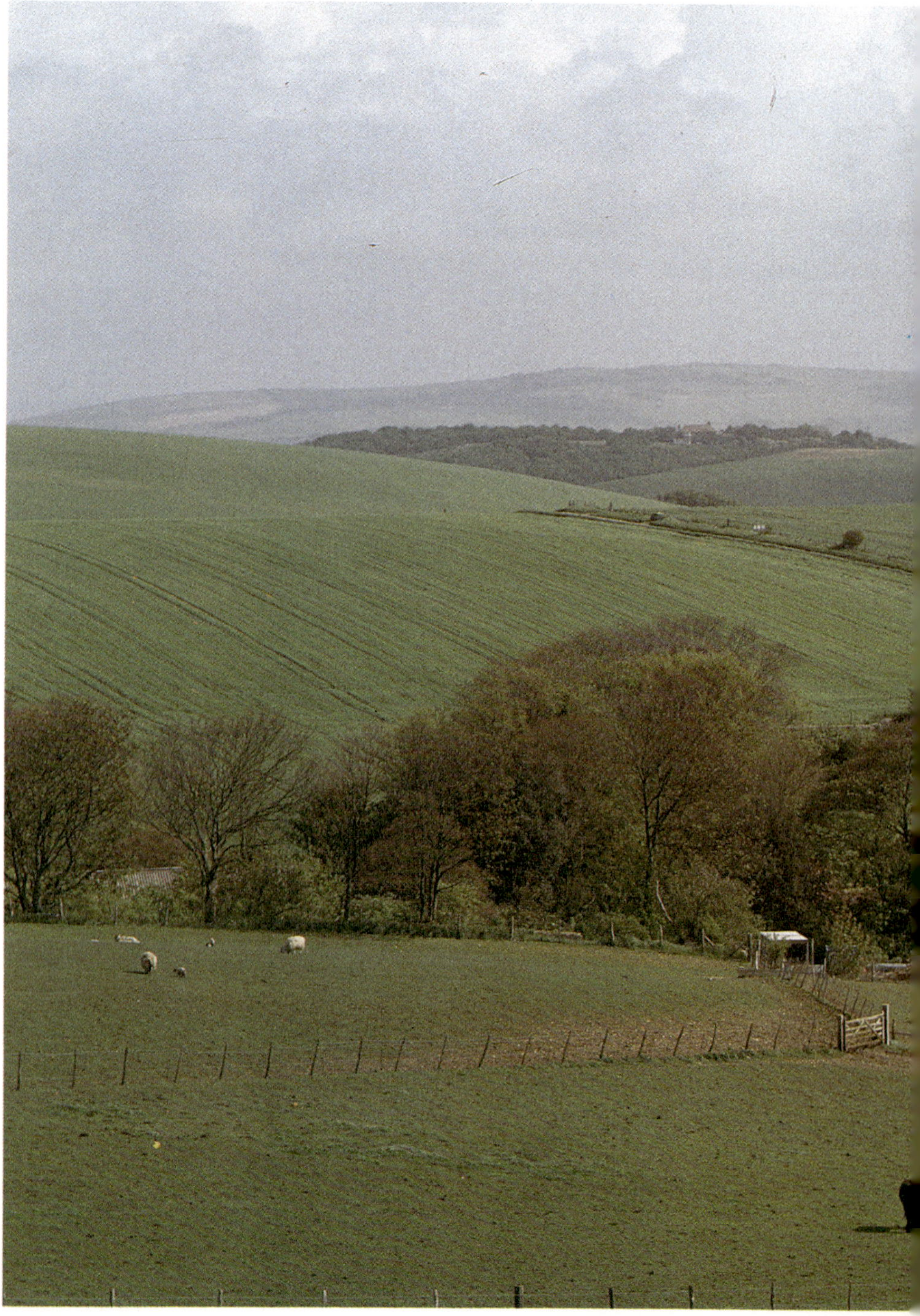

Sussex landscape with farm

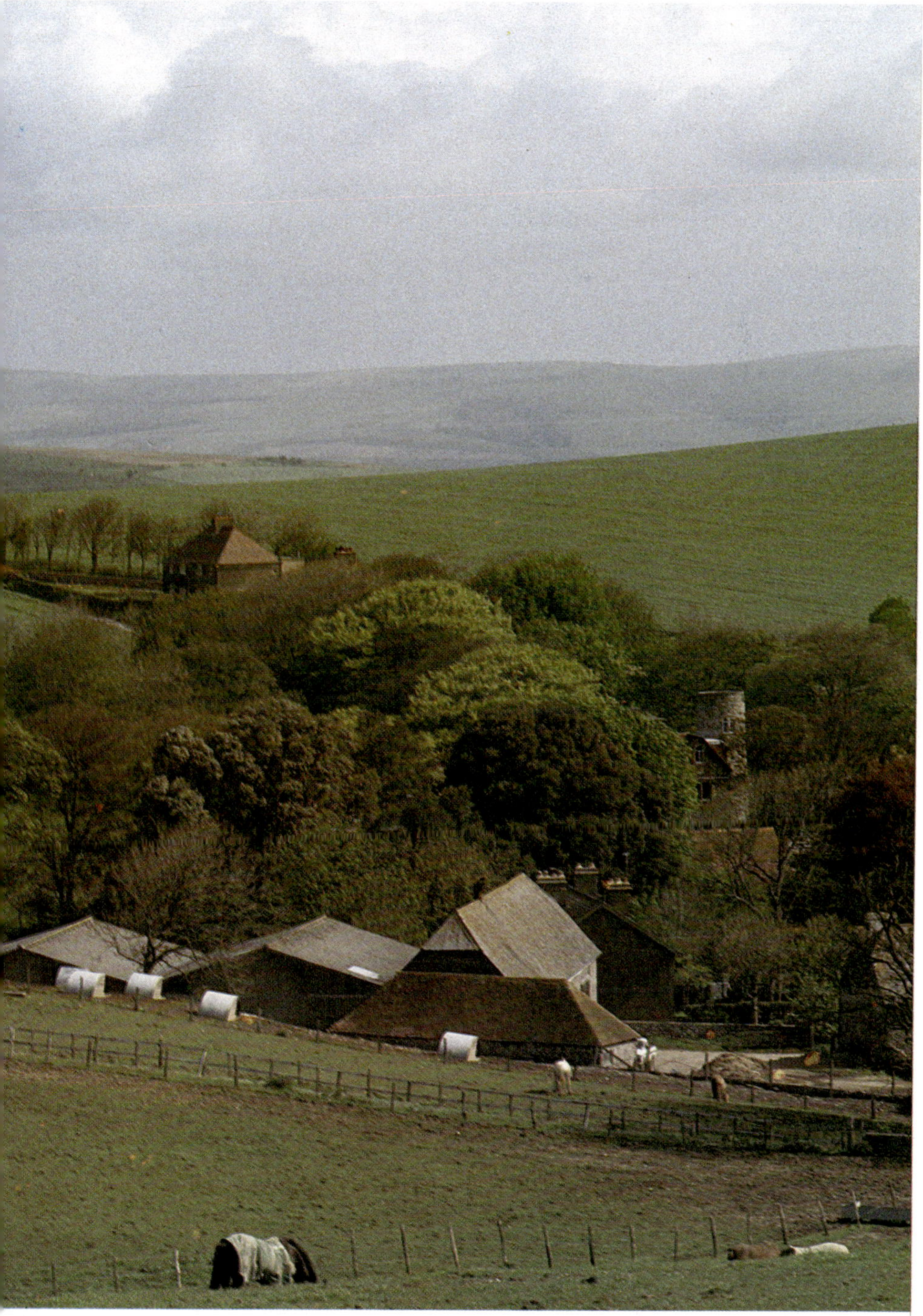

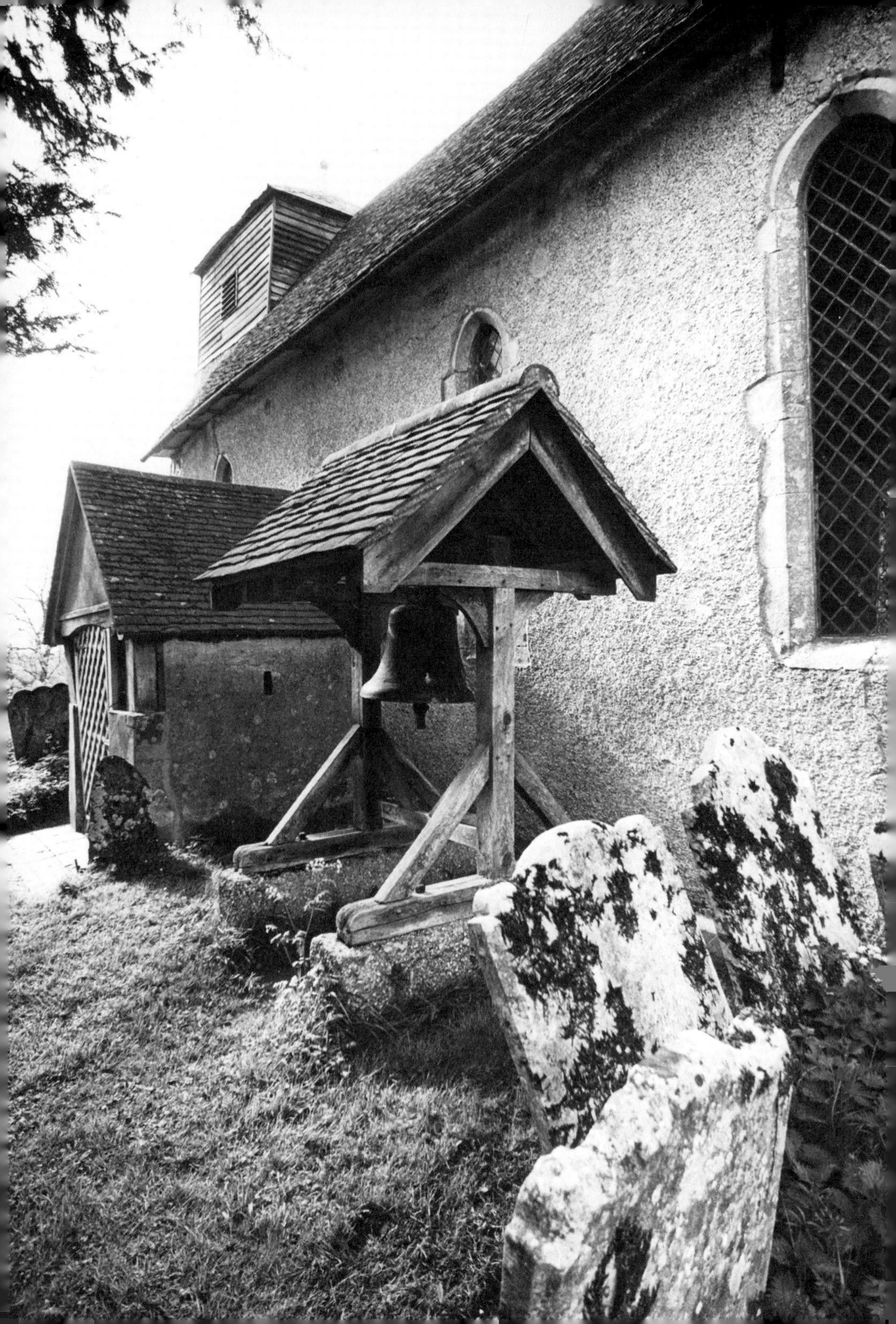

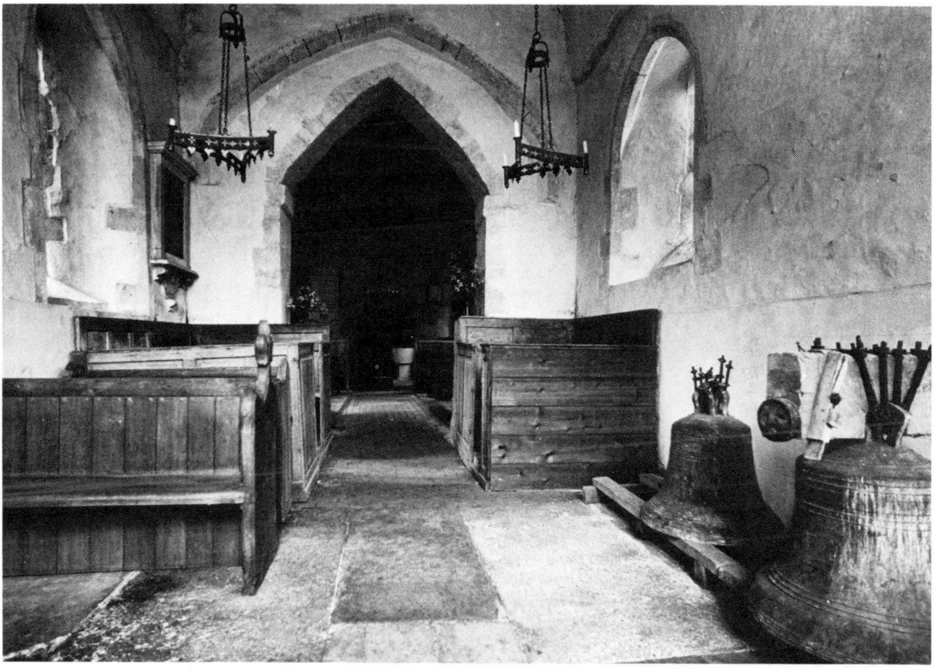

Up Marden Church

There is also a thatched well-head complete with bucket and rope looking disturbingly like the Cornish 'wishing wells' into which you are told to throw coins for luck. Life in every Sussex village once revolved round such a communal well, and an elderly inhabitant of East Marden once told me that before main water arrived it was looked on as the height of snobbery to have your own pump in your garden – such people were getting above themselves.

It is inevitable that the well-head will be included in almost every picture you take, the background varying with the angle. There is usually heavy shadow under the thatched roof and if you give enough exposure to record the detail there the background will be overexposed and burnt out.

Up Marden Church (left)

East Marden is reached by taking the B2141 from Chichester to South Harting and turning left a mile after Chilgrove.

West Marden is pretty in quite a different way. It lies on a turning that runs up a hill off the B2146 that goes from Chichester to South Harting. Just opposite the turning a lane climbs up the opposite slope of the valley and from this, with a lens of around 135mm focal length, you can obtain pictures of the thatched and tiled cottages with smoke rising from the chimneys against a background of trees. I know it sounds like an Edwardian watercolour, but its cosiness is typical of this part of Sussex.

To get to North Marden, the best plan is to take the lane that leads North from East Marden. Just before you arrive at the B2141 the farm and the church can be found if you look hard enough on your left. A rough footpath runs along a muddy farmyard, but the church is well cared for. Small and primitive, everything is in miniature – even the obligatory Royal Coat of Arms, normally so imposing, is made of iron and is only eight inches across.

We have left the best to last. Up Marden is difficult to find by road but well worth the effort. When driving from East to North Marden, you will have passed halfway there a turning on your left. Take this and after three-quarters of a mile turn left again and climb to Up Marden, five hundred feet up. It lies on your right, hidden by trees and a farm.

Some authorities claim that the church has the most beautiful interior in England. I happen to agree with this but you may not – such things are very much a matter of individual taste. Visitors may well ask: 'But what is there special to see?' and the answer is 'Nothing, really'. Its appeal lies in the fact that Up Marden is almost perfect 13th-century – this is how many country churches must have looked before they were 'restored' by the Victorians.

The colouring is subtle – uneven red-brick floor, cream and white plaster walls, dark wooden pews. Plenty of light comes through the clear glass windows and is reflected down from the light-toned wagon roof, but the range of tones is great, and exposure, especially with colour-transparency film, must be spot-on to obtain detail in the shadows without burning out the highlights in the white plaster.

Occasionally, depending on the time of day and the weather conditions, the light inside is fairly even and you can take your photographs by daylight alone, but more often it is patchy. Fortunately, the church is small enough and the walls and ceiling light enough for flash to be used successfully.

If you point the unit at the angle where the wall joins the ceiling behind the camera (as usual, an extension lead will probably

Bluebell Wood (right)
East Marden (below)

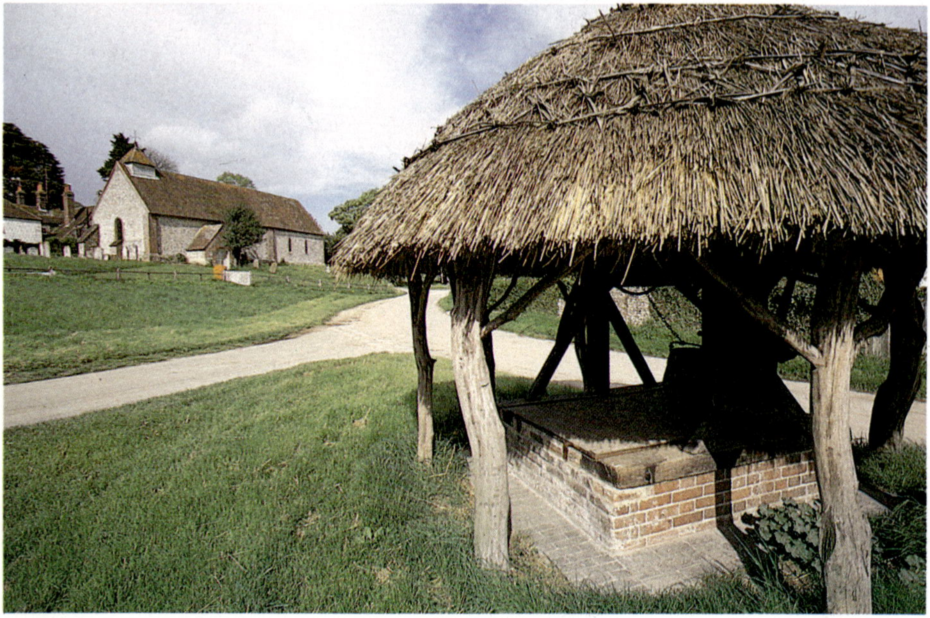

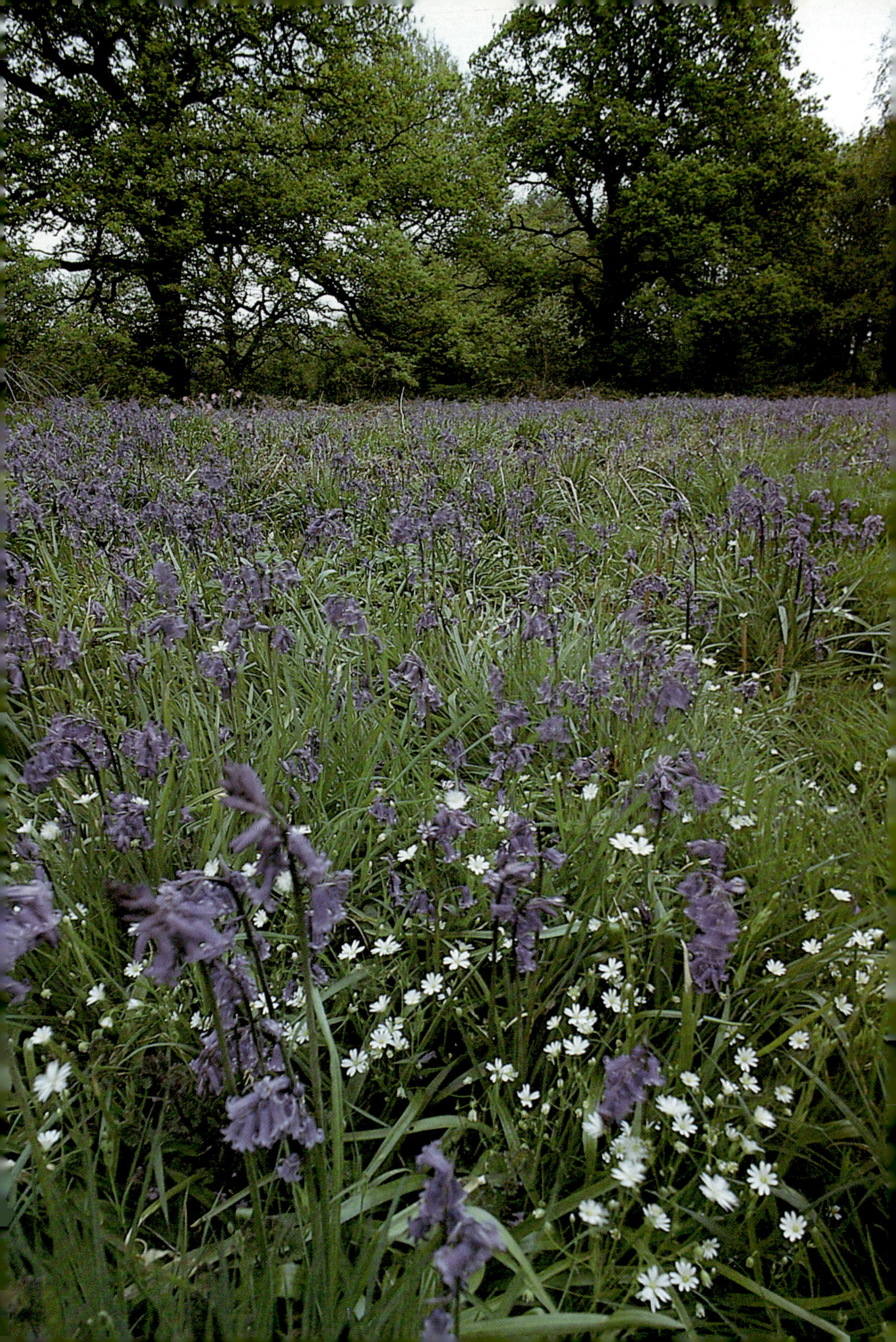

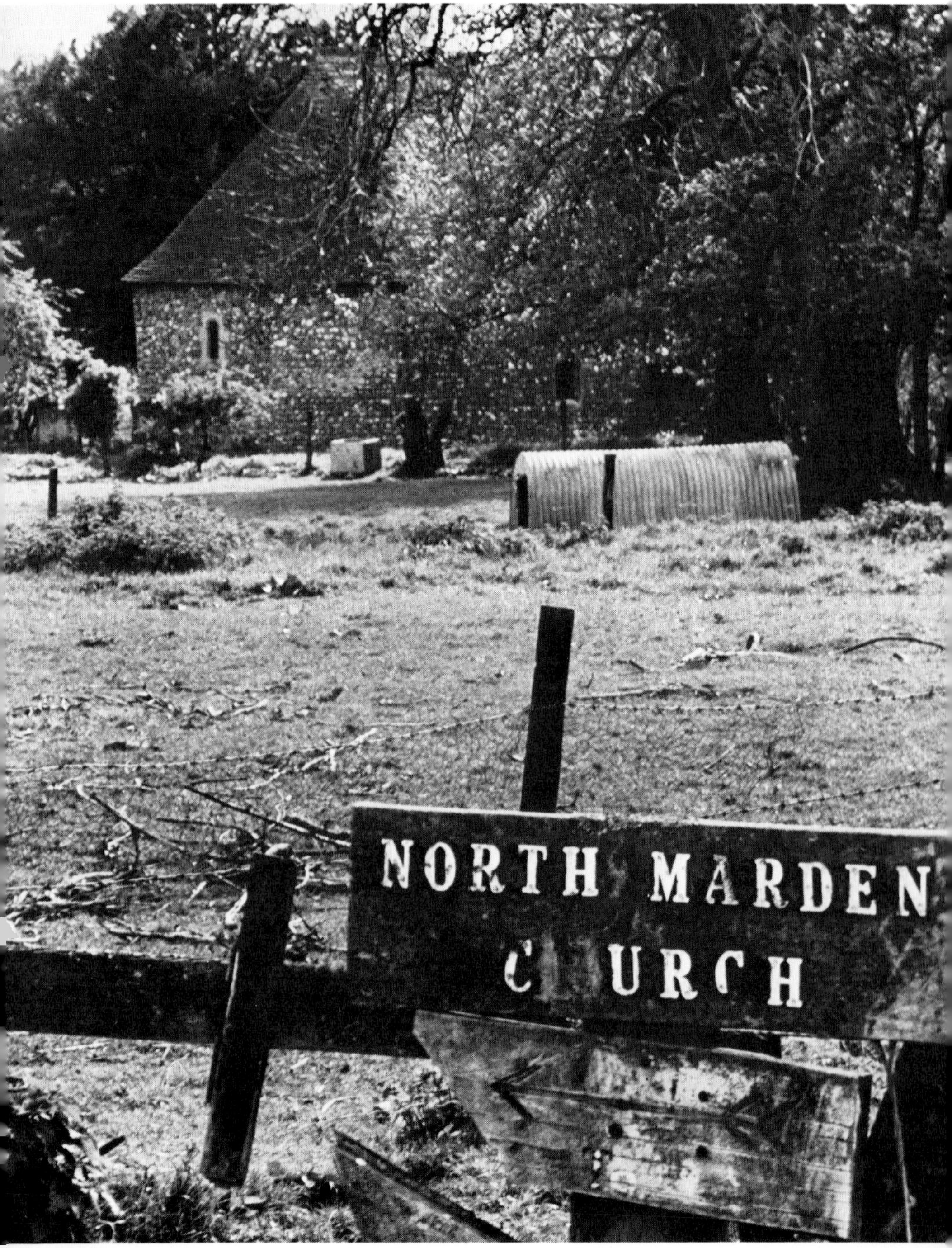
NORTH MARDEN

be needed), the light will bounce from both to give a soft, all-over effect. Alternatively you can work by the existing daylight while pointing a small flash at the darkest shadow area in order to lighten it. However you take your picture, it is wise to 'bracket' the exposure, giving a stop more and a stop less than the exposure you judge to be correct.

Up Marden is a gamble. You may wonder why on earth you ever bothered to go there or you may return over and over again. One thing puzzles me – where did the congregation come from? This part of Sussex seems completely empty of people.

Mayfield

Few places live up to the promise of their names – think of Shepherd Market or Newton-le-Willows – but Mayfield does. The best approach is from Wadhurst. Start off towards Mark Cross but turn left after a mile and a half down a minor road that leads through Tidebrook and Coggins Mill. This will bring you through quiet country to the Eastern end of Mayfield.

As you walk along the raised brick pavement of the one main street, running down the slope of a five-hundred-foot hill, there is hardly a building not worth looking at while on either side stretches some of the best country in Sussex. From a distance the village is not unlike Rye with red roofs crowned by a church, while from the windmill on Argos Hill a couple of miles to the North-West there are tremendous long-distance views over the Weald to the Downs.

Mayfield's most famous citizen was St Dunstan, blacksmith, goldsmith and harpist. While working in his forge one day he was tempted by a beautiful maiden but thinking he caught a glimpse of a cloven hoof under her skirt he seized her nose with his tongs. Had she been simply a young lady wearing a new style of footwear his career would probably have ended on the spot, but fortunately for Dunstan she turned out to be merely the Devil, who promptly fled to Tunbridge Wells.

There can be no doubt about the truth of this legend because if you visit the convent at the East end of the High Street on the North side the good nuns will show you the actual tongs used in the incident. Called the Old Palace, with a 15th-century gatehouse and well house, it is open to visitors at reasonable hours, but try if you possibly can to make an appointment beforehand. It contains the most spectacular mediaeval hall in England, seventy feet by forty feet, with three stone arches and a timber roof; it was the country home of the Archbishops of Canterbury.

After the Reformation the palace became the home of Sir Thomas Gresham, and the sword with which he was knighted by Elizabeth can be seen with the tongs. I have always thought of him as a City shark, but when my school fell into difficulties three hundred and fifty years after it was founded he helped us get back on our feet with a grant, so I suppose I owe his memory a certain respect.

Further along the High Street stands the parish church, set back from the road and looking to the North on open country. It is on the site of a wooden church built by St Dunstan before he became Archbishop of Canterbury in 959 and is very large with a short, broad spire like a hat. Inside, you can photograph as a curiosity a 1620 memorial to Thomas Aynscombe, his wife and five children; it has been violently and garishly re-coloured and has a fair-

North Marden (left)

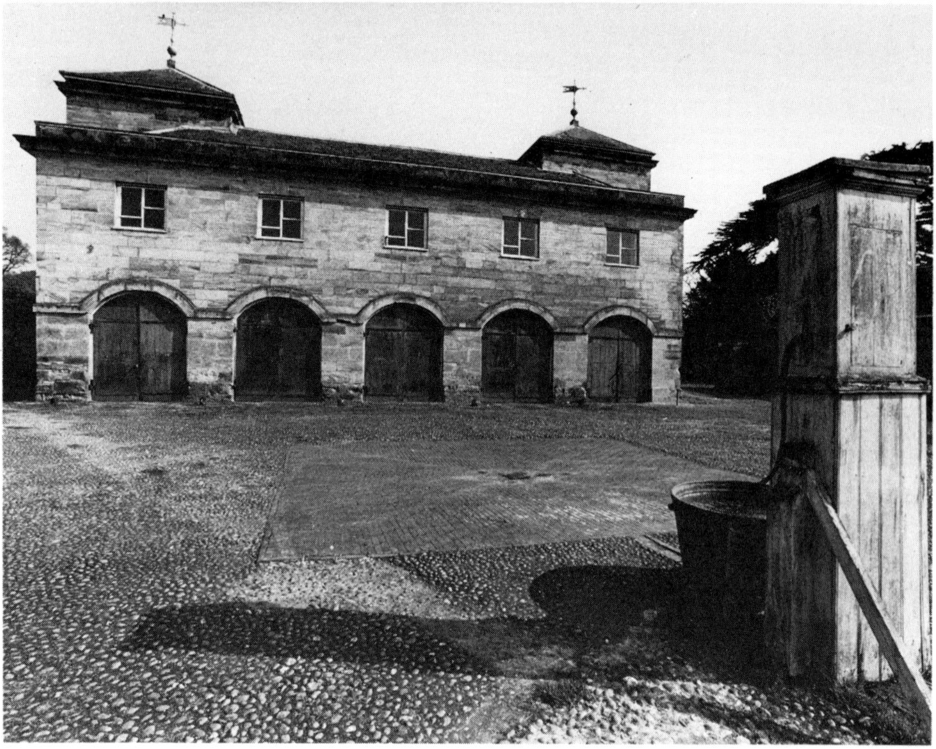

Ashburnham Stables

ground flavour. It is an odd fact that every vicar from 1780 to 1912 was a member of the Kirby family.

The High Street is an extraordinary mixture of architectural styles of every period from the 15th century onwards, but half-timbered, weather-boarded or tile-hung, all the houses nevertheless blend into a whole. Walnut Tree House is 15th century and the Middle House Hotel dates from 1575; both are well worth photographing, but so are lots of other buildings of Mayfield. There are few villages in which you can use so much film in just one street.

It can become far too busy in Summer when people crowd the hotel and restaurants, but in Spring and Autumn Mayfield is hard to beat.

Penhurst

In many ways Penhurst sums up the history of Sussex. Until the beginning of the 19th century it was a busy centre of the iron industry and the hammer from the nearby Ashburnham Forge could be heard for miles across the hills and the valleys. However, the last furnace in the county closed here in 1825 and the whole district went to sleep for a century.

Penhurst Church (right)

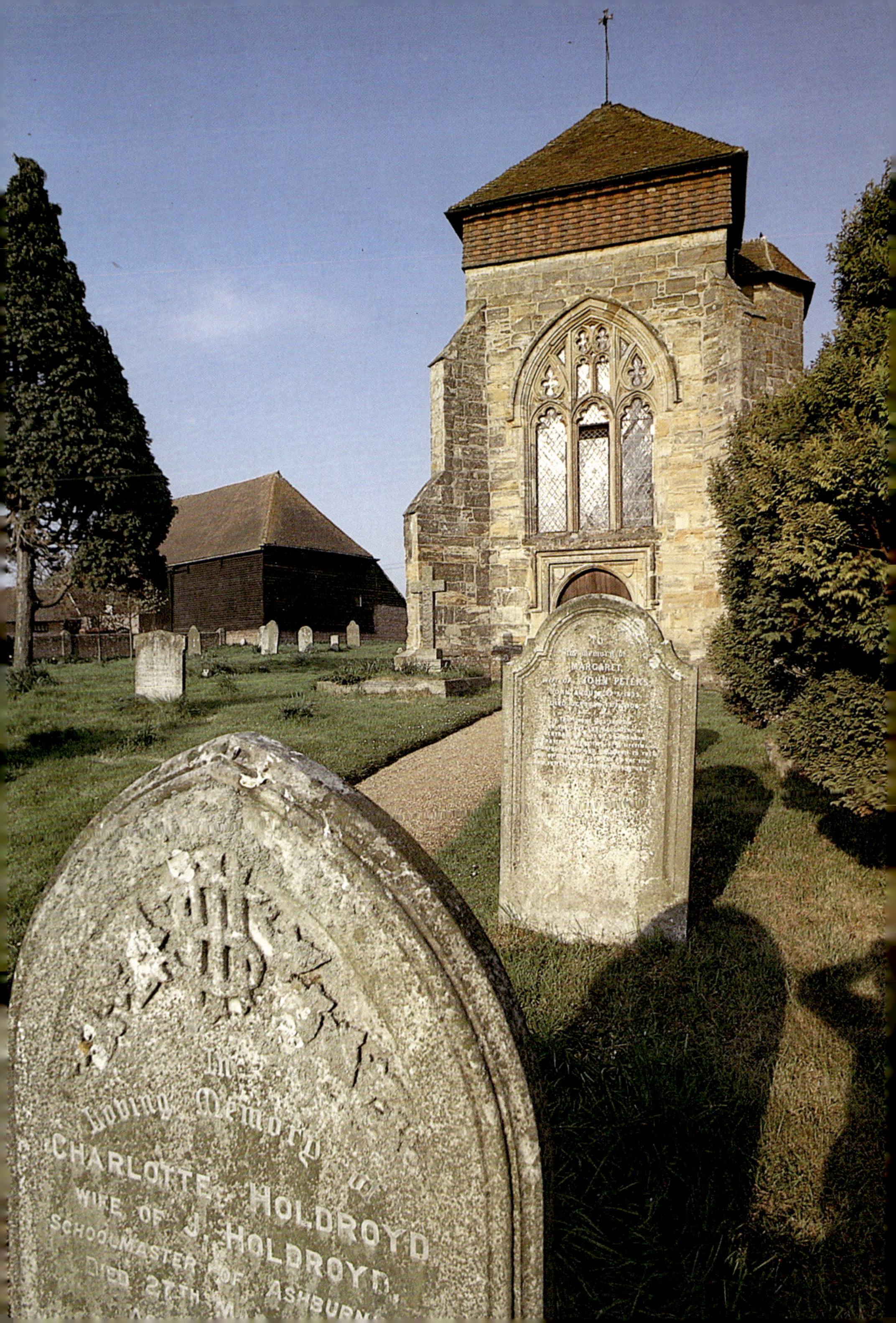
MARGARET
JOHN PETERS
CHARLOTTE HOLDROYD
WIFE OF J. HOLDROYD
SCHOOLMASTER OF

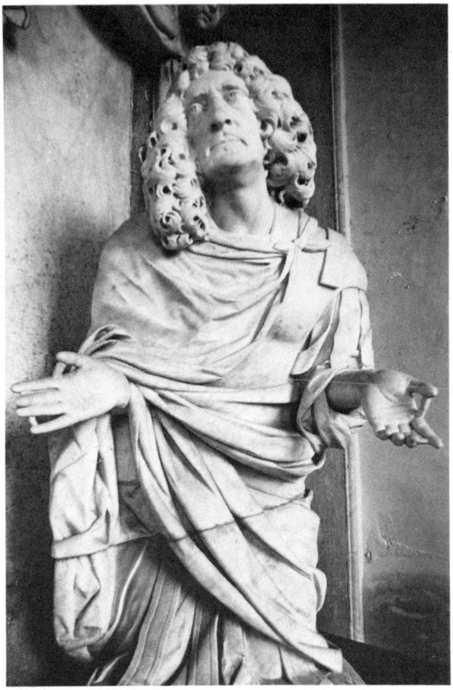

Ashburnham Church

Until quite recently Penhurst was probably the most remote hamlet in Sussex. The lanes leading there were difficult and there were no visitors. The church decayed, the roof collapsed, there were, of course, no services and grass grew everywhere. Then in 1959 the Friends of Penhurst got together and by 1960 the church was miraculously restored and rededicated. In Summer the once lonely place is now popular with tourists from Battle, some four miles away.

Penhurst consists of the church and the Manor House, a farm with a big tiled barn and a pond. When we were there a black and white collie was busily rounding up sheep to be sheared by the church wall, a scene that had been repeated for centuries. The church itself, built in 1340 from sandstone quarried in the Weald, had fresh plaster on the walls, but everything apart from that seemed in its original state. The box pews, the 14th-century screen and the beams were made of oak from the neighbouring Ashburnham estate, while in one of the windows the Pelham arms, three pelicans, were installed five hundred years ago.

The possibly Elizabethan Manor House should be photographed from the South; the entrance on the North side is far less attractive. The lighting is too flat for black and white photography in the middle of the day, though it can be suitable for colour work if conditions are hazy, and the building looks at its best in Summer in the morning or evening when the sun is low. Not far away is a wood with the interesting name of Town Creep, which we were assured had nothing to do with the tourists.

There is a T-junction just below Penhurst; if you turn right here, after a few hundred yards you come to a bend from which a footpath leads off to the right towards Ashburnham Furnace, the one that closed in 1825 to end the Sussex iron industry. If you potter about when you reach the banks of the River Ashbourne you may be able to trace the ditch leading to where a waterwheel once worked the giant bellows; the earth hereabouts is rusty from the ironstone and if you are interested in industrial archaeology you can record the traces of the once great furnace on colour film.

Pett Level

Pett Level is strictly for those who appreciate the off-beat. Pett village straggles along for miles and has little for the photographer, but the road eventually runs down precipitous Chick Hill to the coast. On your right the last cliffs in Sussex, sandstone ones,

Pett Level (right)

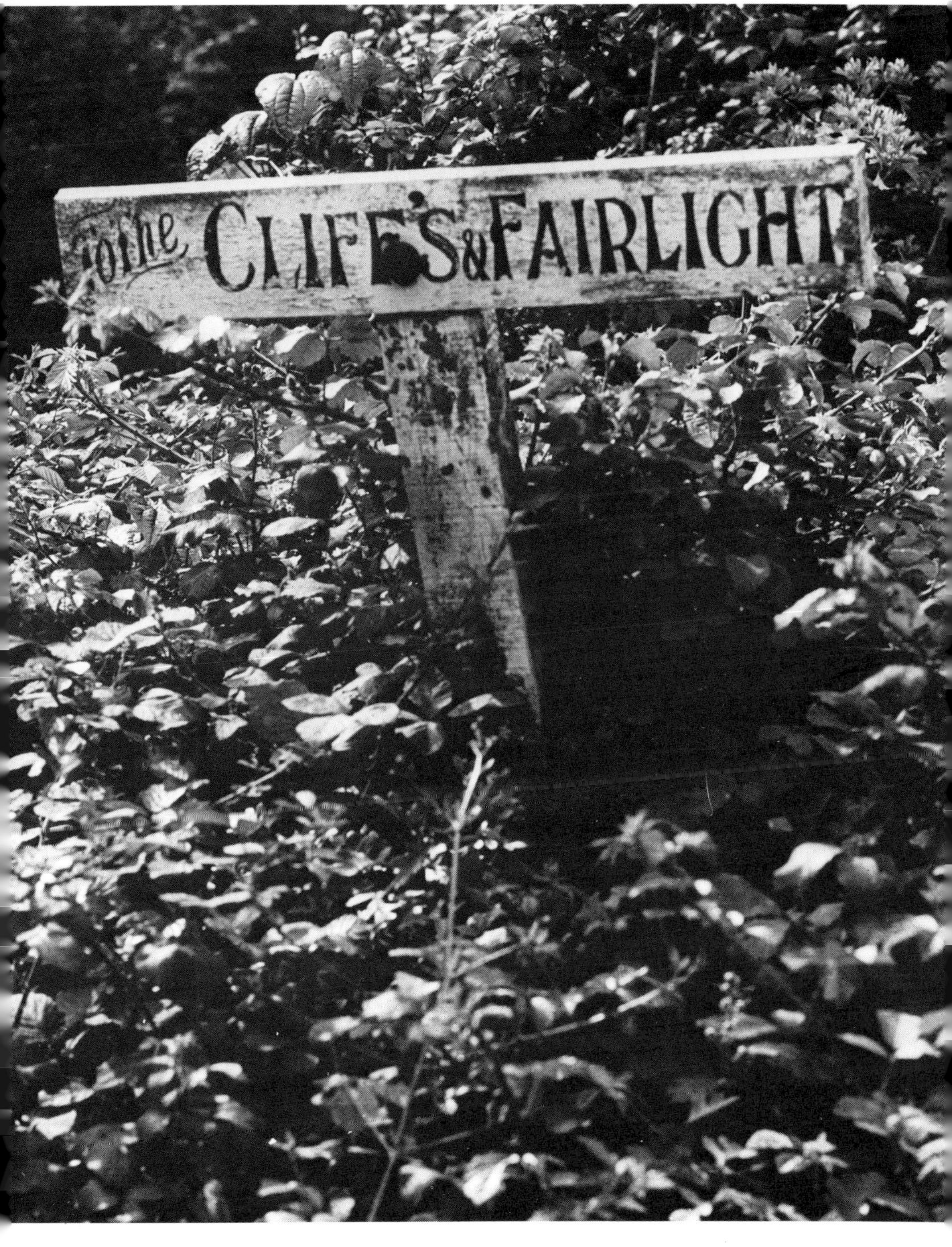
CLIFFS & FAIRLIGHT

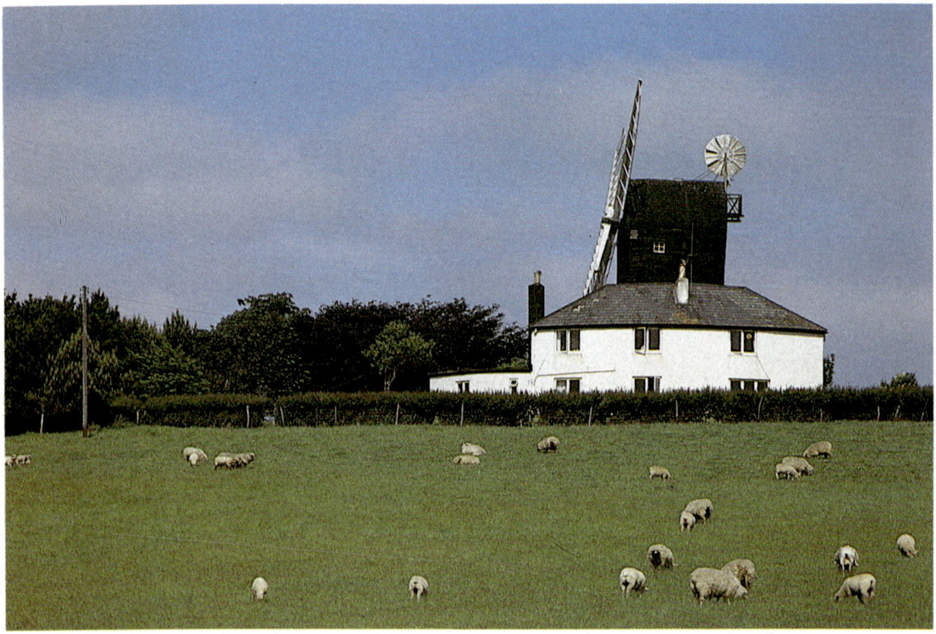

Hog Hill, between Pett and Rye

crumble into the sea; on your left is Pett Level, the oddest collection of eccentric bungalows and caravans, bird sanctuaries and relics of past wars you have ever seen.

Towards the bottom of Chick Hill you will find if you wander about people living in a converted gasometer with crenellations to make it appear romantic, a concrete gun emplacement, a Victorian horse-drawn bus, railway carriages and other dwellings that defy identification. Walk along the sea wall – to the left you can peer into the upper windows of holiday houses while on your right stretches the beach where at low tide there is always the odd fisherman digging for bait.

Look out for the remains of a prehistoric forest of oaks that was submerged by the sea long ago; bathers still stub their toes on the stumps. When the tide is really low you can photograph the outline of the *Anne*, a 70-gun ship sunk in 1690 during the Battle of Beachy Head. There have been horrifying attempts to 'excavate' it with a bulldozer.

Carry on along the sea wall for a mile or so and on the far side of the road that runs along its base you will find a series of shallow lagoons that have become bird sanctuaries (the area was flooded during the War in a rather pathetic attempt to stop a German invasion, and these are the remains of the flooding). Every Summer a pair of pink flamingoes, presumably on the run from a private zoo, come there to make a startling, outlandish picture, but there are plenty of our domestic birds to photograph as well.

If you turn off the main road by a white milestone you come to the beginning of the Royal Military Canal that runs through Kent to Hythe. Even in Summer you will probably have it to yourself apart from butterflies, sheep, cattle, swans, dragonflies, herons and frogs. This is a strange and enchanted part of the world unlike anywhere else in Britain, a place of wide, lumi-

Royal Military Canal (right)

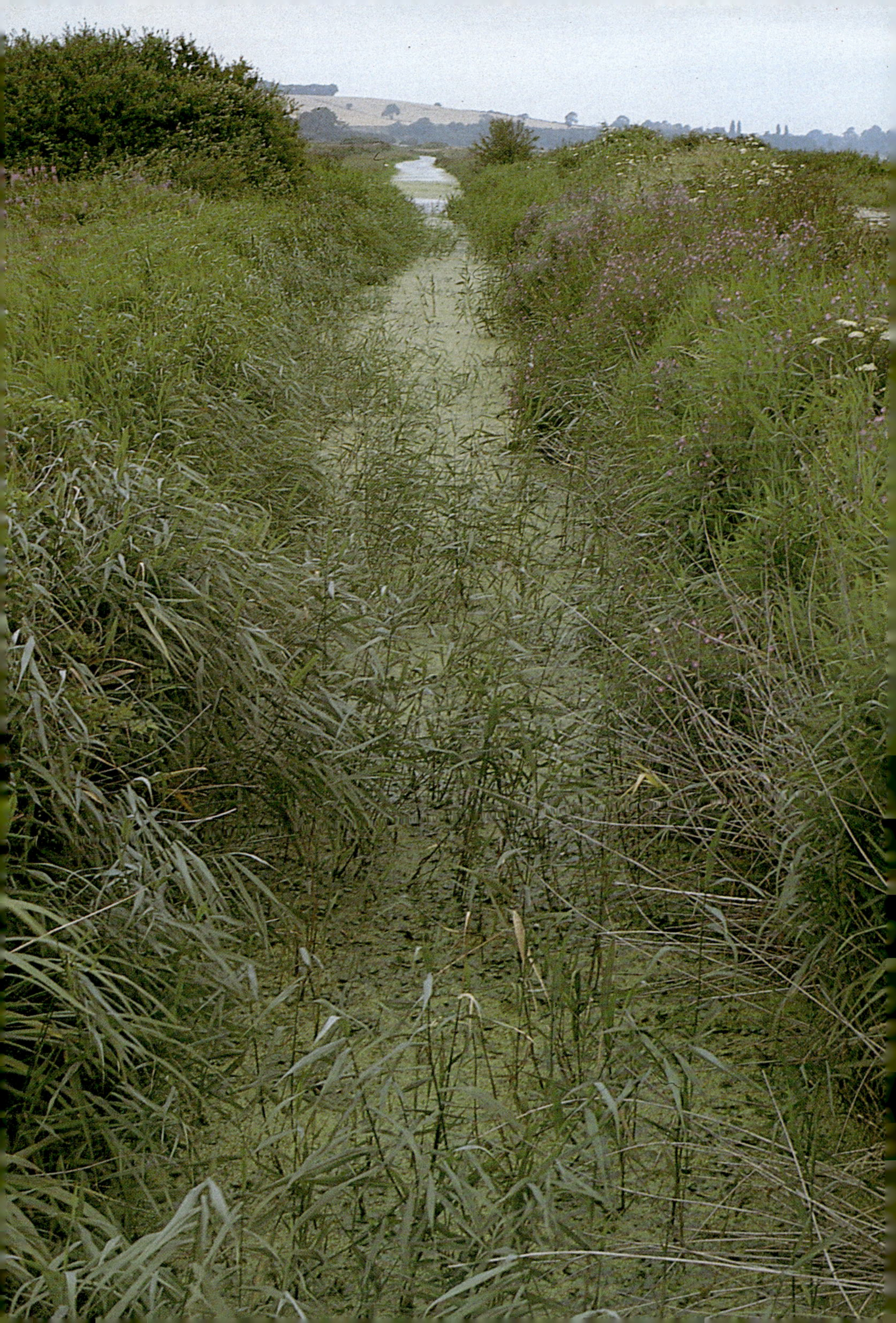

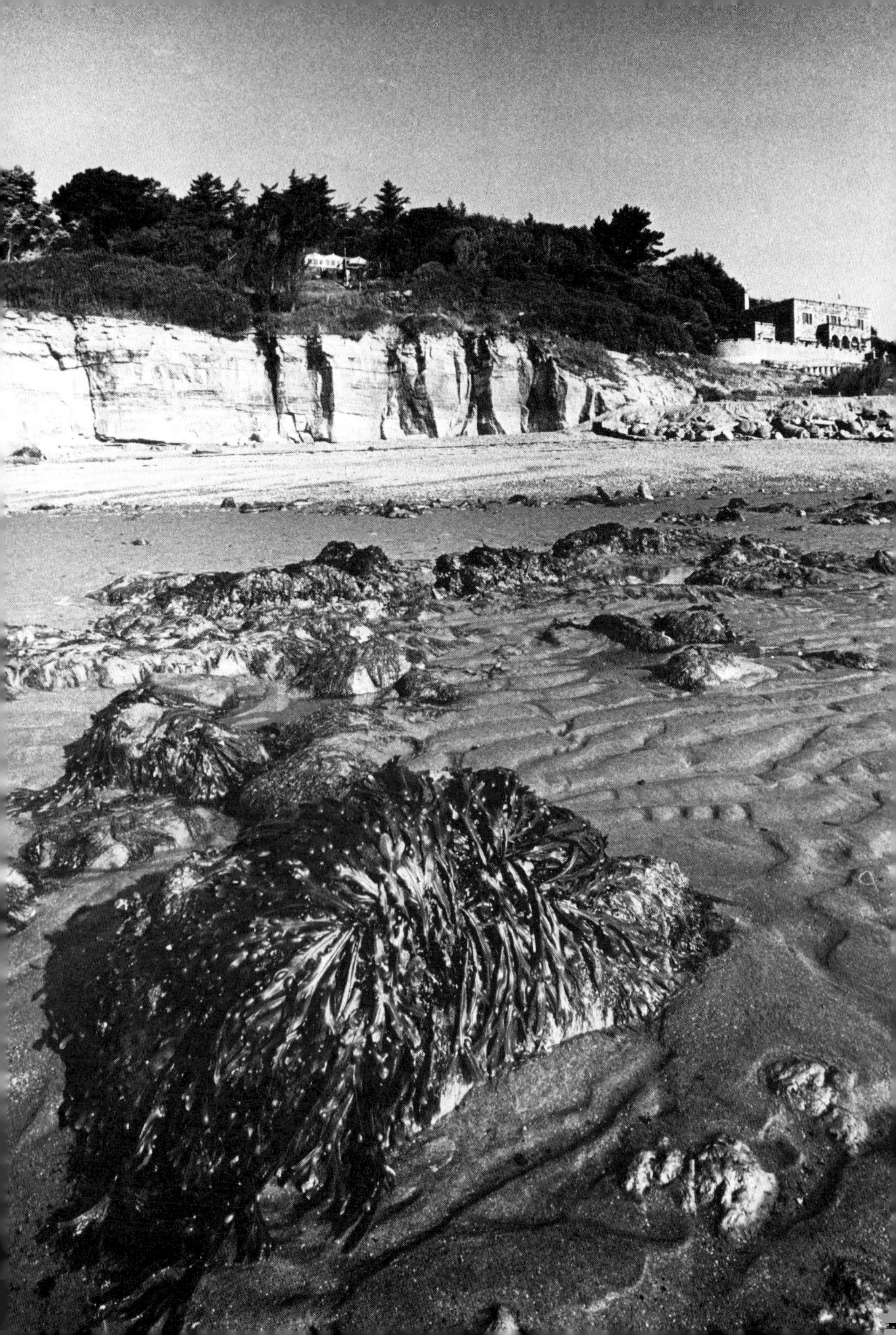

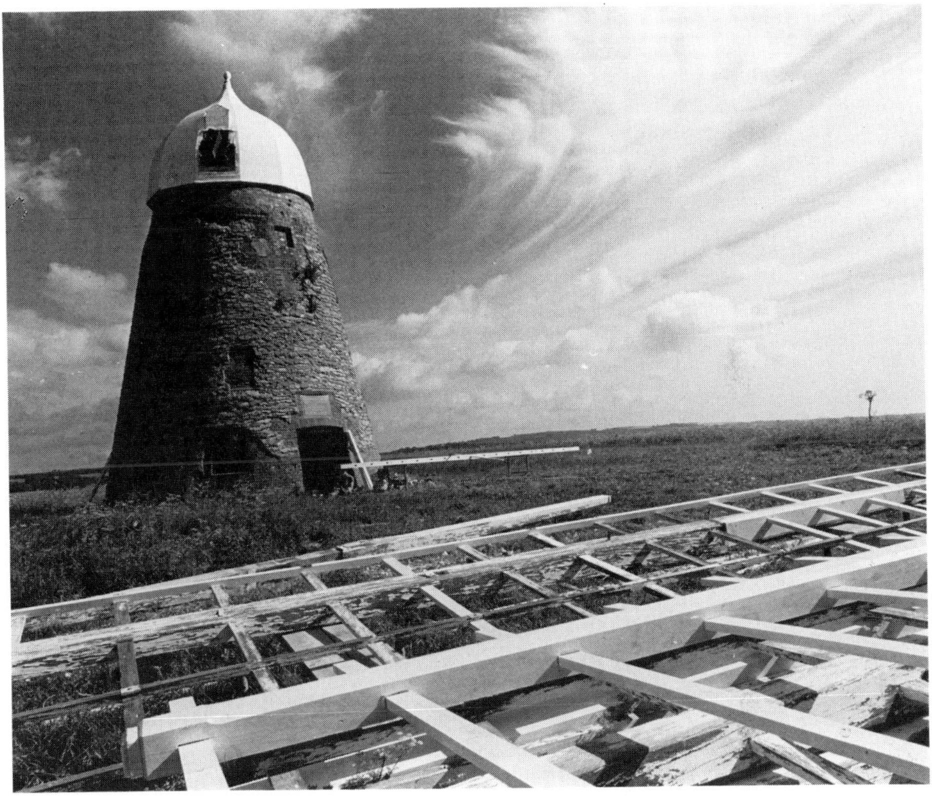

Hog Hill, near Pett

nous skies, reeds, marsh-flowers and an extraordinary stillness.

The path will eventually take you to Winchelsea, a walk that is made more remarkable by the fact that down on the nearby coast there is a mess of caravan parks, supermarkets, hamburger joints and amusement arcades. The contrast between the quiet, beautiful country and the coastal horror is quite incredible.

The canal was, of course, designed to halt a Napoleonic invasion – it was lucky it never happened, because the French Army would have crossed it in minutes. Around here and down on the shore you will find

Cliff erosion, Pett Level (left)

Second World War pill-boxes, brick or concrete, and Napoleonic Martello Towers, designed by one of the Packenhams. Had the Germans invaded, there is no doubt at all that the extremely strong Martelloes would have held out longer than the death-trap pill-boxes. There is a story in pictures waiting to be taken of the defences of this part of England, an obvious landing-place for invaders; you can still find remnants of barbed-wire entanglements on remote cliff-edges and concrete blocks that hopefully would have stopped tanks in unexpected places. In fact, the Germans did plan to land not far away, along the coast to the East of Rye.

The flat landscape calls for a wide-angle lens to capture the feeling of space; the sheep, swans and cattle can be tackled with your normal lens, while the wildlife need something with a focal length between 135 and 200 mm. If you are a naturalist and want to record some of the odd plants and insects that abound, the ability to focus very close to the subject will be essential.

This is a wonderful area for the photographer who doesn't mind leaving the rest of humanity behind for a few hours. There are no very obvious subjects – you have to create pictures for yourself, which is as it should be.

Petworth

Petworth is a sudden town – one minute you are driving through magnificent rolling country with the Downs as a distant background, the next you are inching your way through a complicated one-way system. It has the misfortune to stand on a busy crossroads, and the traffic crams the narrow streets which have many right-angle bends; without the procession of cars and lorries Petworth would be the ideal country town.

Part of the traffic problem arises from the fact that the town huddles up against the very high and very thick stone wall that surrounds Petworth House and Park. I don't think there is such an arrangement anywhere else in the country – the windows of the house overlook the town from behind the wall which runs on out into the country to surround the 2,000-acre estate without a break for ten miles. Inside the wall lies a serene, private world largely unchanged since Capability Brown laid out the park in the late 1750s; outside, the traffic grinds along and the Summer tourists crowd the pavements.

In fairness, out of season and away from the morning and evening rush-hours, Petworth can be very quiet once you are away from the main roads. Leave your car in

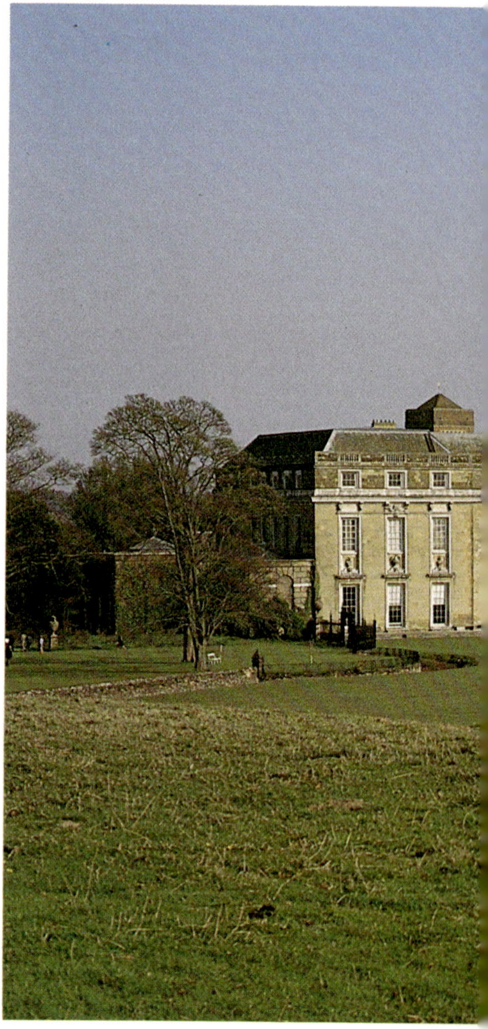

Petworth House

the big car park as soon as possible and walk into the Market Square, surrounded by shops of every period. High up on the Town Hall in the centre is the finest Baroque bust in Britain, a quite remarkable carving of William of Orange full of life and movement. Perhaps one should say it used to be the finest because it has been allowed to crumble and decay – I call it

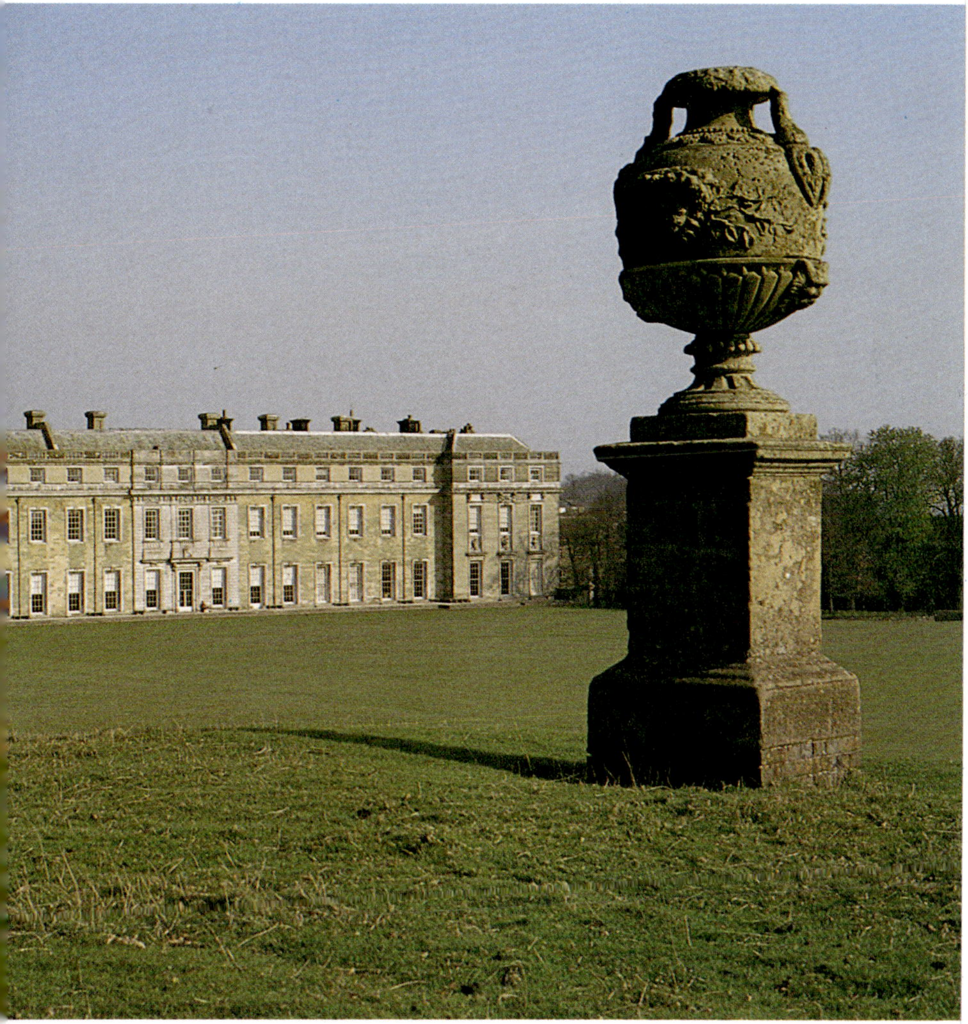

Petworth's Shame. Stand well back and use your longest-focus lens to record this neglected treasure.

To see how the town looked 300 years ago, walk to the North-East corner of the square and go up cobbled Lombard Street; the sun lights it around the middle of the day. At the top stands the church and 'Tudor House' (built actually in 1629); as you stroll up past a series of brick and stone cottages, one composition after another appears in front of you. The walk back to the square is equally rewarding.

More good buildings can be found in the High Street, Middle Street and East Street. Don't be misled by the name 'High Street'; it is a quiet narrow street of small houses and cottages, some of them 400 years old. While doing research for a newspaper we once interviewed a very old photographer who lived in one and he ended up by asking us to share it with

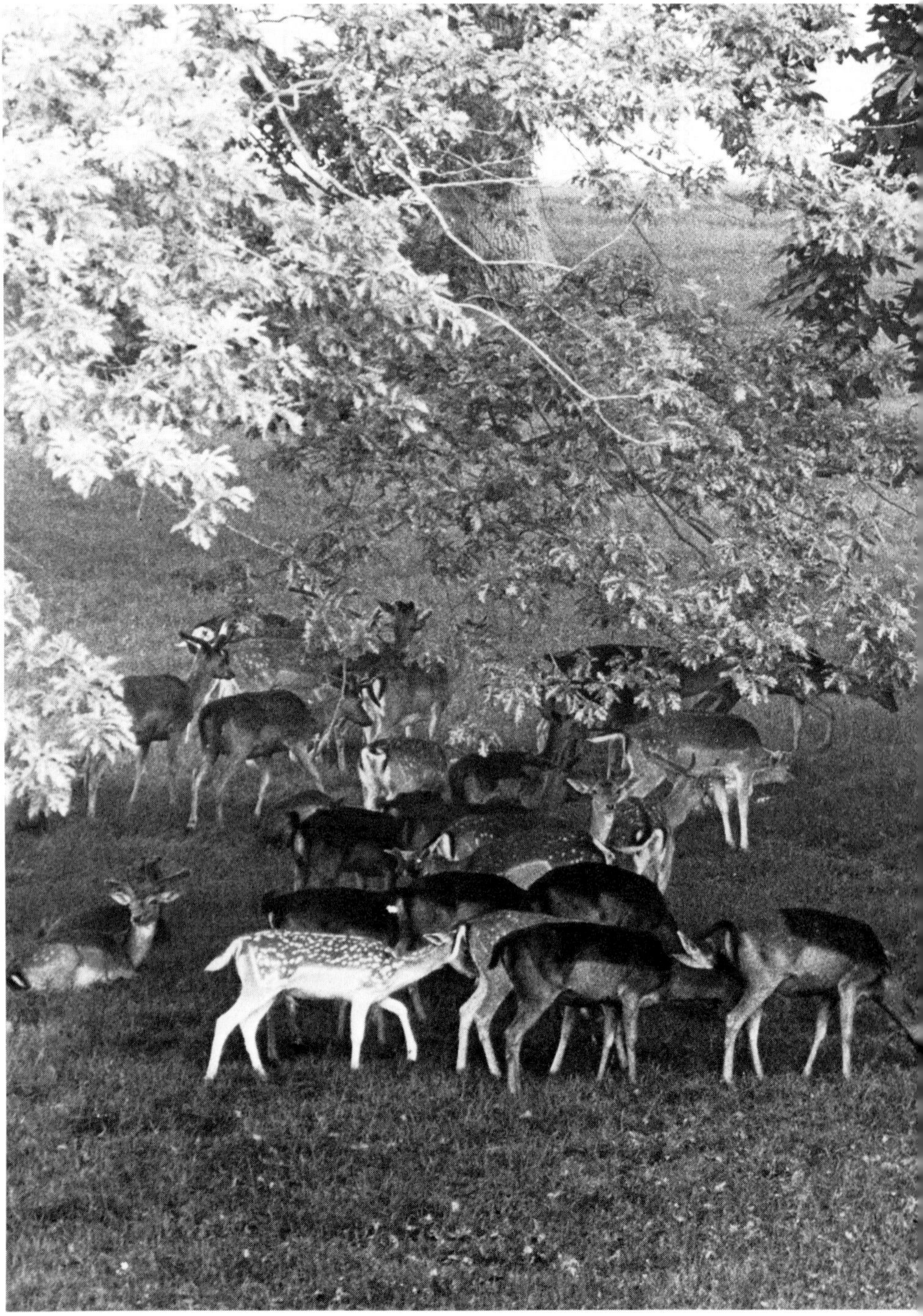

In Petworth Park

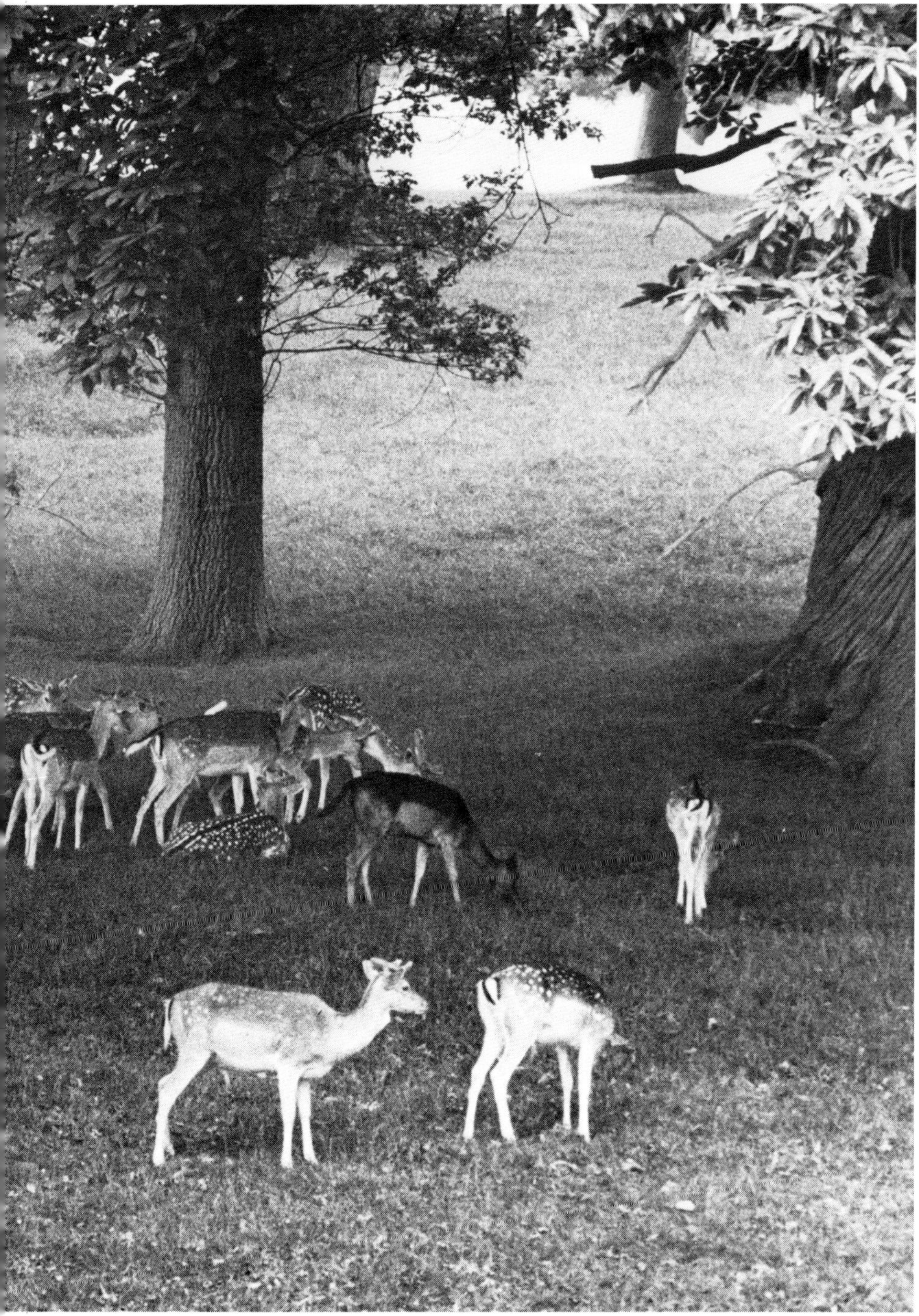

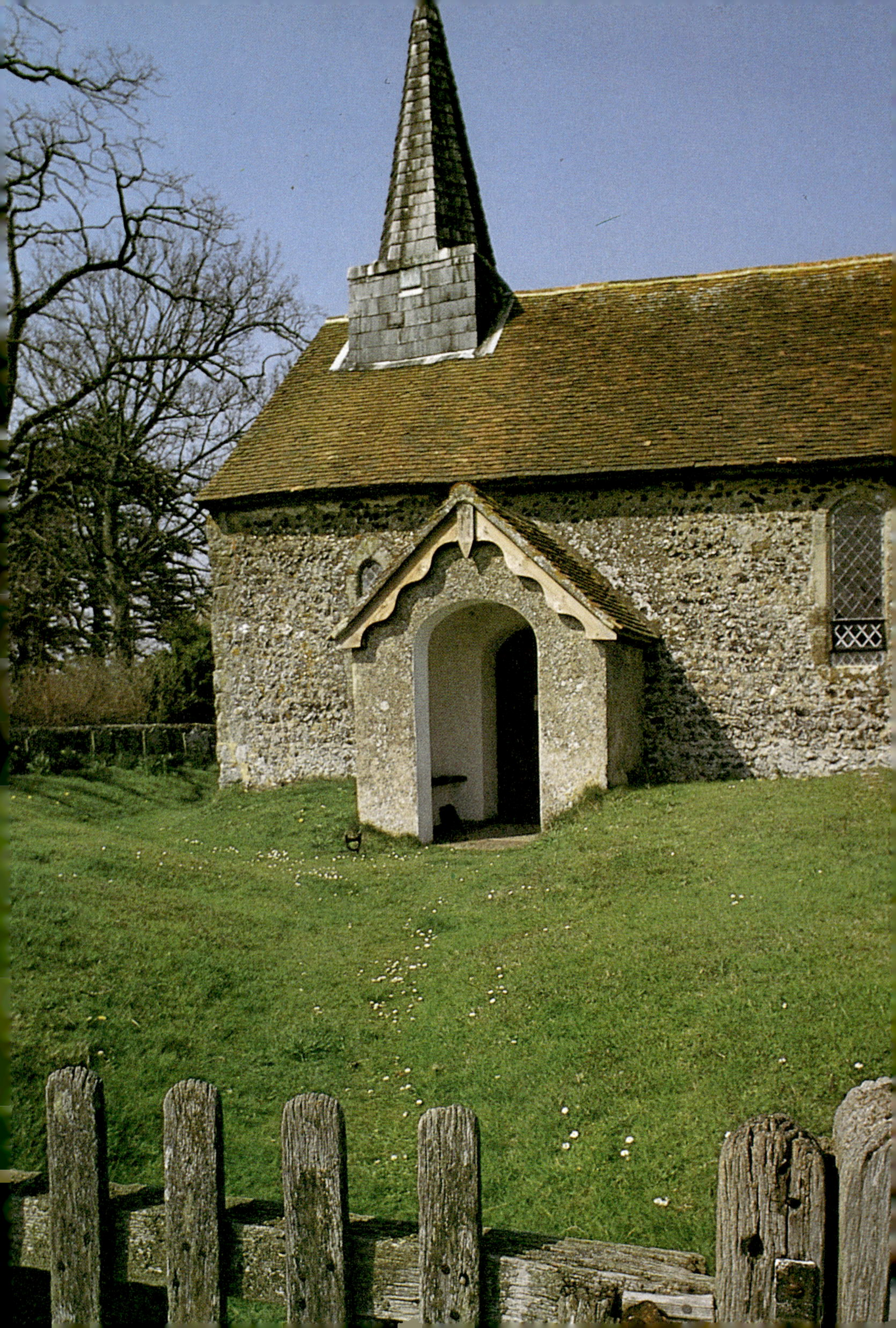

him for the sake of the company – it was very tempting, because the half-timbered house was perfect.

The only way to photograph Petworth is to explore all the streets and alleys for yourself. There are pictures everywhere. Don't miss the entrance gate to Petworth House that is awkwardly placed on a bend – there are extraordinary and very foreign-looking helmets and armour carved on the gateposts. The house is open from April to October on Tuesdays, Wednesdays, Thursdays and Saturdays from 2 till 6; inside the gate you first of all see a jumble of offices and stables. Inside, the best thing is the 'Grinling Gibbons Room', an astonishing riot of birds, musical instruments, flowers, fruit, cherubs and all sorts of things carved in limewood in 1692 with unbelievable skill. It is absolutely unique.

To photograph Petworth House properly you must go half a mile along the road to Midhurst until on your right you see a lodge and a gate in the wall; there is a small lay-by opposite. Enter the park (open from 9 a.m. to sunset all year round) and make for the path that leads to the left along the shore of the lake. Across the water stands Petworth House, long, low and restrained.

As you walk along the lake the pictures compose themselves; any camera can be used with any lens. In the woods you may see some of the three or four hundred fallow deer that live in the park – in summer they tend to go North into the wilder and less frequented parts, but in Autumn when the visitors have left they often come quite close to the lake. To avoid disturbing them use a lens with a focal length of at least 135mm.

Alternative pictures of the house can be taken by entering the gate from the road and walking straight ahead to the top of a low hill. There you will find a

Greatham Church, near Petworth (left)

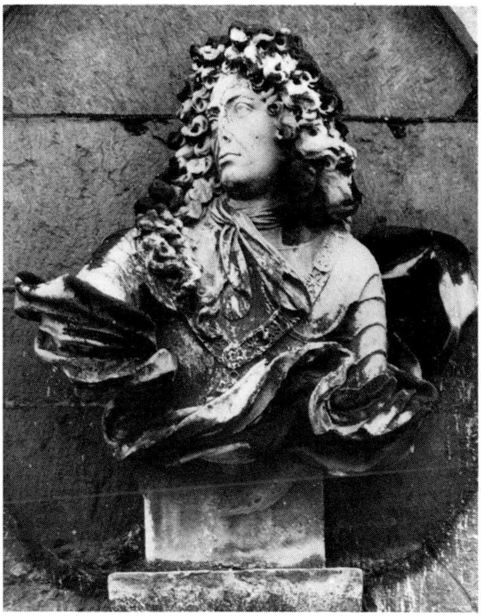

Bust of William III at Petworth

romantic column to provide a foreground.

By following the path along the lake for about a mile and a half you come to an observation tower on high ground with views over very fine country. Few visitors ever go to this part of the park, which is far superior to the rest.

Petworth is one of those Sussex towns that changes character completely around the end of September. Frankly, it is best avoided in Summer when the tourists outnumber the irritated residents.

Pevensey

The history of Pevensey is the history of Sussex. The Romans built a huge fort named 'Anderida' on a peninsular jutting out into the sea; enclosing ten acres of land, it was in effect a walled town. When they left it was occupied by Romano-

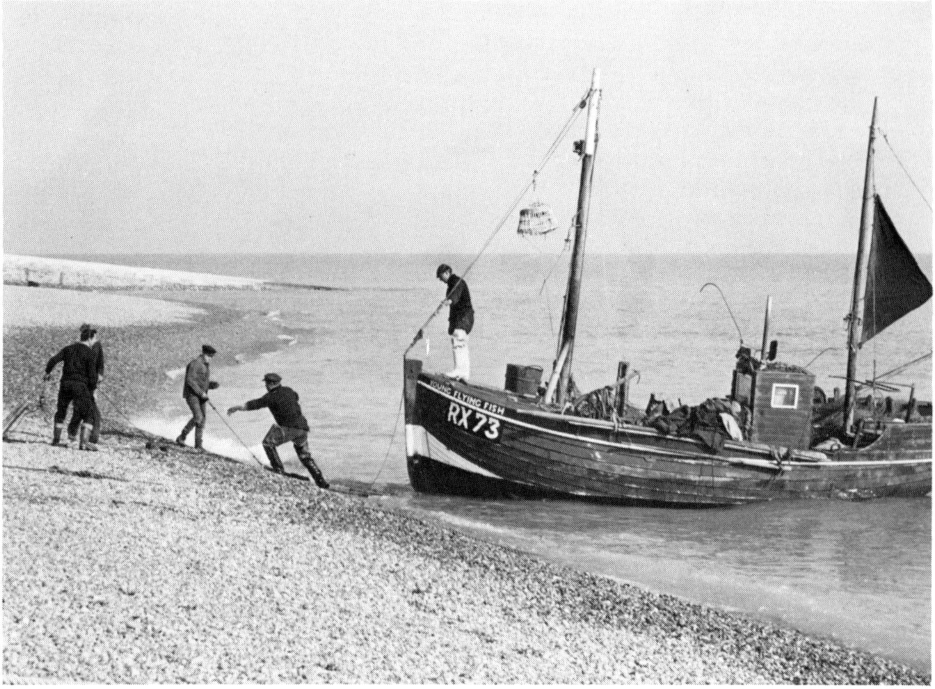

Early morning at the coast

Britons, but one day in 490 the Saxons landed in the area and all the Britons from the outlying districts, terrified, crammed into the fort for protection. It was overrun and everybody inside, men, women and children, was massacred. There were no survivors.

Five and a half centuries later William of Normandy tried to invade this country of Romney, but was driven off. He then sailed along the coast to Pevensey, which in those days had a safe harbour, a gently shelving beach which allowed his troops to wade ashore and an abandoned fort that could be defended. The landing at Pevensey is shown in the Bayeux Tapestry.

His victory changed life in England completely – everyone thinks of him as cruel and ruthless, but he abolished both the slave trade and the death penalty – and castles started to spring up everywhere. One was built in a corner of the Roman walls, strong enough to withstand four mediaeval sieges, but it was gradually allowed to decay. At the time of the Armada it had only two cannon – you can see one of them there today with 'E.R.' and a Tudor Rose on the barrel – and later still the whole fort was sold as a source of stone to a builder for £40. Luckily he found it too tough to demolish.

It once again played a defensive role in the last War, when it was occupied in turn by British, Canadian and U.S. troops as well as by the Home Guard. You can still see some carefully concealed machine-gun positions.

As you stand on the grass inside the Roman fort (open always, free), the sheer size of the enclosure is hard to grasp and certainly presents the photographer with a problem. Though the walls are almost thirty feet high and twelve feet thick, they are so long they appear quite low unless you are close. It's easy enough to take pictures of one of the ten bastions or of a section of the wall, perhaps with grazing sheep in the foreground, but to show the whole fort is almost impossible. From outside the longest stretch of wall is North-facing and in shadow, with a busy road running beside it; better pictures are probably taken from inside.

The Norman castle (open at varying times throughout the year but always in the afternoon) is much more easily photographed. There is a moat to fill in the base of the picture and inside attractions such as a heap of 'Roman Catapult Missiles'. That is what they may indeed be, but it's worth remembering that early cannon were often loaded with stone cannon balls that splintered on impact like shrapnel. Decide for yourself which they are.

It is worth exploring the footpaths that criss-cross the low ground, once covered by the sea, between the castle and the railway to the South. From them you can see both the castle and the church, and there are streams you can use as a foreground.

In the Early English church, look out for 'Pilgrims' Crosses' cut on the inside of the doorway arch. They are said to have been cut by pilgrims on the way to Canterbury, but one wonders how they ever reached their destination – perhaps the Weald was not so impenetrable in mediaeval times as is supposed. There is also a big alabaster monument to the right of the door as you enter.

In the village there is a museum in the Old Court House (open from June to September) and on the opposite side of the road the 'Mint House', said to date from 1342. The home of the original 16th-century 'Merry Andrew', Andrew Borde, it is now a 28-room antique shop but can be visited from July to September.

Though the Roman Fort at Pevensey is not easy to photograph, it is of such very great historical importance that an attempt should be made. Perhaps you'll be the one to discover the secret of how to do it.

Rodmell

Rodmell attracts two very different types of literary pilgrim – one comes because the cricket field was the setting for the match in *England Their England* which even non-cricketers still find hilarious, others because the weather-boarded 'Monk's House' near the church was the home of Leonard and Virginia Woolf, the Pride of Bloomsbury, from 1919 to 1941. It is now preserved by the National Trust.

The single street runs North towards the Ouse and then peters out into a footpath from which you can look back at the church surrounded by the cottages. There is no through-traffic and during the week the village can be very quiet indeed. To reach the Norman church you have to pass a little school; once as we walked by in the utter silence, the children inside suddenly started to sing like a choir of angels, an enchanting introduction to Rodmell.

At the end of the mainly flint-built street there are some good thatched cottages and a church with a Norman font made from Sussex marble; it was in Rodmell that the first mulberry trees were planted in England at the start of the 17th century, resulting in a flourishing silk industry; apart from this there is nothing outstanding about the place. It is just one of the most pleasant and relaxing villages in East Sussex to visit with a camera.

On the other side of the Lewes-Newhaven road from the main village, a lane rises up a hill and then becomes an up and down track which after a mile leads to Fore Hill on the Downs, where you can find a group of tumuli and a couple of dew ponds which are supposed to fill themselves by condensation from the air, though some say they merely held rain water. They used to be used by sheep, but there are few sheep left on the Downs these days; however, you might be lucky.

Rye

A compact hilltop town, Rye is very beautiful, very atmospheric and in Summer very crowded. On the surface it is a tourist-trap, the bait being the cobbled streets, the haphazard jumble of superb buildings of all periods, the boats and the historical associations. Tea-shoppes sell expensive cakes, antique-shoppes expensive junk, while the Old Tucke Shoppe unexpectedly sells very good bread. No part of Rye is much more than five minutes' walk from the 12th-century church on the top of the hill, and the visitors crowd the streets as they wander round and round, peering from side to side.

Beneath the surface there are other Ryes, one of which (with its art shows, chamber music, pottery and poetry) resembles Hampstead Garden Suburb and protects the town from exploitation and 'development', resulting in very little change for the last century. Then there is the Rye of hard-working people who fish and produce all sorts of goods.

No matter where you go the buildings are remarkable and, unlike Winchelsea, Rye is full of life. No wonder photographers have been coming here ever since photography was invented.

If you are driving, dump your car in the big car park at the foot of an old windmill and make for the Quay that runs beside the River Tillingham. Half-way along, turn left and make for the steep, cobbled Mermaid Street – everybody does, and it's as well to get it over as soon as possible so that you can concentrate on the less well-known parts of the town.

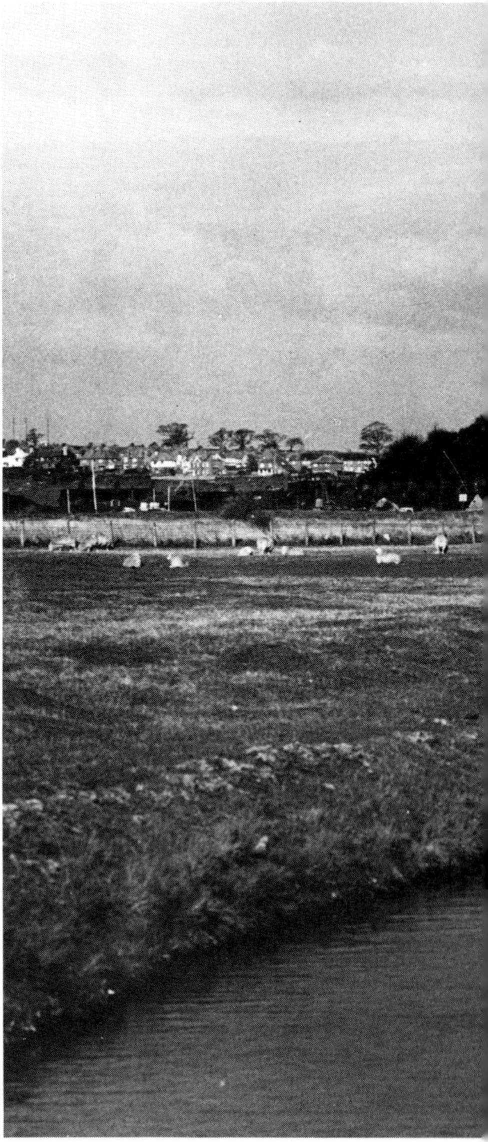

Rye from the South

The standard picture is of the 15th-century Mermaid Inn. When photographing the front use a wide-angle lens and

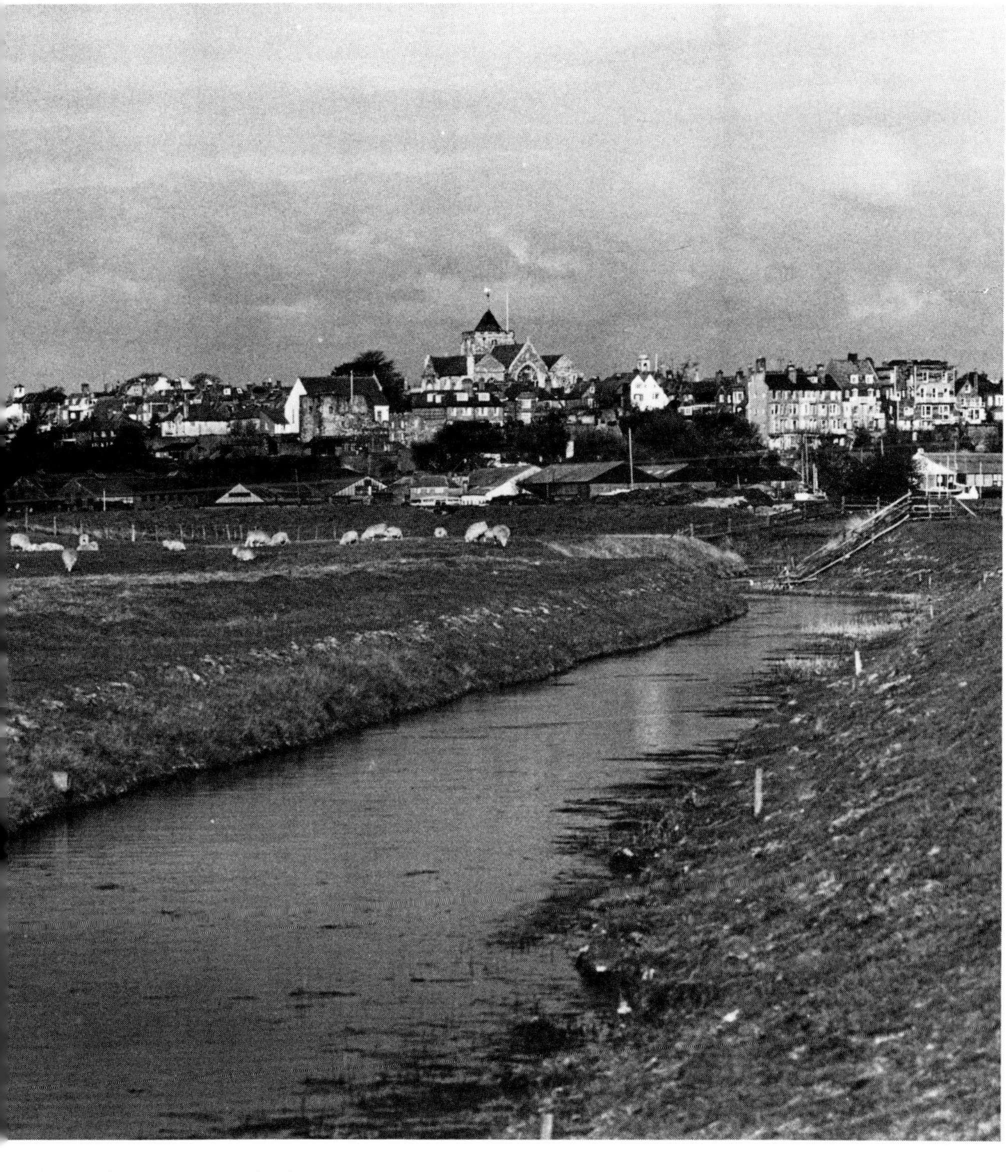

keep the camera really low so that you can include a close-up of some of the cobbles in the foreground; go through the passage at the side and you may find more interesting pictures at the rear. The light is behind you if you walk up the street in the evening, but the morning backlighting will probably give better results. To avoid competition, come in Winter – Rye is then so pleasant we used to drive there all the way from London to do our Christmas shopping.

At the top of Mermaid Street, turn right past Lamb House, where lived that old bore the writer Henry James, and then left to the church and the Town Hall. The latter is open at certain times and inside you can photograph a gibbet containing the skull of a butcher, an assassin of all-time inefficiency. Fined by the Mayor, a Mr Lamb, for giving short weight, he decided to kill him but by mistake stabbed the wrong man in the dark. He then ran around shouting: 'Butchers should kill Lambs', which aided detection considerably. Try to fill the viewfinder with the skull and its frame and use a flash on the end of a long lead from a low angle to get the right sinister effect.

Nearby is the church, the churchyard and Church Square. All are superb. Though painted and photographed thousands of times, the temptation to try your own individual interpretation of them is irresistible. In any weather, at any time of day and with any camera there's no excuse for not producing good results.

Don't wait for the fat gilt cherubs called 'quarterboys' on top of the tower to strike the bell over the clock on the hour – as you would expect, they only strike the quarters. They are fibre-glass replicas of the originals but look genuine enough, even if you climb the tower for the view of the red roofs and the marsh.

A short walk brings you to the Ypres Tower, which contains an interesting museum and the Gun Garden; the view of the flat river estuary is not very inspiring, but you can photograph the Ypres Castle pub from an unusual angle.

Walk down Church Square to Watchbell Street, cobbled and both quieter and in many ways more attractive than Mermaid Street. Turn right at the bottom into Traders Passage and return to the Quay by way of Mermaid Street. The big black wooden warehouses can form compositions that are almost abstract.

Now that you have covered some of the standard photographic subjects, your best plan is to deliberately lose your way in the side alleys and see what chance brings in front of your camera. The street plan at first seems a maze but becomes clear when you realize that they either run from the top of the hill to the bottom or else encircle it.

However, don't confine your photography to the buildings – some of the inhabitants are just as quaint. In the 18th and 19th centuries Rye had a reputation for wickedness rivalling that of many far bigger seaports, and if you believe the gossip in the seventeen taverns in the town (population 4,500) you'd think that little has changed; Rye is indeed a lively place. The market, held on Wednesdays near the station, should be visited and if the tide is right you may also be able to take pictures of the fishing fleet setting out – Rye Bay plaice is famous.

Perhaps, like so many photographers, you have visited Rye for the first time in Summer, seen the coaches depositing their loads of tourists, been jostled in the streets by bored holiday campers, found the car parks full and have left without even unpacking your camera, deciding it is a town to be avoided. If so, return in Winter. Rye is then probably the most interesting and pleasant town you can photograph in the South of England. Give it another chance.

To do justice to the hilltop situation and the surprising lack of suburbs, Rye is best photographed from a distance. If you turn right off the A259 to go to Camber, after about a mile the road crosses a stream. This makes a good foreground, especially since cattle are usually grazing there, but a lens with a focal length of at least 135mm will be needed to bring the town into proportion. Alternatively, start out from Rye on the A259, but immediately you have crossed the Rother, after about a

Rye cobbles (right)

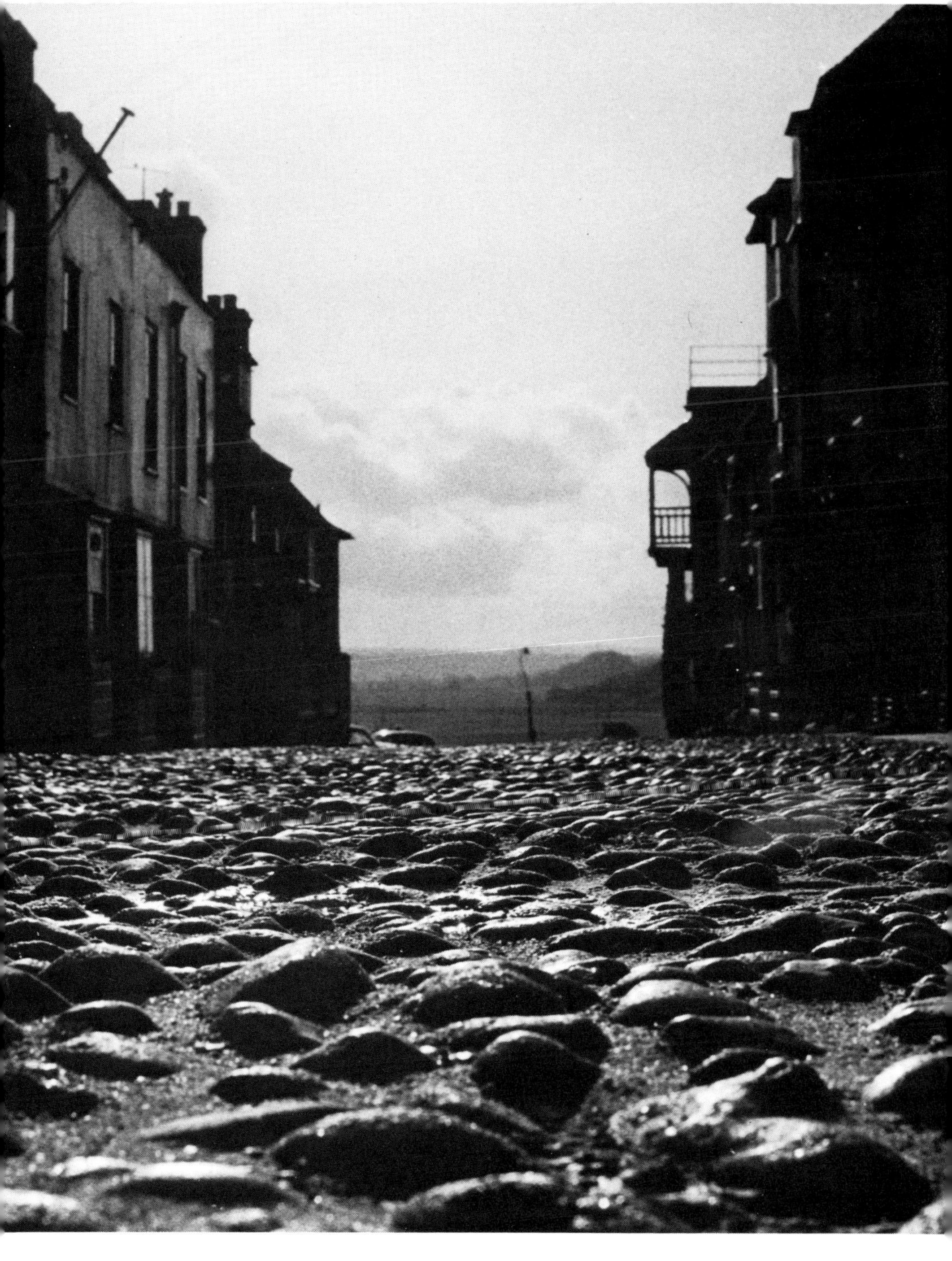

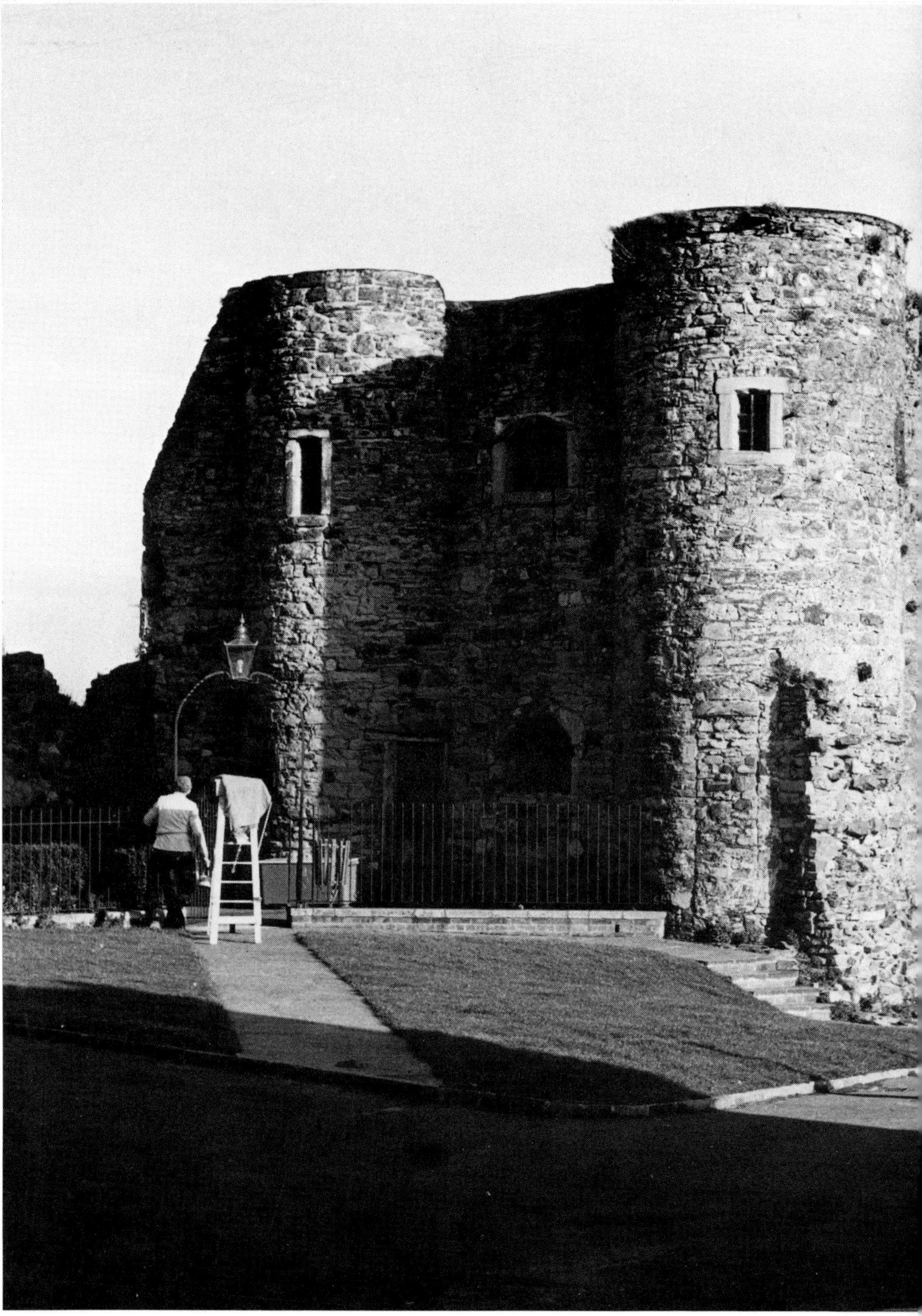

quarter of a mile, take either of the two footpaths leading South-East. In the morning the light comes from behind you, but when the lights come on in the town at dusk and the sun is setting behind it, more emotive pictures can be obtained.

Singleton

Singleton lies in a valley surrounded by hills and trees. A compact, well-kept flint village full of chestnut trees, it is a pleasant place to walk around but has nothing special to offer the photographer. The Saxon church is set back and you may like to record the mediaeval and Tudor graffiti on an archway in the porch.

The great attraction is the Weald and Downland Museum, on the right of the road leading to Goodwood Racecourse. This really is something special and must be visited if you are anywhere near the area. It exists to save buildings that were falling to pieces or threatened by demolition and has rebuilt them on a grassy slope with woodlands above.

It sounds as though it might be something out of Disneyland, but it isn't at all like that. No building is ever moved from its site unless it would otherwise disappear, and houses have been saved and brought here from as far away as Kent and Hampshire as well as from Sussex. There is nothing like it anywhere else.

Winkhurst, a timber-framed wattle-and-daub house, dates from the 14th or early-15th century; Bayleaf Farmhouse is a little later but has similar construction. Neither has a chimney, the smoke escaping through a hole in the roof, but fires are kept burning in them so that you can get a good idea of the living conditions of the period.

Up in the woods there is a charcoal

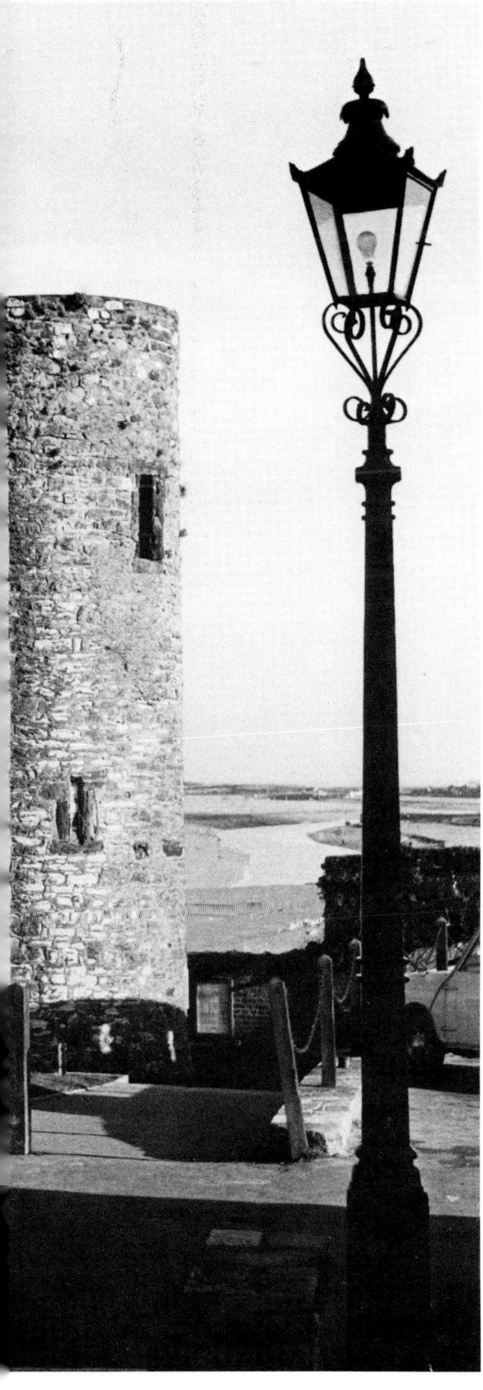

Ypres Castle, Rye

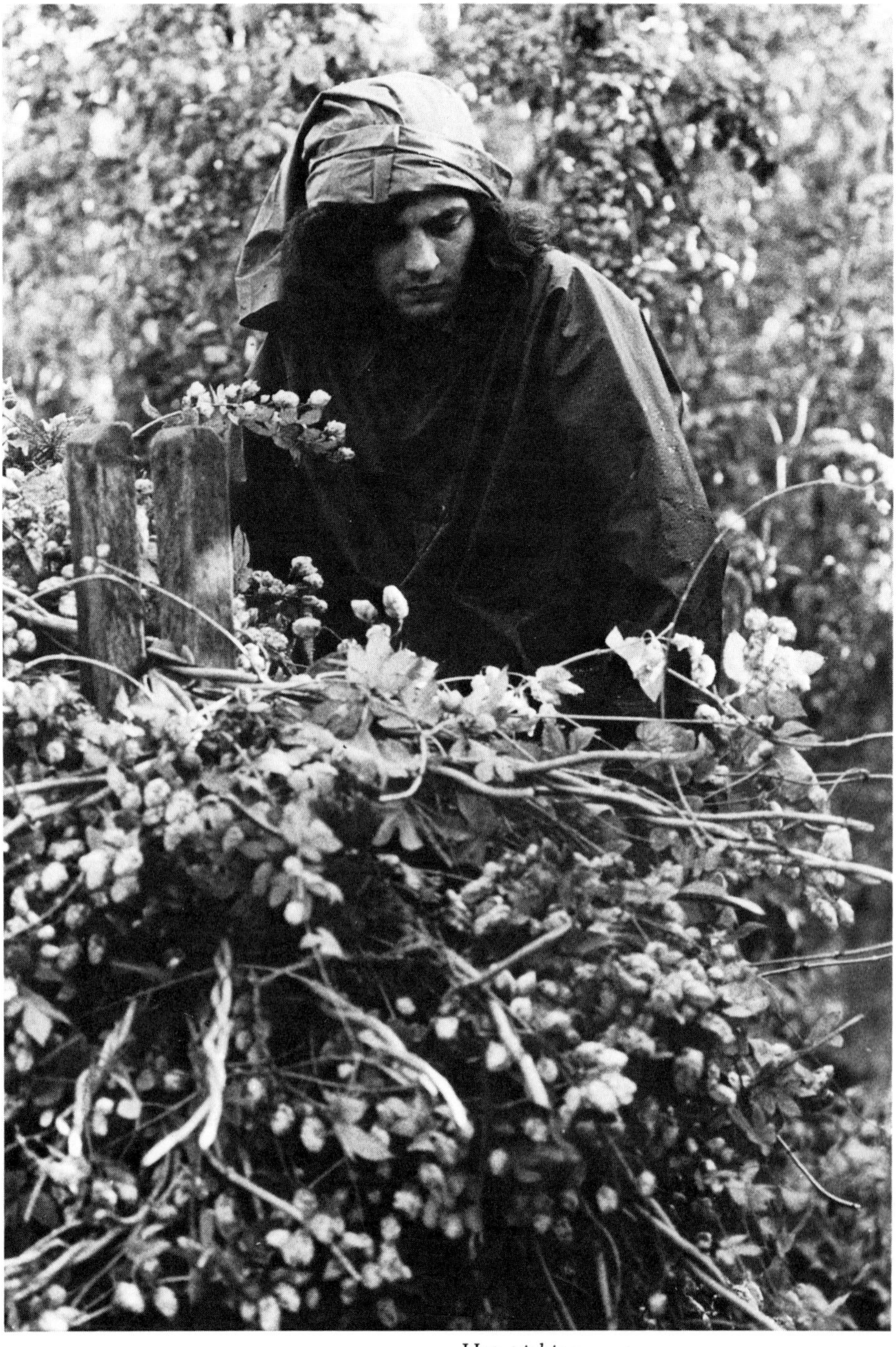

Hop picking

burner's camp with a kiln and a turf hut. A Saxon weaver's hut has a working loom – if you are lucky someone may be using it. There is a pottery and a smithy where craftsmen and women work, a saw-pit, a granary supported on stone mushrooms designed to keep out mice, and the Market Hall from Titchfield which will eventually have a market square of houses built round it. One day there will be a working water-mill, once lakes and a millstream have been constructed.

All the buildings can be entered; and since they are constantly being added to, you never know quite what to expect when you visit the museum. Everything is worth photographing, but some of the interiors present a challenge. To record the effect of the smoke, it is probably best to back-light it either with sunlight coming through the doors or windows or else with a flash on the end of a long lead (flash on camera merely gives a picture that appears to have been taken in fog). Flash will also be needed for the craftspeople at work.

As usual, when photographing the buildings keep the back of the camera upright and try to include something to fill the foreground. In most cases you can get far enough away to use a normal or even a long-focus lens, when the danger of 'converging verticals' is very much reduced. If using black and white film, a deep-yellow or orange filter will help show the texture of the the wooden beams and the thatch and will provide a background for the roofs by darkening the sky.

Opening times are a bit complicated. From April to September the museum is open from 11 to 6, but it is closed on Mondays. In October it is open on Wednesdays, Saturdays and Sundays from 11 to 5, and in January, March, November and December on Sundays only from 11 to 4. In other words, if you go there before lunch on any Sunday you'll find it open. Don't miss it.

Sompting

The village of Sompting has become a suburb of Worthing and is cut off from the church, fortunately, by a busy bypass. There is nothing in the village worth photographing, but Sompting Church and the country to the North should not be missed.

The church is unique. There is nothing else like it in England and you have to go to the Rhine Valley to see anything similar. The tower, topped by a wood-shingled roof that can with some imagination be compared in shape to a helmet (which is why the design is known as a 'Rhenish Helm'), is Saxon and is one of only twenty buildings throughout all England that definitely date from the 10th century. A hundred feet high, it incorporates Roman bricks from some lost villa.

The Knights Templars took over the church in 1154 and rebuilt it completely except for the tower. The order was accused of black magic – they had in fact accumulated too many enviable possessions – and was supressed in 1306. The Knights Hospitallers replaced them and were themselves supressed in 1540.

Though the church is so close to the over-developed coast it has managed to preserve a rural atmosphere. A farm on the North side rests against the churchyard and beyond that lie unspoilt Downs. It is best photographed from the South side, good camera angles being found to both the left and right depending on the time of day and any foreground interest you can find. The latter will be necessary because, as when photographing most buildings, the camera back must be kept as vertical as possible and inevitably you will include more foreground than you really need. A wide-angle lens will probably be required and this makes it even more important to keep the vertical lines in the subject parallel to the sides of the viewfinder.

Inside, St Mary's is just as interesting as it is outside. When the body of the church was re-built, some of the Saxon carvings were saved and incorporated in the new Norman fabric. Look out for an abbot with a book propped up on a stand beside him – it makes the thousand years between then and now shrink to nothing. Flash will be needed, but if you keep it on the camera the pictures of the carvings will be flat and lifeless.

The best solution to the problem is to connect the flash to the camera by means of a six-foot synchronizing lead. This is normally kept coiled up with the loops held together with an elastic band so that the correct length can be pulled out as needed. Ideally a companion will hold the flash back and to one side of the subject so that the carving is shown in relief, but if this is not possible the camera can be held in one hand while the flash is extended at arm's length with the other – it is easier than it sounds.

A Sussex well

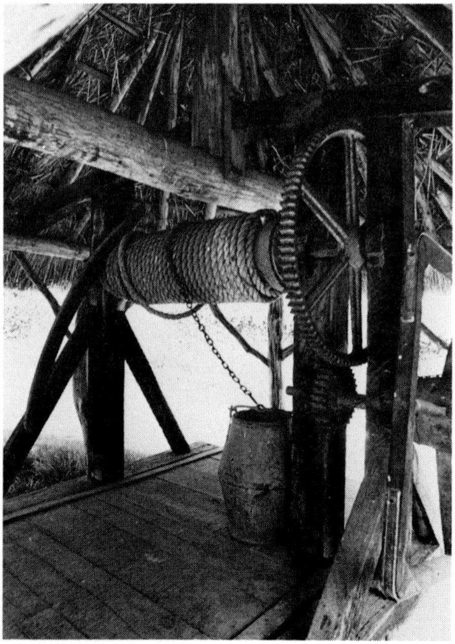

The farmhouse North of the church was lived in by Trelawny, the friend of Shelley and Byron. Joining the Navy in 1805 at the age of thirteen, he deserted in Bombay on his first voyage and lived in the East until he was twenty-one. Back in England he wrote an extraordinary account of his adventures, much of it true, was lionized in literary circles, watched Shelley drown in Italy and cremated his body on the beach, snatching his heart from the flames to give to Mary (*Frankenstein*) Shelley. Going with Byron to Greece, after further adventures he married a Greek woman.

In his old age he lived in this peaceful place, growing flowers and vegetables until dying at the age of eighty-nine. For its associations alone the farmhouse is worth photographing.

A narrow lane passes the church to climb over the Downs to Steyning, a pleasant five-mile walk if you don't mind encountering the odd car, but alternatively you can branch left off the lane after a mile and a half at Beggars Bush on to footpaths that lead to Cissbury Ring or to the prehistoric settlement of Park Brow.

South Downs Way

Once upon a time if you wanted a mildly adventurous walking holiday you would start at one end of the Downs, perhaps at South Harting, and then find your way with the help of Ordnance Survey maps to the other end at Eastbourne. Much of the fun lay in working out a route, in taking wrong footpaths that led only to remote farms and in the fact that you seemed to have the whole of the Downs to yourself.

However, people who like to organize

South Downs Way from Didling Hill (right)

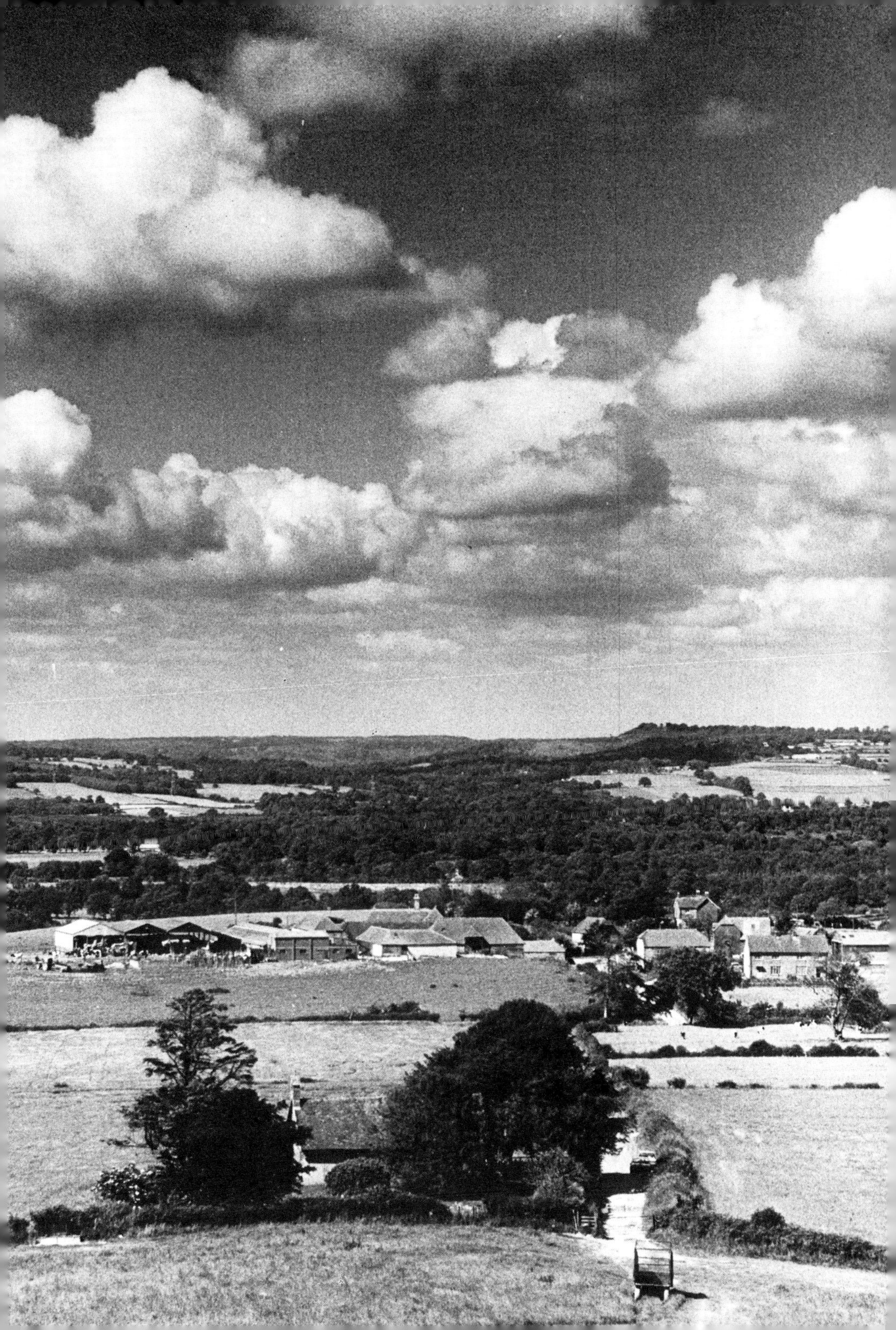

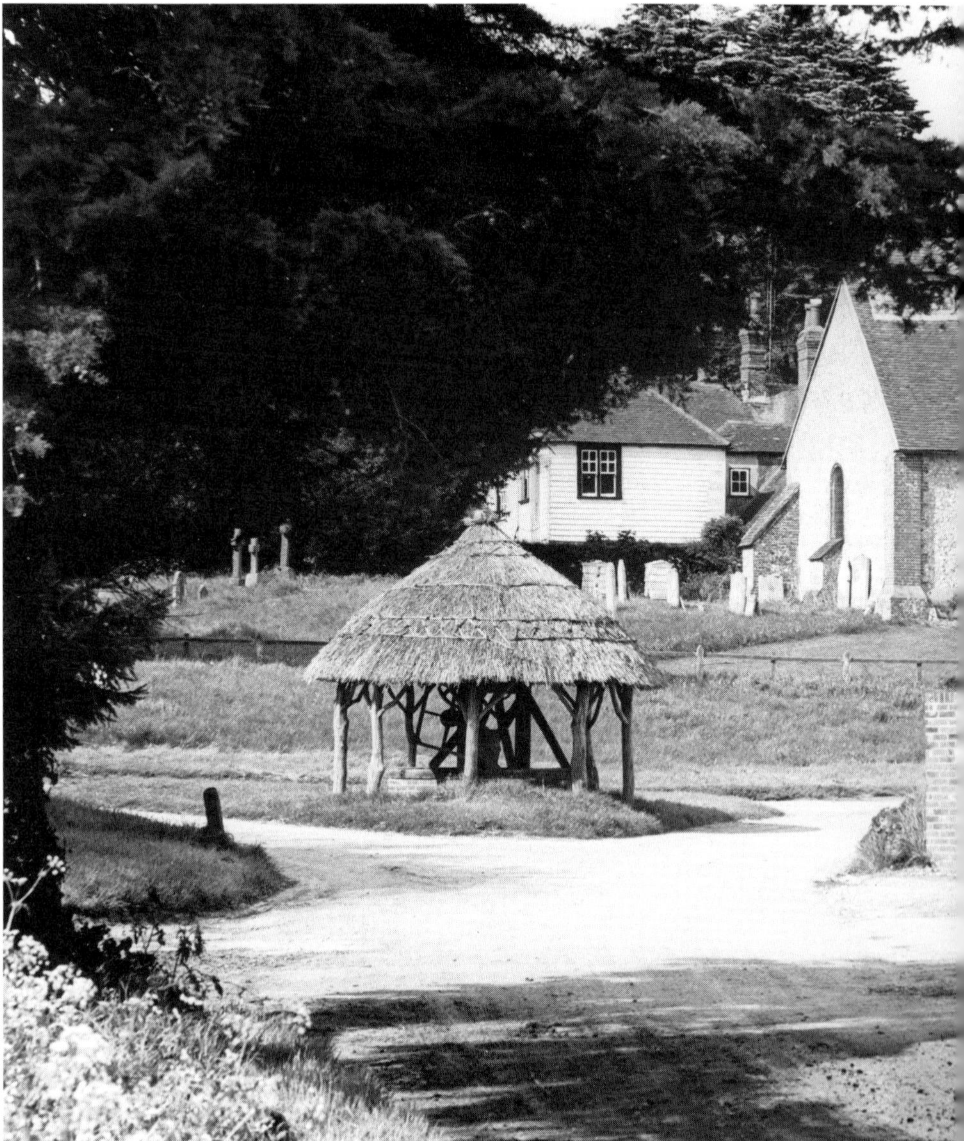

A typical Sussex village scene

and control others decided on and sign-posted a 'South Downs Way' along which pedestrians should walk, and all sense of adventure and exploration disappeared. The once deserted track becomes very busy in Summer with back-packing walkers dressed to climb the Matterhorn; fortunately they never swerve from the official line and the other Downland paths remain empty.

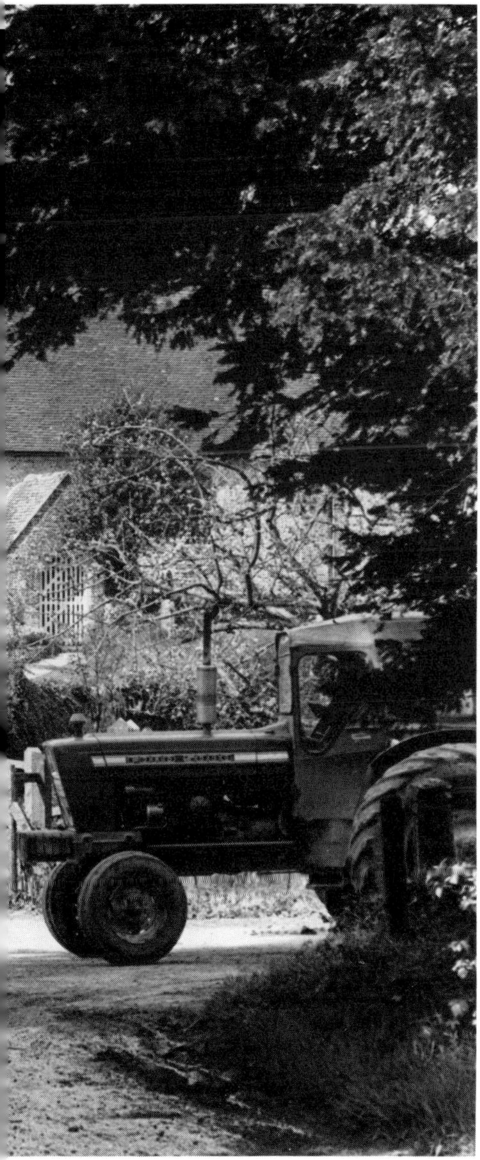

The way is still worth following in Spring and Autumn and provides superb views of the Weald and its villages. The snag is that you have to climb down from the heights in the evening to find somewhere to spend the night and then toil up again in the morning; lunch must be carried to avoid having to do this in the middle of the day.

Though photographic equipment should obviously be kept to a minimum, a light-weight long-focus lens will be needed to concentrate on distant subjects (a 70-200mm zoom would be useful), together with a 'haze' or 'skylight' filter for colour and a red or orange one for black and white to penetrate the long-distance haze which can be very heavy. I have on occasion used infra-red film from the top of the Downs, and the results showed clearly objects quite invisible to the eye.

The ideal method of following the way, or for that matter any other long-distance footpath, is to arrange for a friend to drive you to the start of a section in the morning and to pick you up again when you phone from wherever you have reached in the evening; you can thus cover the whole route on foot over a period of perhaps a week with the minimum of inconvenience. I realize this sounds like cheating, but it's really a very practical system.

Stopham

On the way from Pulborough to Petworth you will probably be halted by traffic lights at a bridge that is so narrow it can only take one vehicle at a time. This is the famous Stopham Bridge, a standard subject for generation after generation of photographers. Just before the bridge there is a pub on your right; on the left some rowing boats are usually moored by the bank of the Arun. These have supplied the foreground for the tens of thousands of pictures that have been taken from this spot.

Though the bridge is a cliché, it is a very beautiful one. Built in 1423 to replace an earlier structure (though the central arch

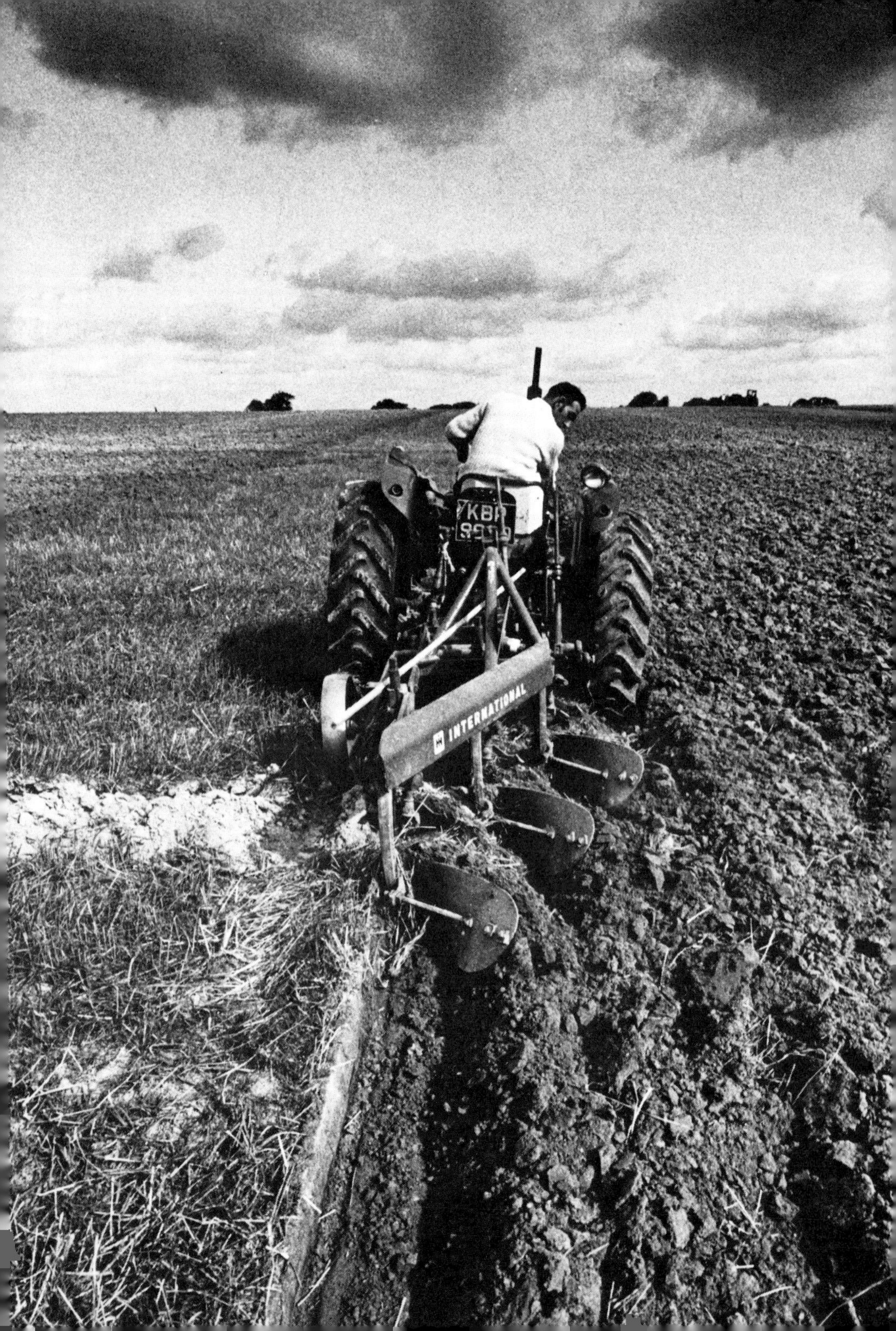
INTERNATIONAL

only dates from 1822), the seven arches with their cutwaters, the still river and the boats make a mellow colour composition, especially if taken on a day with hazy sunlight. Having taken the conventional picture, try walking up the muddy and overgrown path that runs North from the pub beside the river to see if you can find a different angle, which admittedly will be against the light. In both cases, be careful not to spoil the effect by including the traffic lights.

If you persevere along the path you eventually come to a mound where once stood a 'motte and bailey' castle, a wooden tower encircled by a ditch and a stockade, quickly run up by the Normans as a temporary measure.

Before the first bridge was built, probably in 1200, there was a ford where a Saxon family had the right to collect tolls. They became so rich they adopted the name 'de Stopham' and told everyone that their ancestors had come over with the Conqueror – typical *nouveau riche* behaviour.

Cross the bridge and after half a mile take the lane to the right marked 'Stopham'. This leads to some cottages, a couple of farms, an unrestored stone-built manor house, a Norman church – and then goes no further.

In Spring there are daffodils in front of the rather squat church. Inside, it is a perfect example of how most Sussex churches must have looked after the Conquest, traces of the original Saxon building remaining but all the rest except for the windows being pure Norman.

The district was dominated by the Barttelot family whose land at one time ran in an unbroken line from Stopham to Horsham. Their brasses in the church cover four hundred years and there are memorials to a Barttelot who was killed leading the 'Petworth Volunteers' in the Boer War and to his brother who died in Africa on an expedition with Stanley to find Livingstone. It would be charitable to think he was driven mad by the conditions, for he flogged some natives to death and committed other acts of extraordinary cruelty before his servants came to their senses and killed him. There is also a drum and a bugle in a recess commemorating one of the family who died in the First World War.

This is a great part of Sussex to explore with a camera since even in the Season there are few visitors. You can find magnificent half-timbered farmhouses with spectacular views of the Downs, old barns, thatched cottages, bluebell woods in Spring and all kinds of other delights.

Ploughing under a Sussex sky (left)

Telscombe

Travel from Lewes to Newhaven along the A275 and at Southease take the turning to the right. As you go towards Telscombe you pass through some of the best Downland scenery in Sussex, a rich mixture of browns and greens which changes according to the season. If ploughing has been recent there may be flocks of seagulls which can make an extraordinary picture as they take off simultaneously.

Telscombe itself lies in a hollow. In late March and early April the flint Norman church and the handful of houses and cottages are surrounded by a wealth of daffodils, a conventionally pretty subject, but inside the church the restoration is embarrassing.

Though pleasant and well-kept the village is best photographed from a distance, when it can make a typical Sussex subject with its screen of beech trees. Go there in the morning and take the track that leads due East from the church. The village with the church in the centre can then be photographed from various distances with varying lenses, the background and the composition changing as you move.

Though Telscombe appears to be utterly remote, a couple of miles away lies Peacehaven on the edge of the cliffs looking over the sea. Built after the First World War to attract ex-servicemen (it was first called New-Anzac-On-Sea), it is a grotesque collection of bungalows and houses, each in its own little plot, arranged in a gridiron pattern.

A story in pictures can easily be made about this Suburbia-on-sea, and people laugh at the twee names of the dwellings, but I can't help feeling sympathy for the men who after the horrors of Flanders wanted to be on their own with the sea on one side and the Downs, then white with sheep, on the other. If you take your camera to Peacehaven, do so with understanding.

Ticehurst

A typical Wealden village, Ticehurst stands on high ground surrounded by very beautiful country with fine views over the Rother Valley. A little square is surrounded by weather-boarded cottages, the village store has a canopy supported by elegant Victorian cast-iron pillars, there is a good 16th-century inn, the Bell, and several old houses and shops. For me, however, the main interest lies in the church.

To the left of the altar you will find the remains of a 15th-century 'doom' window, intended to remind sinners of the fate awaiting them. There is a wonderful hell-cauldron and an even better over-loaded hell-cart, pushed by a poor disgruntled devil who is obviously fed up with the job. The whole of the window is worth photographing in either black and white or colour, but I like to concentrate on sections, each one a picture in itself.

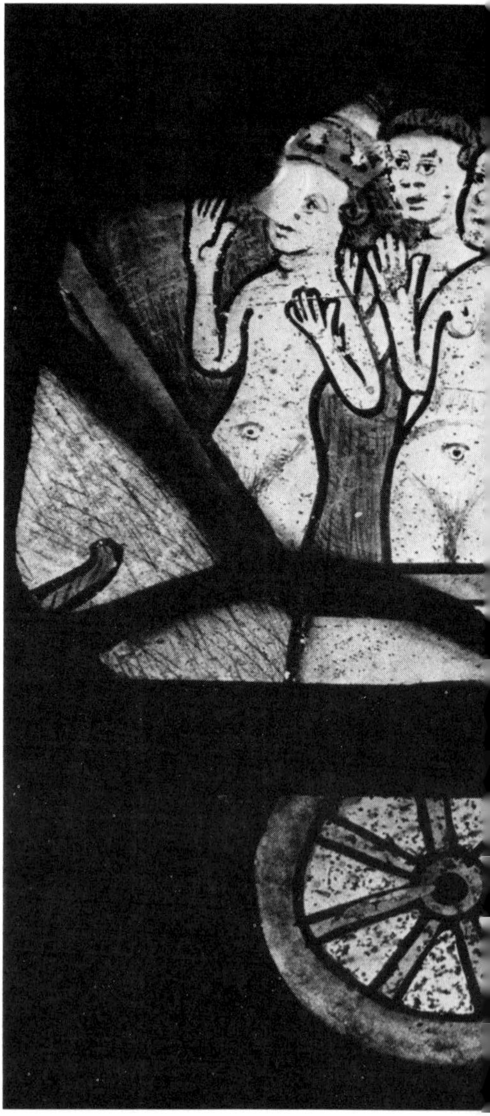

The Hell Cart, Ticehurst

A tripod or monopod will be needed and a close-focusing zoom lens (it will let you fill the viewfinder with the subject) with a maximum focal length of at least 150mm, though 200mm is really needed.

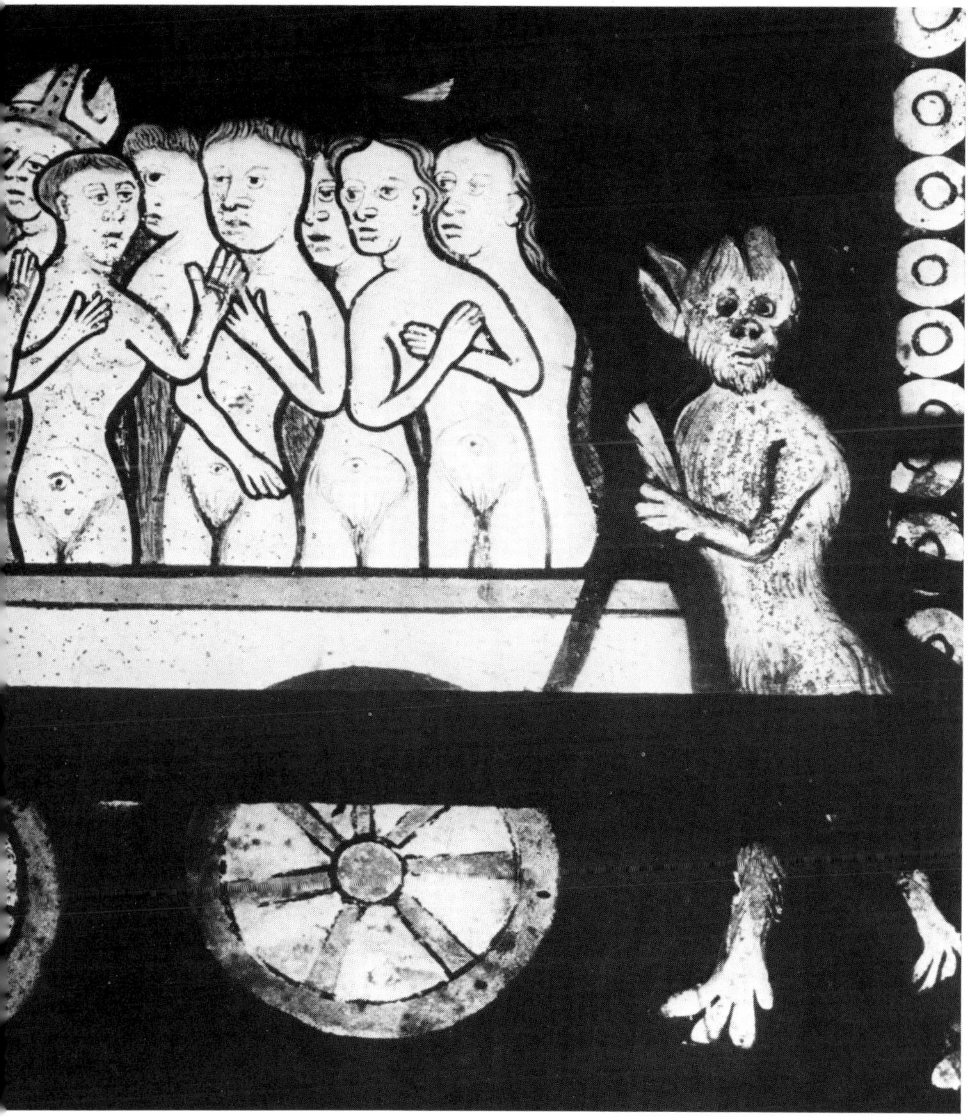

Choose weather conditions and a time of day when the light coming through the painted glass is soft and even, otherwise shadows may give a patchy effect.

I doubt if the congregation took the picture very seriously; they were probably too busy trying to identify the souls in torment with their neighbours.

Uppark

The fact that there are very few old houses on the Downs is due to the difficulty of raising water to the necessary height. Uppark is an exception; in 1650 a pump was invented that could cope with the task, and the water-wheel that drove it can still be seen beside the road that leads to the house from South Harting.

The North entrance at which the visitor arrives does not give the correct impression of what is a simple and dignified Wren design, and the photographer should go round to the Southern side from which there are wide views as far as the Isle of Wight. The front of the building on this side is best taken when late-afternoon sun glances across it, showing up the details and curves of the steps; in the middle of the day it can appear flat and dull.

It is not easy to make an interesting picture out of the exterior. In showery or stormy weather a dramatic sky background will help, aided by a red or orange filter if using black and white film, but the bold foreground interest that is badly needed is hard to find.

Though the design may not be visually exciting, the house has certainly seen life. The rakish Sir Harry Fetherstonhaugh used to entertain his guests, including the Prince Regent, by getting his mistress, the beautiful fifteen-year-old Emma Hart, later Nelson's Lady Hamilton, to dance on the dining-room table (still there) and perform her 'Pose Plastique' strip – she would have been greatly appreciated by H.G. Wells, son of the housekeeper of Uppark a century later.

At the age of seventy-one Sir Harry reformed, married his head dairy-maid, who rejoiced in the name of Mary Ann Bullock, and lived happily ever after. The interior of the house and the furniture are unchanged since the 18th century, which makes them almost unique, and the tiled dairy in which Lady Fetherstonhaugh worked until her lucky break can be photographed (a wide-angle lens will be needed).

Until comparatively recent times the country to the North was largely covered by the remains of the ancient forest of Anderida. Within living memory dramatic changes have taken place throughout the county, as in the rest of England, and I once met a very old man near Uppark who in September 1916 took a load of oak to 'the new hospital they were building at Palmers Green'. Day after day his horses dragged the heavy load through Sussex, Surrey and London, but he realized he must have missed the hamlet of Palmers Green when he came upon the remains of the Zepplin just shot down at Cuffley by Leafe Robinson. He retraced his steps, delivered his load and plodded back to Sussex. Now there is little oak, the hamlet is a busy part of London and a truck could deliver the timber within hours.

Uppark is owned by the National Trust and is open from April to September on Wednesdays, Thursdays, Sundays and Bank Holidays from 2 until 6.

Upwaltham Church

These days few people visit Upwaltham Church, for the stretch of the Petworth-Chichester road that passes it is very fast and you are past the track that leads to the church before you realize it unless you know exactly where to stop. Careful study of an Ordnance Survey map is essential before you go there.

It is one of those Sussex churches that merges into a farm. You open a ricketty, string-tied gate, walk uphill across a field that is muddy after rain (there is no clear path) – and there stands the small, lonely church with tombstones at all angles. Small as it is, the area which it serves is so empty these days that when it was built in the 12th century and even up to comparatively recent times there must have been many more people around to form a congregation;

Upwaltham Church (right)

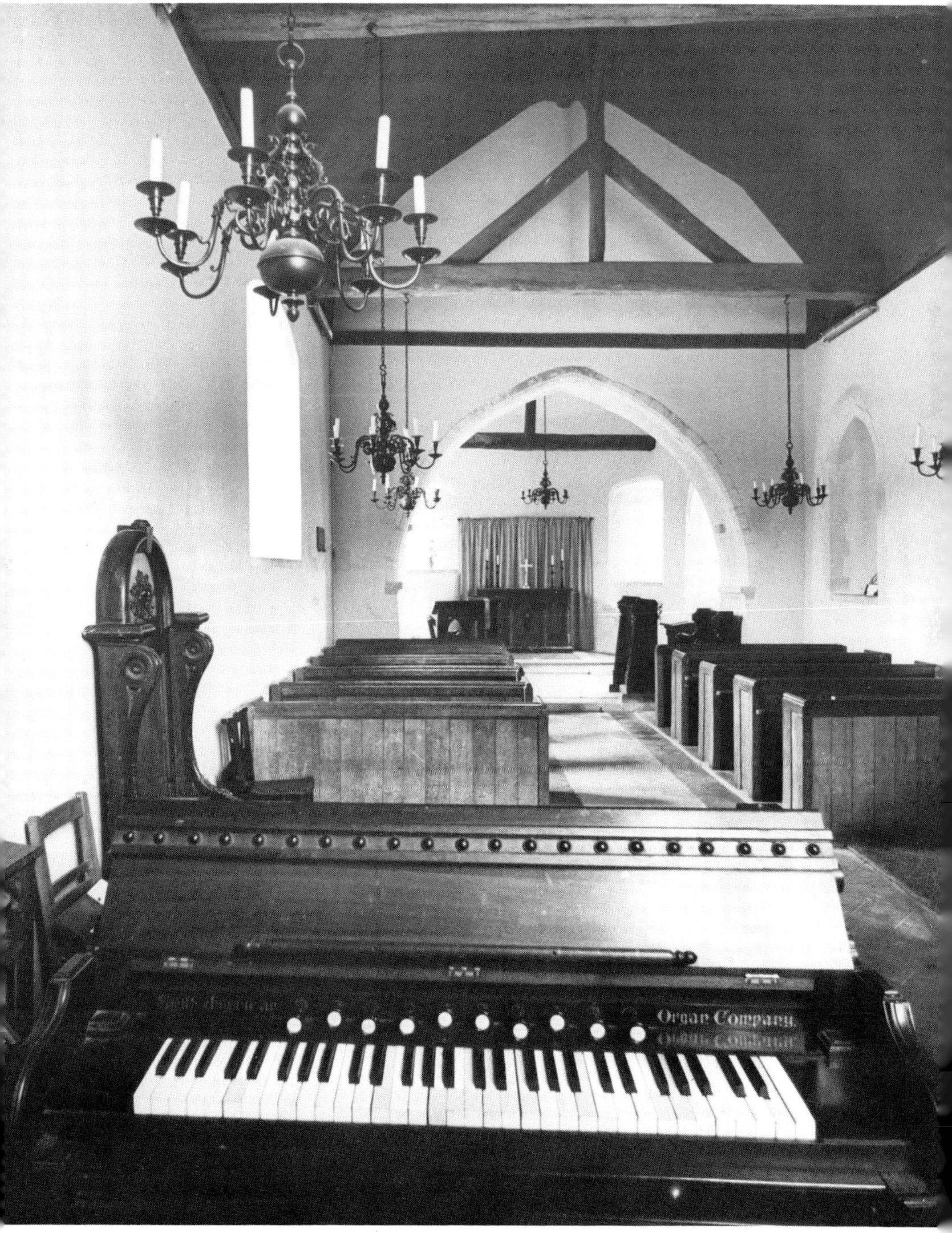
Organ Company.

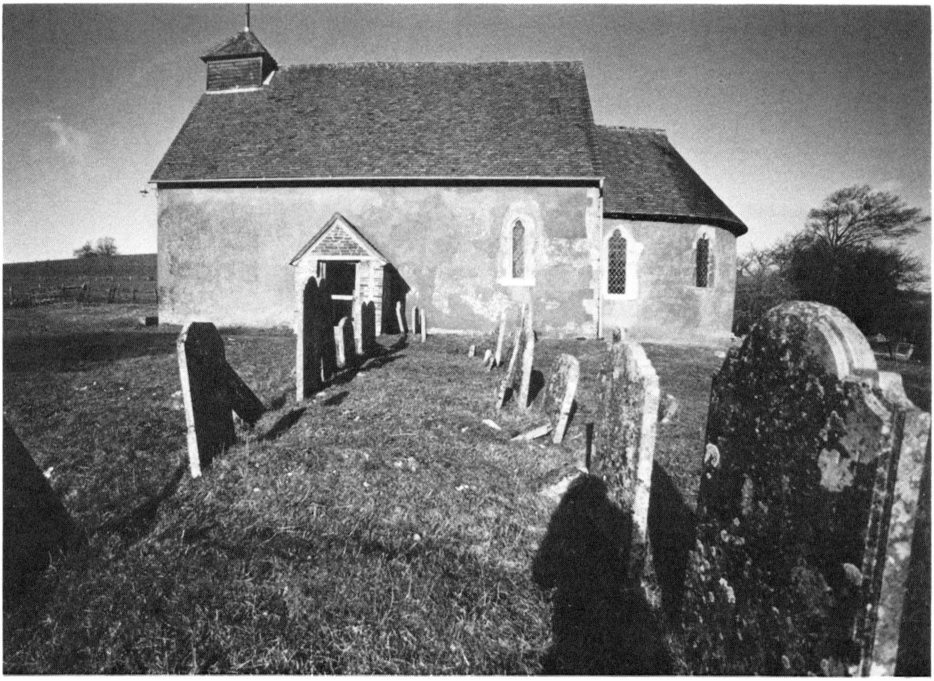

Upwaltham Church

thanks to mechanization the countryside has never been more depopulated than it is today.

As you approach you will see changing compositions of church, farm, barns and the Downs (some fine pictures have been taken when the snow was on the ground), and close by you can use a wide-angle lens to exaggerate the effect of the slanting tombstones. Don't rush things; walk around and study the lighting and the ever-changing background.

A public footpath leads past the West side of the church through the farm down to the road in one direction and up towards Waltham Down, over 800 feet high, in the other. In Winter it is probably the most rutted and muddy path I have come across in Sussex, a throwback to the days when wagons had to be drawn by oxen and photographically interesting in itself.

Its only connection to important events is that Cardinal Manning, who caused such a Victorian uproar by changing sides at half-time in his career from the Church of England to the Church of Rome, preached his first and last sermons at Upwaltham. He used to toll the bell himself to summon the farm workers to the services and when he later reached high rank probably sometimes regretted having left such a simple, beautiful place.

Wiggonholt

Wiggonholt is one of the hidden treasures of Sussex and like all good treasures it's hard to find. Let's hope it stays that way and never becomes casually visited by bored tourists.

If you are travelling from Pulborough towards Storrington, after a couple of miles you pass what looks like a farm track on your right. It isn't signposted and for some reason the church isn't even marked on the latest Ordnance Survey map. Going down the track you come first to a farm and then to a little, hidden Norman church next to a huge, over-powering 18th-century rectory.

It was April when we first walked down the track to find the church surrounded by a sea of cowslips and daffodils; undulating waves of country led away from it towards Amberley Wild Brooks and the distant Downs and we were torn between the church and the landscape. The whole area seemed deserted except for a self-confident Persian cat with a fox's brush of a tail who showed us around in a condescending manner; his black and white fur looked remarkably like a surplice and he was obviously a reincarnated Victorian vicar. The very simple, very plain interior of the church, now alas locked, was lit by four oil lamps.

You'd have to try really hard to produce a bad photograph with any camera, but you are most likely to obtain the right impression of the flowery church with your widest-angle lens. The view towards the Downs on the other hand needs a long-focus one to compress perspective. Visit Wiggonholt with gentleness and respect; it has the kind of delicate charm that is easily destroyed.

Wilmington

Everyone goes to Wilmington to see and photograph the Long Man, 230 feet high and the biggest representation of a human figure in Europe. The theories about its origin are countless; is it a Roman surveyor with two measuring staves, the Norse god Baldur opening the Gates of Summer, a prehistoric fertility symbol, something done by the monks for recreation, or an 18th-century joke? No one knows. My personal guess is that it is Bronze Age and that it looked very different when it was first carved on the hillside by someone with an advanced knowledge of perspective.

Seen from the air the figure is tall and thin, but from Wilmington he appears normally proportioned. I wonder if aerial pictures taken on infra-red colour film would show any trace of his original shape?

Most visitors stop when they first see the figure, take a snap and move on. It pays to wander around for a while before you take your first picture, trying to find an angle that will show the figure in an appropriate setting. Some photographers get well away and then use a long-focus lens, others include a nearby object to give depth; if you're lucky, someone may be ploughing at the foot of the hill, emphasizing the size of the huge figure above. The surrounding country is beautiful and it's no hardship to spend an hour or so exploring.

If using black and white, an orange filter will increase the contrast between the grass and the white bricks with which the Man has been outlined.

Wilmington has a good church, partly 12th-century. Hidden away behind the organ is a window showing St Peter surrounded by a series of small panels each containing a butterfly, moth or bee – each makes an attractive colour picture. In the churchyard there is a yew said to be over a thousand years old – if true, this makes it the oldest tree in Sussex.

The Priory Ruins (open April to September, weekdays except Tuesday 10-6; Sunday 2-5) are a jumble of several different periods from the 11th to the 16th century and are not easily photographed. You may find the agricultural museum in the adjoining Tudor house more interesting, with its mole- and man-traps, ox-goads and yokes (oxen were used for ploughing well

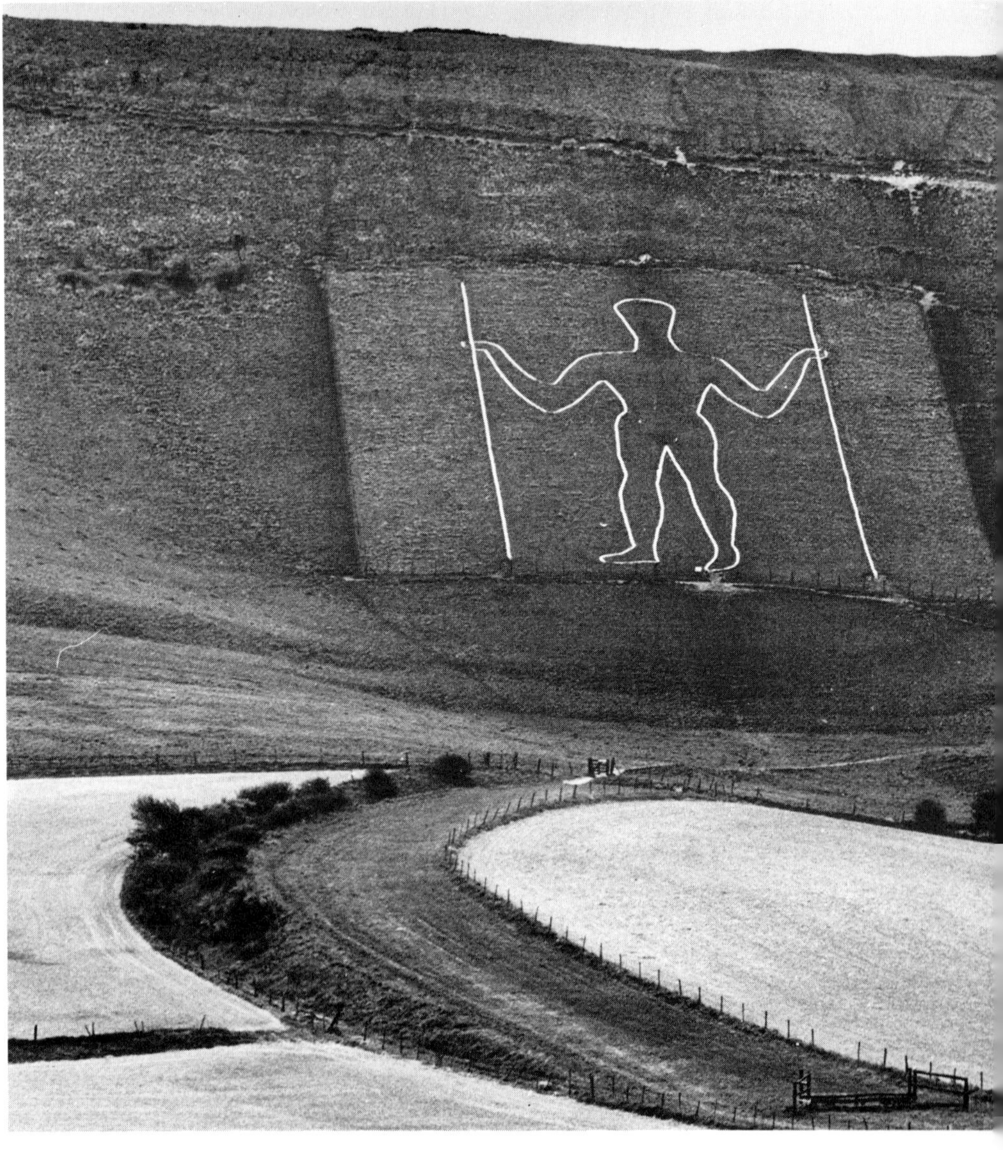

The Long Man, Wilmington

into the Twenties), old guns, tubs used by smugglers, early ploughs and all sorts of bygone odds and ends.

Need it be said that, as with all places popular with tourists, Wilmington is best visited in the early Spring or late Autumn? The pleasant village street is then peaceful and if you climb up above the Long Man to Windover Hill, with its prehistoric burial mounds, and walk along the crest of the Downs to Jevington, you'll think you are the only person in Sussex.

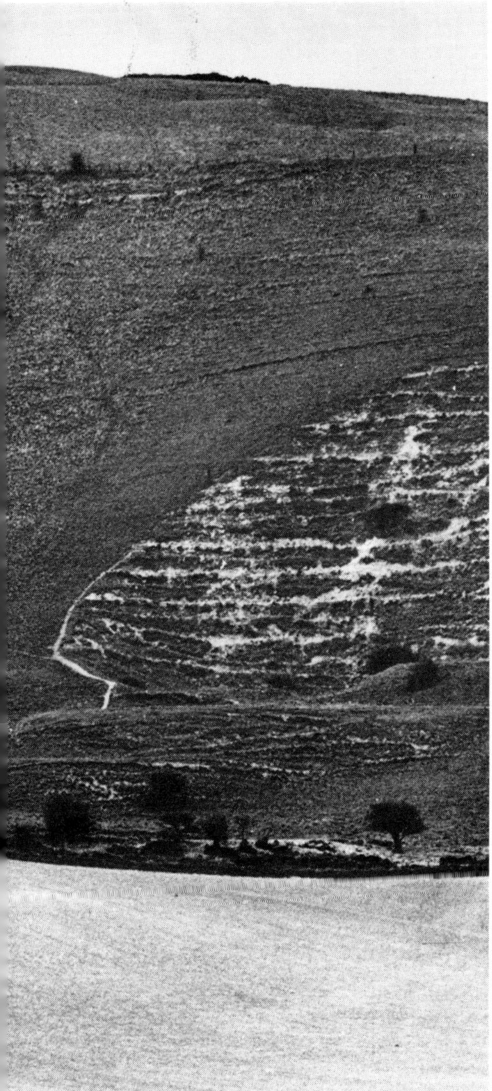

Winchelsea

Winchelsea resembles a very beautiful corpse carefully embalmed by an expert undertaker. The streets run East to West and North to South in a gridiron pattern like a town in the Middle West and every house in them, white weather-boarded or tile-hung, is perfect. There are few pavements, just carefully mown grass verges; hollyhocks and roses frame the doors and windows; there are three mediaeval gates, views over the Channel to France on a clear day, a superb church with unique tombs – what more could a photographer want?

Perhaps because of its very perfection, it is not easy to produce interesting pictures of Winchelsea. You walk along an East-West street, turn into a North-South one, turn once more at the end and so on, all the time passing superb 18th-century houses (many of them are late-19th-century reproductions but look none the worse for that). There are none of the crooked alleys or haphazard placing of buildings that make the exploration of English towns and villages so interesting, and the effect is strangely sterile and subduing.

I once took a pointer bitch, a wilful and defiant creature who spent part of her life dancing on her hind legs and the rest galloping in all directions at once, into Winchelsea. She took one appalled look and for the first time in her life walked sedately by my side with her muzzle pressed against my knee until we left, when she became once more her usual lively and disobedient self.

This sounds very unfair to what is possibly the most beautiful town in Sussex (it elects its own Mayor, though I know of many much bigger villages), but the straight, deserted streets do have a soporific effect – it must be a great place to retire to after a stressful life.

Like Rye, three miles to the East, it is built on a hill and, also like Rye, was devastated by the French during a series of raids in the 14th and 15th centuries. But while busy Rye, bursting at the seams with tourists, has prospered, Winchelsea seems never to have recovered from the shock and to this day remains in a trance.

Planned by Edward I in 1283, obviously using a ruler, it was intended to be a much bigger place. The New Gate, for instance, is a long way out of town. By far the best approach to Winchelsea is to turn right at Icklesham on the main A259 trunk road into a lane that passes Hog Hill and eventually goes through the New Gate, standing all by itself in the fields. You'll probably want to photograph it, but wait until something appropriate passes through – a farm tractor, a cyclist, a walker or perhaps a flock of sheep. Cars seem very out of place.

If, on reaching the centre of the town, you walk West from the church, past Rectory Lane, you can reach an 18th-century mill, minus its sails, but to get there you pass humps and hummocks in the fields that mark the sites of the buildings destroyed five hundred years ago; no attempt has ever been made at re-building. They are best photographed when a low sun casts long shadows.

The church of St Thomas is itself only a fragment of a once huge building, as can be seen from the surrounding ruins. Inside, the main attractions are the unique 'Alard Tombs', individually lit by a low-powered bulb and calling for an exposure of perhaps 1/30th of a second at f2 on 400 ASA film; you wouldn't dare use a tripod, but a monopod could be very useful. The ghost of a black man in a red uniform does his best to enliven the churchyard.

In the main street, the only one down which traffic passes, is the smallest bank I have ever seen, straight out of Toytown – it's worth photographing as a curiosity. People with an interest in literature will want to record the cosy, weather-boarded house in which lived Ford Madox Ford, while if you are photographing the side streets, from some of which you can see the open country, try to include some of

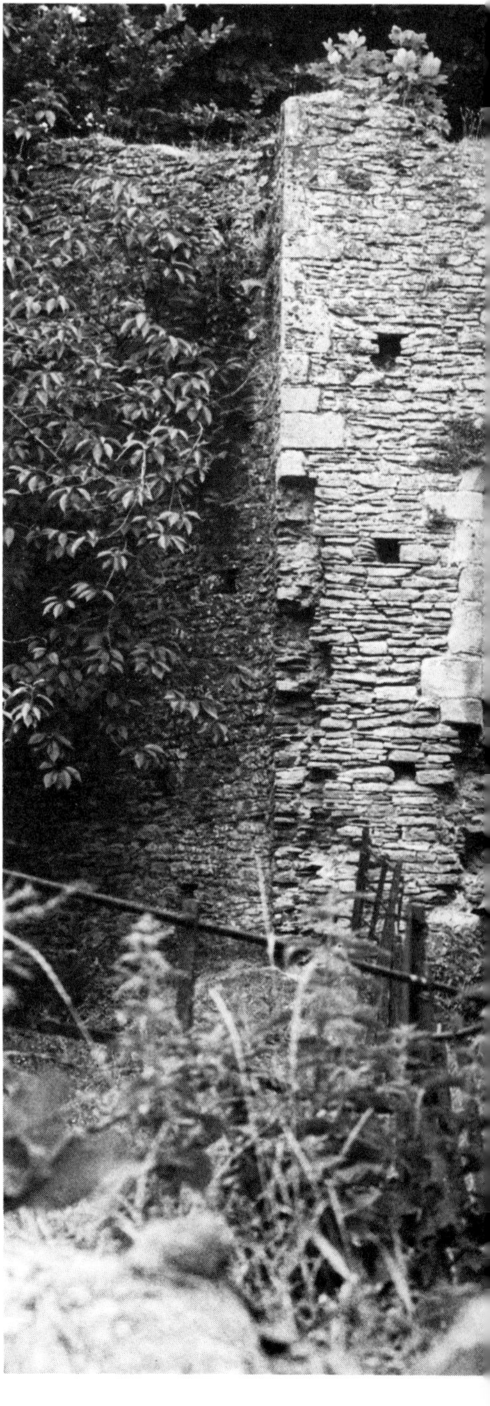

The New Gate, Winchelsea (right)

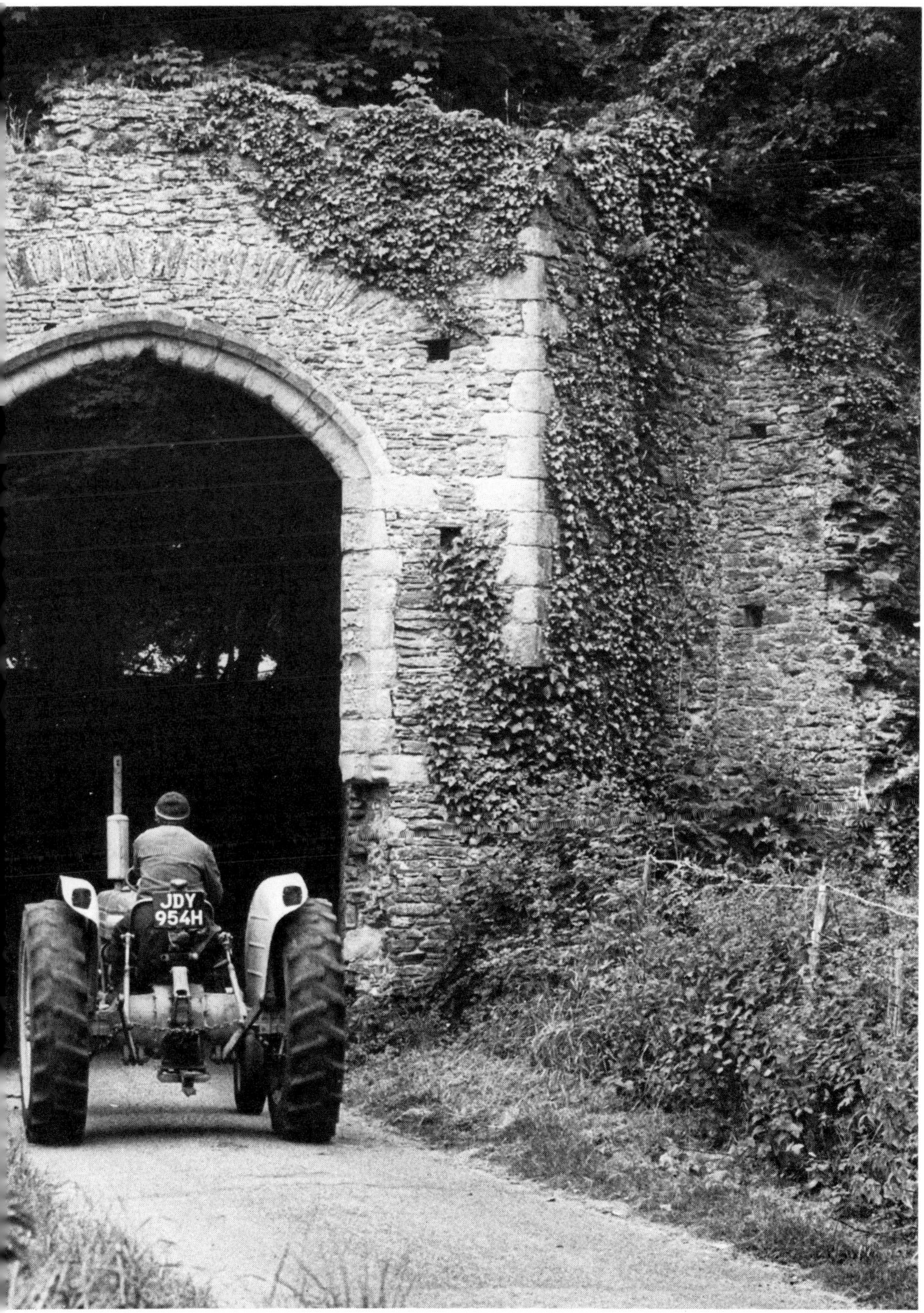
JDY
954H

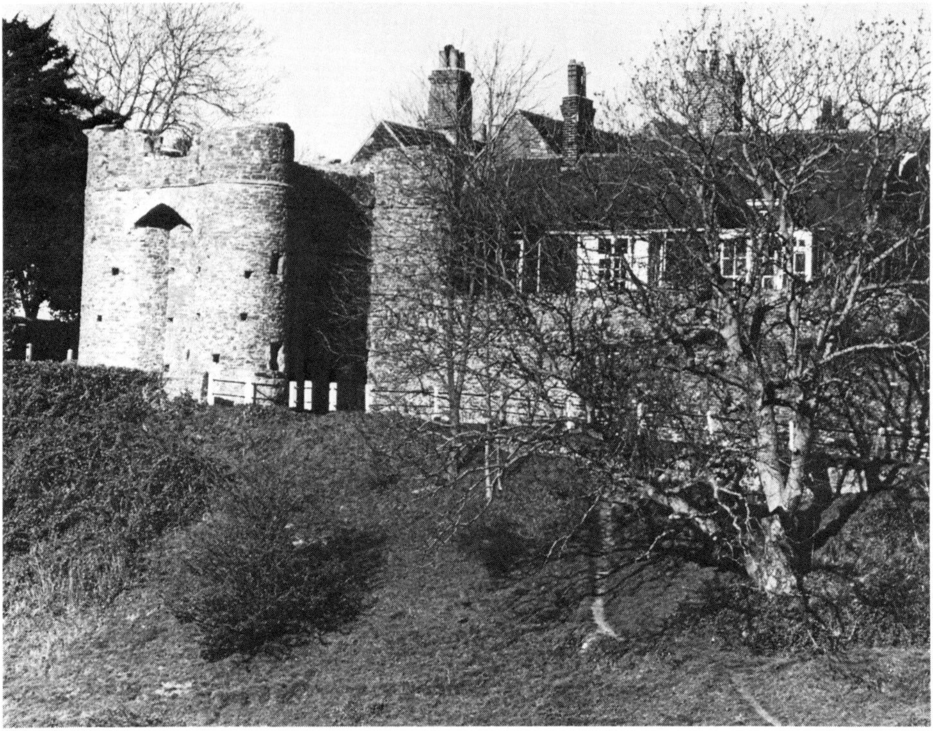

Strand Gate, Winchelsea

the ever-present flowers and shrubs close to the camera to give foreground interest and depth.

The Strand Gate is best photographed from the 'Look-out', a miniature terrace on the right of the road from which there is a good view over Romney Marsh and, in ideal conditions, to the coast of France. To the left of the gate is the pleasant cottage in which lived Ellen Terry, the beautiful gooseherd and model who became the country's leading actress. A lens with a very wide angle is needed to include both the gate and the cottage.

If you have been in Rye, you will find Winchelsea a complete contrast. Even at the height of the Season it is utterly peaceful, but to capture its unique atmosphere with a camera is remarkably difficult.

Wisborough Green

If a visiting photographer from overseas ever asks to see a typical Sussex village, take him to Wisborough Green. It's by no means typical, but it is what he'd hope to see.

A huge rectangular green is surrounded by chestnut trees and half-timbered, tile-hung or weather-boarded cottages. On a Sunday in Summer there'll probably be a cricket match going on; the low, red-roofed, welcoming Three Crowns is set back in one corner, while in another there is a perfect group – a pond with water-lilies, barns, a stone-built village hall (once the workhouse) and the 11th-century church.

From the church you cannot see the road or its traffic; instead there is a view of the distant Downs. To the right of the chancel arch there is a remarkably well-preserved mural of St James of Compostella with his staff and cockleshell, and another of the Crucifixion, both dating from around 1275.

As you walk around this corner of Wisborough, the buildings, the pond and the trees form one composition after another. From the photographer's point of view, it really is the perfect village, and to the West, towards Petworth, lies what is probably the best stretch of country in Sussex.

Try taking the road that runs North of the green through Kirdford and Balls Cross, past farms and giant oaks through a dream landscape. It's usually deserted and is the drive of a lifetime.

Withyham

Climb the steep slope up to Withyham Church, but pause and look back before you enter. The view is straight out of an 18th-century engraving – sheep graze, ducks swim on the pond, the sun glints on the spire of Hartfield Church in the distance. Everything is peaceful and civilized.

Once inside, the memorial to Thomas Sackville, who died in France in 1677 at the age of thirteen, grips your attention. C.G. Cibber was paid £350 – a vast sum in those days – to carve this masterpiece, perhaps the finest in the country, out of white and grey marble. The boy lies on top of his tomb holding a skull while his parents kneel at either side. The whole work is so uncannily natural and lifelike you feel you are intruding on their grief.

You must decide for yourself which angle pleases you best, but on the whole a lens with a focal length between 85 and 105mm will be most useful. It would be a sin to use flash since the natural lighting is perfect.

All around there are less spectacular

The Sackville Monument, Withyham

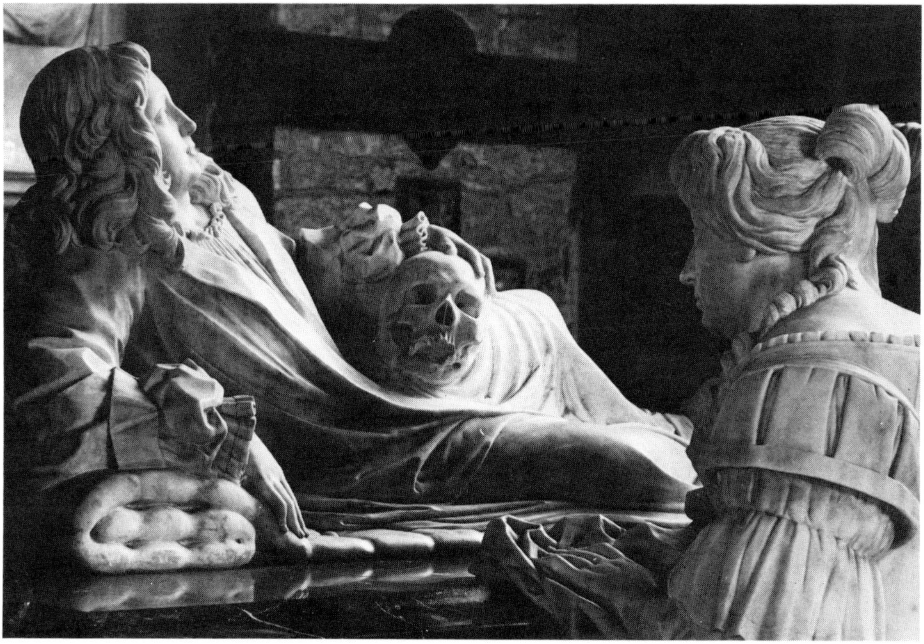

memorials, while tattered banners hang from the roof. The East window of the chapel shows the line of descent of the Sackvilles from a Herbrand de Sauqueville who came over with the Conqueror – cynics will wonder why such a window was necessary.

Not far away is the comfortable white weather-boarded Dorset Arms (the Sackvilles were Earls of Dorset). A turning at the side leads to the village cricket ground, backed by trees and making with the pub a perfect picture.

Further along the road to the East, on the same side, is Duckings, a half-timbered house dating from 1507 – there is a hammer-pond nearby and it must once have belonged to an ironmaster. Simple and perfect, you'll never see a better example of a Tudor house in Sussex.

Local Events

As you travel through the less frequented parts of Sussex you will see from time to time a notice pinned to a tree or telegraph pole. Hand-written or set in some 19th-century type by a country printer, they announce ploughing matches, flower shows, church bazaars and all the minor events that mean so much to the often widely scattered community.

These little local affairs are always worth visiting with a camera since they represent rural life in Sussex much more accurately than the big, organized agricultural shows. The people taking part are seen as indivi-

Ploughing North of Rye (right)
Corn Auction at West Burton (below)

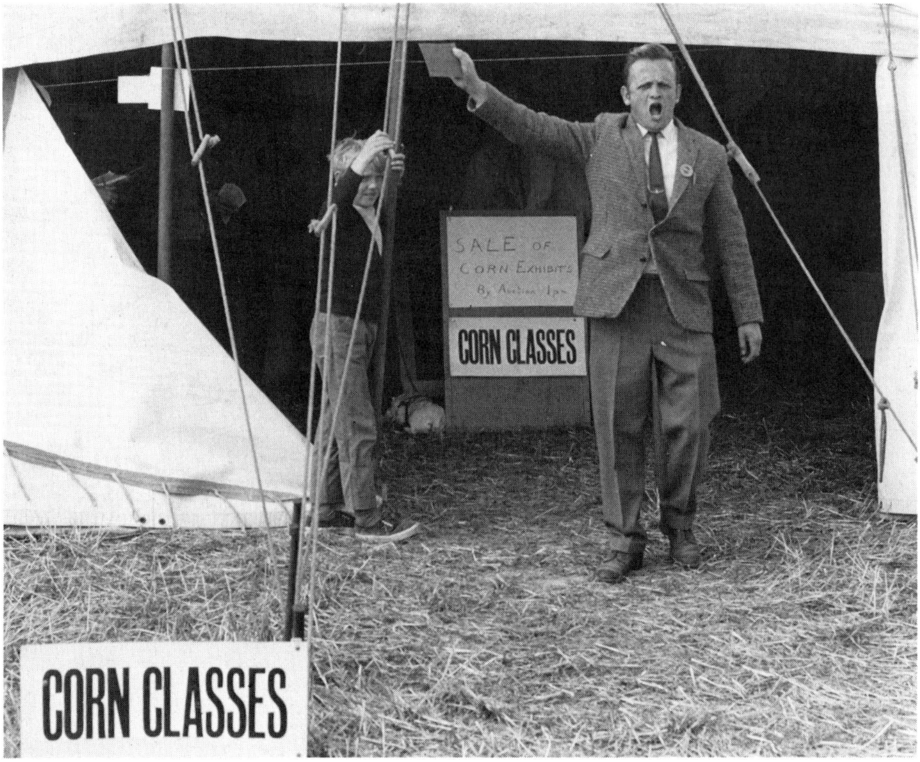

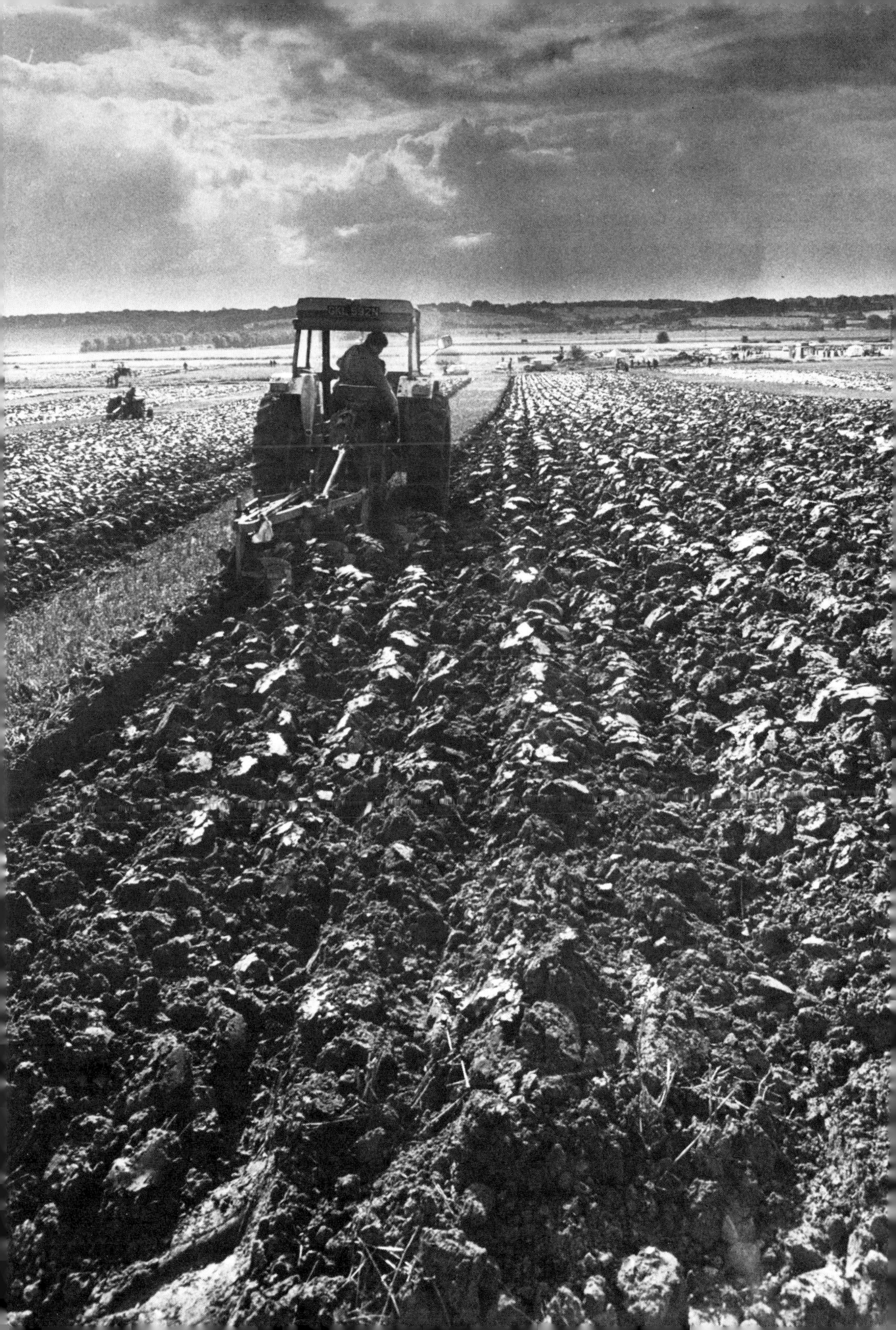

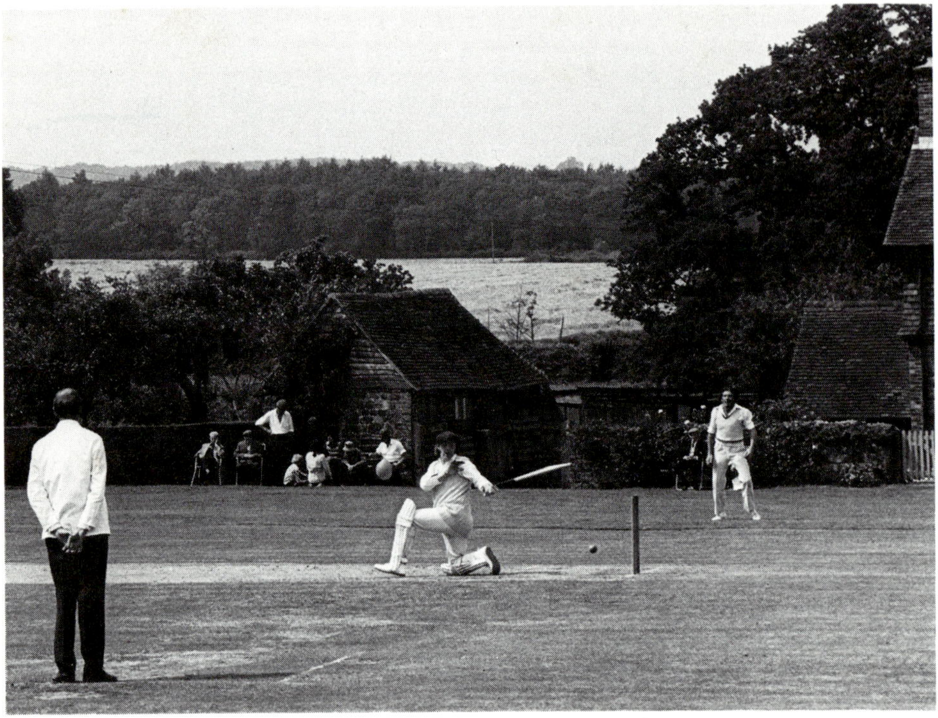

High summer in Sussex

duals, not as part of a crowd, and rivalries are intense. Everyone knows everyone else and the whole thing is like a family gathering.

Bad weather is ignored and good pictures of ploughing can be taken in heavy rain provided your camera has a lens-hood deep enough to protect the lens from the drops. Sales of jam and chutney are often held in the open if the day is fine; when photographing these, try to include something in the background, perhaps the church, that will provide a setting for the scene. If an event such as a flower show is held in a marquee, do not use flash, which will destroy the atmosphere. Instead fit a semi-wide-angle lens, perhaps a 35mm, and set it at a large aperture; 400 ASA material may be needed.

For ploughing pictures I like to use a wide-angle lens – the shorter the focal length the better – to get a close-up of a furrow in the foreground with the plough in the background moving away from the camera, but every photographer has his own technique. For pictures of people at the event a medium long-focus lens, something between 85 and 105mm, will let you fill the viewfinder with the subject without getting too close.

When you pass a notice telling you of a coming happening it is only too easy to say: 'That sounds fun – I must go there'; by the time you have returned home you find you have forgotten both the location and the date. It really is essential to write down the details at the time; from the photographer's point of view a ploughing match or a jumble sale for repairs to the church is much more interesting and likely to produce good pictures than any of the standard tourist subjects.